OXFORD *Children's* ANCIENT HISTORY

OXFORD
Children's
ANCIENT HISTORY

Roy Burrell

with many illustrations by

Peter Connolly

Oxford University Press   1994

Oxford University Press, Walton Street, Oxford OX2 6DP

Oxford University Press, Inc., 200 Madison Avenue,
New York, New York 10016

Oxford New York Toronto
Delhi Bombay Calcutta Madras Karachi
Kuala Lumpur Singapore Hong Kong Tokyo
Nairobi Dar es Salaam Cape Town
Melbourne Auckland Madrid

and associated companies in
Berlin Ibadan

Oxford is a trade mark of Oxford University Press

© Text: Roy Burrell 1991
© Illustrations to Parts 2 and 3: Peter Connolly 1991

Library of Congress Catalog Card Number 93-85651

A CIP catalogue record for this book is
available from the British Library

ISBN 0 19 917243 9 (UK edition)
ISBN 0 19 521058 1 (US edition)

Typeset by MS Filmsetting Limited, Frome, Somerset
Printed in Hong Kong

Contents

Part 1

On the threshold of history

All the early civilisations shown here emerged in the past 10,000 years. They had all mastered the art of writing. The prehistoric period before that stretched back over **3,000,000** years to mankind's earliest ancestors.

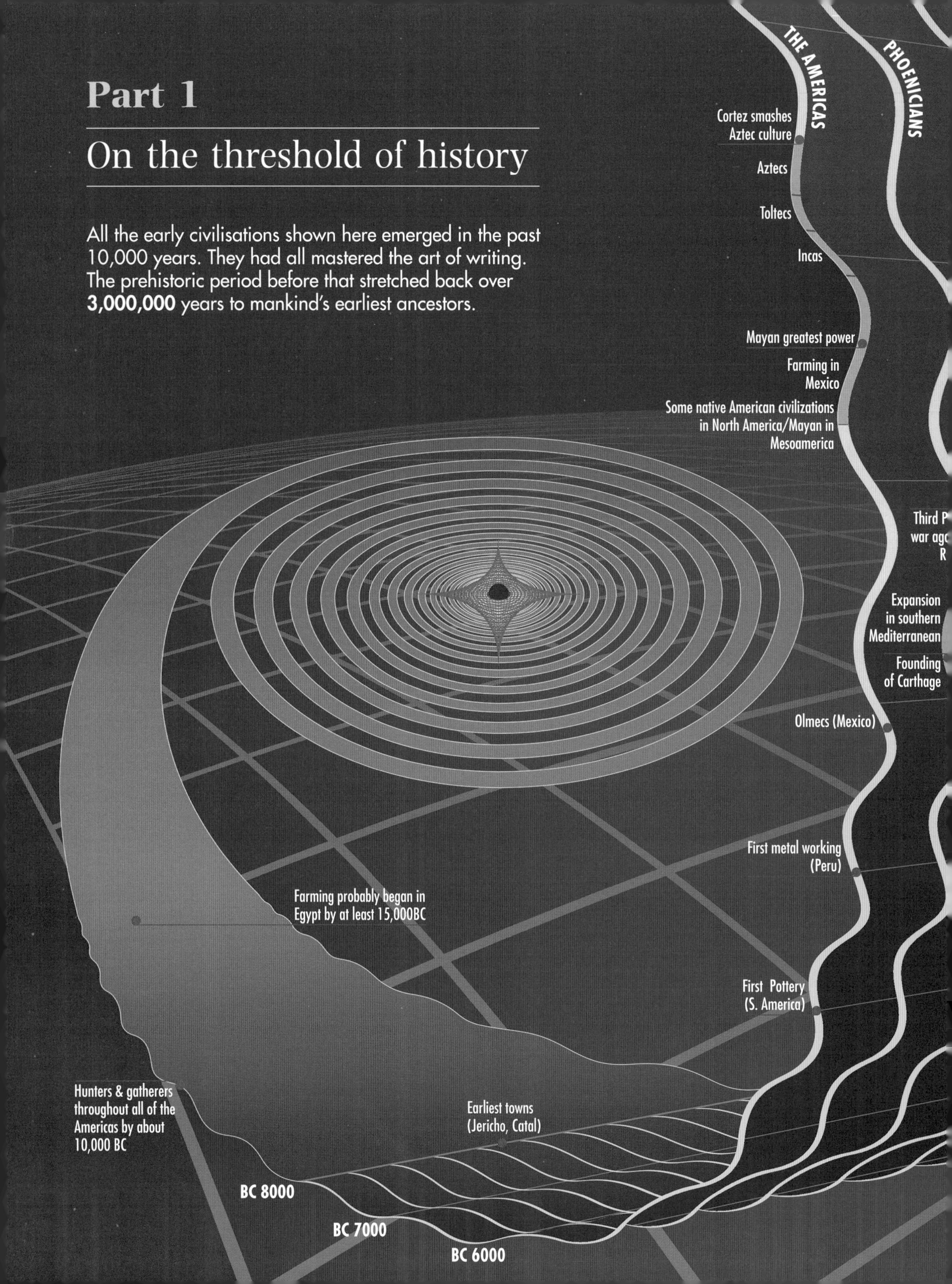

THE AMERICAS

PHOENICIANS

Cortez smashes Aztec culture

Aztecs

Toltecs

Incas

Mayan greatest power

Farming in Mexico

Some native American civilizations in North America/Mayan in Mesoamerica

Third P war ag R

Expansion in southern Mediterranean

Founding of Carthage

Olmecs (Mexico)

First metal working (Peru)

Farming probably began in Egypt by at least 15,000BC

First Pottery (S. America)

Hunters & gatherers throughout all of the Americas by about 10,000 BC

Earliest towns (Jericho, Catal)

BC 8000

BC 7000

BC 6000

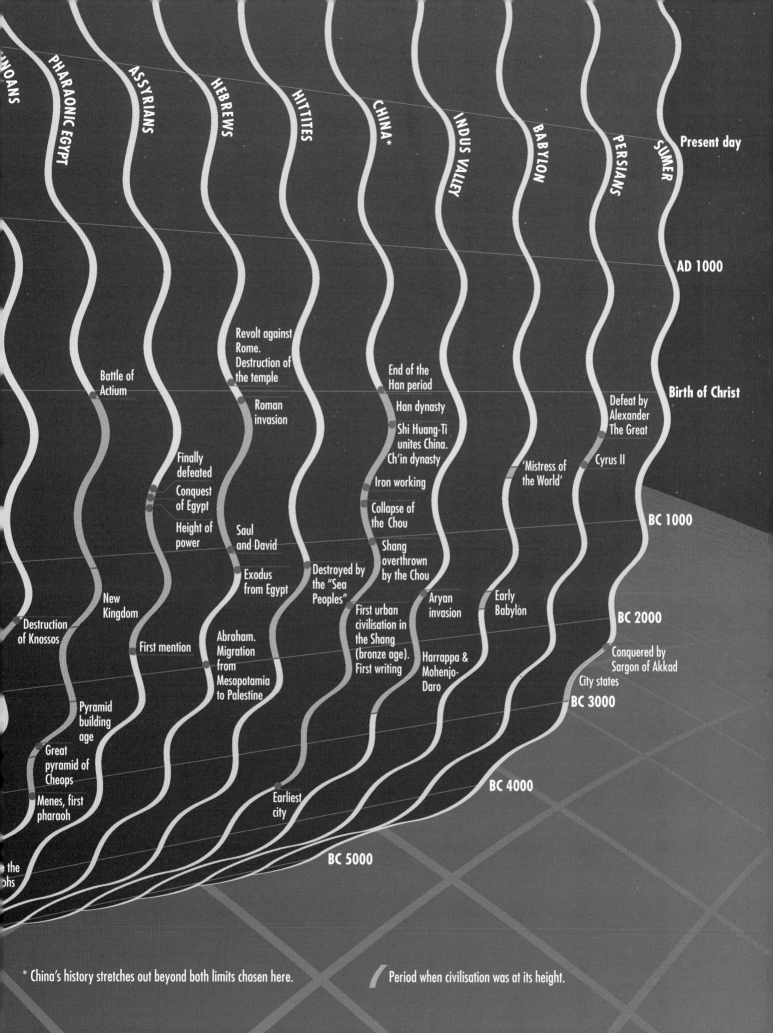

MINOANS

PHARAONIC EGYPT

ASSYRIANS

HEBREWS

HITTITES

CHINA*

INDUS VALLEY

BABYLON

PERSIANS

SUMER

Present day

AD 1000

Birth of Christ

BC 1000

BC 2000

BC 3000

BC 4000

BC 5000

Revolt against Rome. Destruction of the temple

Battle of Actium

Roman invasion

End of the Han period

Han dynasty

Shi Huang-Ti unites China. Ch'in dynasty

Defeat by Alexander The Great

Finally defeated

Conquest of Egypt

Height of power

Iron working

'Mistress of the World'

Cyrus II

Saul and David

Collapse of the Chou

Exodus from Egypt

Destroyed by the "Sea Peoples"

Shang overthrown by the Chou

New Kingdom

Aryan invasion

Early Babylon

Destruction of Knossos

First mention

Abraham. Migration from Mesopotamia to Palestine

First urban civilisation in the Shang (bronze age). First writing

Harrappa & Mohenjo-Daro

Conquered by Sargon of Akkad

City states

Pyramid building age

Great pyramid of Cheops

Menes, first pharaoh

Earliest city

the
hs

* China's history stretches out beyond both limits chosen here.

/ Period when civilisation was at its height.

Introduction

The Stone Age

Did the thought ever occur to you that you are descended directly from ancestors who lived at the same time as all the exciting events of history?

Your parents are (on average) about 25 years older than you. With the same age gap in your family, only four ancestors would take you back a century. Sixteen ancestors ago, your distant forebears were living at the same time as Shakespeare.

When you read about the Stone Age, you realise that some of the people then were heading a line leading directly to you – even though the time that has gone by since the appearance of Man on earth may be as much as two million years.

Why do we call it the Stone Age? It's because stone was the only thing known from which to make tools and weapons. At first, stones were used as they were – to be thrown at a bird or animal in order to provide food for the day.

Eventually, Stone Age Man found that he could chip stones into spear or arrow heads, into knives or scrapers. Some animals are known to use tools but never to the extent that early Man did. The latter's intelligence was tested as the weather began to get worse.

At first, it was no more than a case of the summers getting shorter and the winters colder. Man (or more likely woman!) had the idea of using animal skins to protect the bodies of her family from the Arctic conditions.

Sooner or later, the time came when last winter's snow was still lying as the next winter's first snow fell. The fourth immensely long ice age had set in. For thousands of years huge sheets of ice covered much of the northern parts of the world. Nothing grew on the ice and there were few animals about.

A difficult life for early Man was to be had on the freezing fringes of the glaciers. The animals he hunted included musk ox, reindeer, woolly rhinoceros and mammoth.

This life style went on for thousands of years and then the climate began once more to change. Winters grew less severe, summers warmer.

Inch by inch the mile-thick layers of ice melted and retreated northward. Plants made their appearance on

the now ice-free margins. Our ancestors had always depended on nuts, roots and berries to plug the gaps in their meat intake but unfortunately, as the weather warmed up, the animals they had mostly hunted moved away to be nearer the ice. You couldn't expect beasts with thick furry coats to remain where temperatures were higher, so early Man had to look for other kinds of prey – antelope, horse, bison and so on.

However, a few Stone Age men actually trailed after the cold-loving animals and followed them right across Asia and over the Bering Strait (then dry land) into what is now Alaska.

By about 10,500 years ago, the forerunners of all modern native Americans had colonised the 'new world' from Alaska to the tip of South America.

In the 'old world' the alteration in the climate was to lead to an even more dramatic change in the way that our distant relations got their living. As the Old Stone Age gave way to the New Stone Age, and eventually to the Age of Metals, human beings learnt how to grow plants when and where they needed them and how to domesticate animals.

How this happened you can see in the next sections.

The Northern Hemisphere showing the extent of the ice sheets.

Model of a mammoth

Chapter 1 First civilisations

The climate changes

How the rain belt moved from North Africa to Europe

An oasis in North Africa

As the ice disappeared towards the Arctic in Northern Europe about ten thousand years ago, the snows of winter turned mostly to rain. The rainfall on which the people, animals and plants of N. Africa and the Near East had depended for centuries gradually moved away towards Europe.

The rain did not go completely but it was much reduced. Plants die if they don't get water, and over the years the less hardy ones simply disappeared from some regions. Often it was a case of the parent bush or tree surviving for a while but whose seeds did not take root and grow owing to a lack of rain.

The grasslands of North Africa began to develop patches of bare earth where nothing could flourish: the dry heat sucked from the soil what little moisture there was, leaving it to be blown about as a fine powder. Gradually the patches grew larger and started to join up with other patches. As the centuries went by, plants could grow only where a lake, river or oasis provided the water they needed.

Animals have to drink too, so they also had to live near the water. Human beings who depended on the animals for their hunting were naturally confined to the same places.

Oases and river valleys could not support the same amounts of animal and plant life that a whole region had once provided for. There were probably fewer human beings too and for the same reasons.

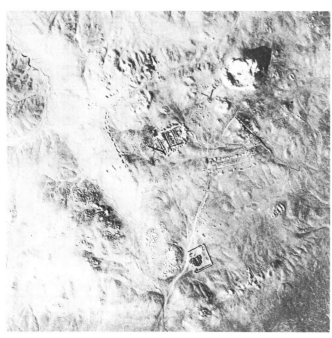
An aerial photograph showing the traces of an ancient village

In the foothills of the mountains which run from the eastern Mediterranean to the Persian Gulf, traces of villages and even small towns begin to appear. Here, in the wooded valleys, rainfall was still sufficient to support life. Many of these early settlements can be dated to around eight or nine thousand years before Christ. During the next two thousand years, many such towns were started. Their names are mostly unfamiliar to our ears – Hacilar, Catal Huyuk, Jarmo, Jericho – but they are almost certainly among the oldest towns in the world.

Here, careful burials were not unknown, often under the floors of the huts in which the people lived. Sometimes the walls of the houses were made of rammed mud, some were of stone and later on mud bricks were used. A common type of dwelling was round or square with high window spaces and no doorway at ground level. If you wanted to get in to your house, you had to climb a wooden ladder and get home by way of a smoke hole in the roof.

Food containers of wood and stone were made at first, then baskets waterproofed with animal skins or tar, if locally available. These were followed by the first pottery of clay.

Civilisation was on its way but what had brought about this tremendous change? Man had been a wanderer, hunting and gathering his food – now he had begun to settle permanently in one place. Once he had owned only what he could carry on his back: now he could own as much as he could protect in his house. On the next page we shall see what had started to alter our ancestors' way of life.

From food gathering to farming

We saw that, even back in the old stone age, human beings did not live entirely on meat. They had all kinds of nuts, seeds, and roots depending on what was in season.

Hunters probably took some of this 'gathered' food with them when they went out searching for prey. It might have consisted of several handfuls of tasty seeds in an animal skin bag slung over the shoulder. If they were unlucky and did not manage a kill, at least they wouldn't go hungry. Some of the seeds in question came most likely from the ancestors of our well-known cereals such as wheat and barley. The villages and towns mentioned on the previous page owed their existence to the fact that in their neighbourhood the cereals grew wild and in abundance.

Corn grinder

We are fairly sure that Man began to harvest the heads of these plants long before he knew how to grow them for himself. Sickles were made by setting small sharp stone chips into handles and examples have been found with plant stem scratches, still identifiable after several thousand years. If there were enough collectable seeds nearby, town life became possible.

The collection of plant seeds was one thing, the eating of them quite another! It was quickly found that grinding the seeds between two stones was better than grinding them with your teeth. The result was flour from which a kind of bread could be made. The stone grinders, or querns, have been dug up on many Near Eastern sites.

The biggest step in Man's advance was still to be taken however. This was the change over from collecting the cereals to actually growing them. How was the new idea discovered? Probably by accident. Perhaps the hunters might sit to eat their unground seeds on a fallen log. They had been unlucky in the hunt all the morning but they knew about the log from previous expeditions and they chose this as their place to eat at midday because there was also a stream nearby.

The scene may be imagined. The men and boys sit on the log and open their food bags. A few seeds are scattered as they eat. One of the hunters notices the plants growing by the log and points them out to his companions. 'There are always a lot of this sort growing here,' he says.

Of course, if he and his friends come back in a few months, some of the seeds they dropped at their picnic will have sprouted into new plants. All this is obvious to us – you sow seeds in your back garden, mark the row with a wooden peg, keep the weeds down, water the ground and up comes the plant you want. It wasn't so obvious to the people of those days. The scene round the log with the hunters and their scattered lunch had to be repeated time after time until something clicked in someone's head and the connection was made.

After that, it was a matter of putting the seeds in the earth deliberately, clearing away the unwanted vegetation and protecting the growing crop from the animals which would have eaten it until it was ready to gather.

Before planting, the weeds had to be removed and the soil loosened. This was done at first with a stout pointed stick. Such a slow process could be speeded up if two people co-operated, like this:

Eventually, a tame animal would take the place of the second person. But the taming of animals belongs on the next page.

From hunting to stock farming

In the same way that Man changed from being a gatherer to a crop farmer, he also gave up hunting and took to animal farming. It didn't happen overnight, of course. Hunting and gathering continued to be important at least in some settlements for centuries after the great switch was made. In the case of certain animals, Man found herding more efficient than hunting them. Again, the alteration in our ancestors' way of life was gradual, not dramatic.

The beasts first domesticated were sheep, goats, pigs and cattle. It probably happened like this: a tribe of hunters began to depend on two or three herds of animals to provide the meat they needed.

If the herds wandered in search of food and water, then the hunters had to move too – at least to be within striking distance of their food supply. It was a good deal easier to take animals that tend to crowd together in herds or flocks, rather than those which prefer to be on their own. In the latter case, you have only one chance of a kill but with a herd, if you miss one animal, there are plenty of others.

It took some time before Man realised he could prevent the flock from moving away and keep them in good health if only he could provide them with food and water.

He may have co-operated with his friends and relations to drive a herd of cattle into a steep ravine from which there was only one exit – the way they had gone in. The next step was to put a fence or thorn hedge across the mouth of the ravine. If they had chosen well and the valley had a stream and extensive areas of grass, the herd could be kept alive.

Driving goats into a ravine

Meat goes bad after a while, especially in a warm climate, so it was a great advantage for Man to keep live animals and to butcher one just before it was to be eaten.

Other ways in which a tame herd could have been built up were: 1. some single wild animals were captured instead of being killed, or 2. the young of some species were taken in and reared after the parents had been killed.

Other animals were also tamed or domesticated. These included not only dogs which had been helping Man to hunt since the old stone age but also goats, sheep and pigs which were, at least to begin with, solely meat animals. The idea of shearing sheep for their wool or milking cows probably came later.

Some species were eventually pressed into service as draught or riding animals. Oxen were trained to help with the ploughing and after a long while, horses were broken for use, both for hauling and riding.

Donkeys were also caught and tamed. In other parts of the world, camels, elephants, alpacas and llamas were forced to help Man's slow climb towards civilisation.

CHAPTER I

Attraction of river valleys

Over the centuries it was gradually noticed that the great river valleys of North Africa and Asia were ideal places in which to grow food. There was plenty of water for the crops, and the weather was hot enough for the farmer to produce two, or (if he were lucky) even three harvests a year.

Another advantage was the fact that the surrounding countryside was fairly flat. With steeply sloping ground the farmer has problems. Ploughing vertically up and down the slopes is a quick way to invite the rain to wash all your soil away. Sometimes, hillsides with abrupt slopes can only be worked if a great deal of labour is spent on making terraces, or flat steps in the rising ground. None of these problems faced the river valley dweller.

The earliest settlements in the Nile valley can be

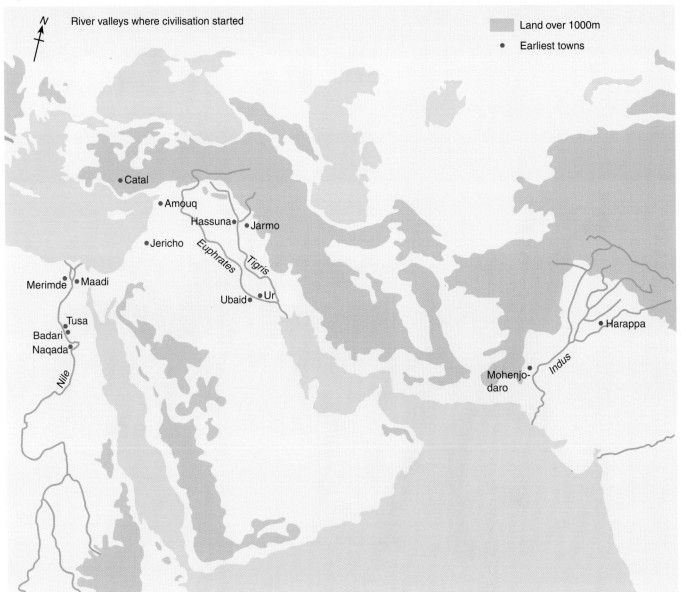

N — River valleys where civilisation started

Land over 1000m

● Earliest towns

The flood plain of the River Nile, where farming probably began.

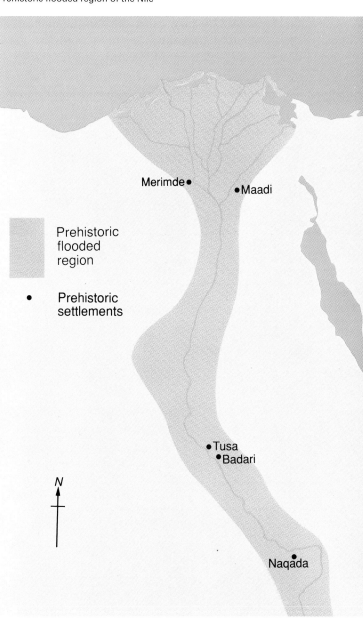

Prehistoric flooded region of the Nile

Merimde •
• Maadi

Prehistoric
flooded
region

• Prehistoric
settlements

• Tusa
• Badari

N

Naqada

dated to a period about 30,000 years ago but no one knows whether the first farmers to live in Egypt were descendants of these old stone age men or newcomers from elsewhere.

It seems certain that wild plants were harvested along the banks of the river long before anyone set out to grow them deliberately. Sickles for reaping and stones for grinding the seeds have been found. Peoples who used them couldn't at that time depend on plants entirely, or even mainly, for the food they ate. There were fish to be caught in the river and animals to be hunted.

The Nile plain was wetter and wider some 10,000 years ago than it is now and there would have been more game, particularly along the little tributary streams which fed the Nile. Nowadays they are dry watercourses or wadis, with no wild animals to hunt.

We know for sure that these early settlers used stone-tipped spears and arrows, many of which have been found in modern times. Their existence proves that the tribesmen of those days still depended on hunting for much of their living.

However, river valley farming was beginning to provide a growing share of what they ate. There was another advantage to this sort of life. The soil was easily worked and there was a large area which could be cultivated.

In the early days of farming up in the foothill valleys of the northern mountains, a family would have to move every few years because the soil was exhausted. It was far easier to find a place to settle in the great river valleys of the Nile, Tigris-Euphrates and the Indus. And, of course, once you were there, you could stay as long as you liked, for the soil never became exhausted. You'll find out why on the next page.

Irrigation and flood

In all the great river valleys where early civilisations started, there were periods of the year when the water levels began to rise until the rivers overflowed. This was particularly noticeable in the Nile valley. In Egypt there was just one great annual flood – not a series of minor, irritating ones.

The Nile is the longest river in the world and rises far to the south. Spring rains and snow melting from mountain tops thousands of miles from the sea flow down into the lakes and streams which feed the Nile.

The water level rises slowly and travels – just as slowly – down to the Mediterranean. The flood water spills over the banks on both sides – sometimes hundreds of yards to right and left.

The waters scour the hillsides and stream beds, picking up a great deal of mud – so much that the colour of the river changes from green to brownish red. By mid-summer, the swollen Nile has spread out over the fields bordering it. The farmers wait anxiously for the waters to go down.

Diagram showing the variation of the height of the River Nile during the year

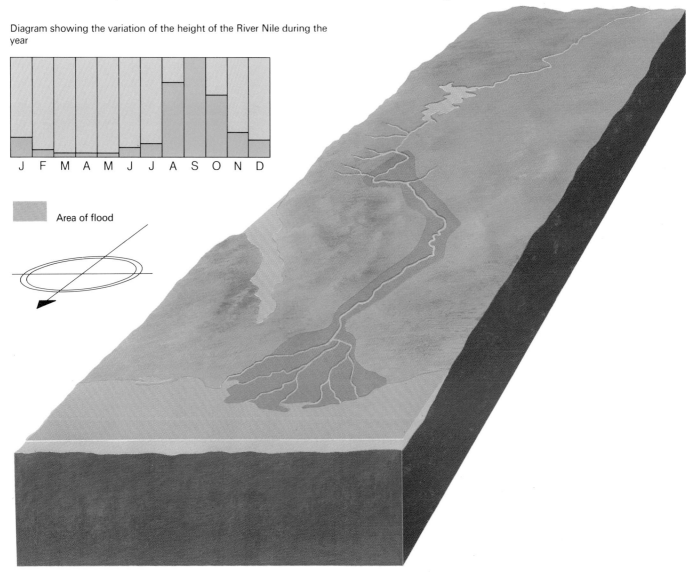

J F M A M J J A S O N D

Area of flood

When the land emerges once more into the light and air, the peasants can see that their farms and small holdings are thickly plastered with fertile mud. Now we can see why, in the Nile valley, the soil is never exhausted and why farmers don't have to move on to a better site every few years.

Every mid-September the level starts to drop and when the river has returned to its normal course, the farmer sets out to plough or hoe his fields. Provided he doesn't let the mud dry to a hard crust in the hot sun, not too much effort is needed to get the soil ready. When it is, the seeds of rye, wheat, barley, peas or beans are scattered on the sticky mud.

The next step is to drive the sheep or goats over the fields, their hooves burying the seed and covering it up. Of course, the baking sun sends the shade temperature up to over 100 degrees fahrenheit, so it doesn't do to allow the ground to dry out completely, or the plants would wither and die.

Somehow or other the farmer has to find a way of watering his growing crops. One method is to irrigate his fields. He must dig out small channels all over his land and arrange them so that they slope down away from the river.

Unluckily, by the time the flood is over, the Nile is probably many feet below the level of his farm, so he has to use a machine to get the water up. This is called a shaduf: the water bucket is on one end and the other is plastered with clay to balance it. The farmer dips the bucket on its rope down into the Nile and uses the counterweight to lift the water to the right level. When the bucket is just above the earth bank, the farmer swivels it round and tips it into the channel that supplies his crops.

A shaduf

Raising water using an Archimedes screw

The rise of the leaders

In most of the early civilisations, leaders arose naturally – they usually do. Even a small group of people will normally split up into the leader and the led.

This was important in Egypt, Sumer and ancient Pakistan – particularly in the first mentioned. It was vital for the farmers to grow as much food as they could, so as large an area as possible was cultivated.

To irrigate the largest farms, long and deep water channels were needed. It was all very well for a peasant and his family to scrape shallow ditches through the dirt of his small-holding but for a canal which had to reach to the farthest limit of a great estate, many men had to be employed.

This meant dividing them up into gangs, giving out tasks and getting them to work together. Those who gave the orders were the ones who seemed to know what was to be done and how to do it. One way of becoming a leader was to show that you knew things that the others didn't. For example a man who was able to foretell the coming of the annual flood would be very important indeed. It's all very well to say, 'The Nile floods once a year, so it's easy to say when it will be.' The difficulty is that although *we* know there are just over 365 days in a year, the earliest settlers didn't.

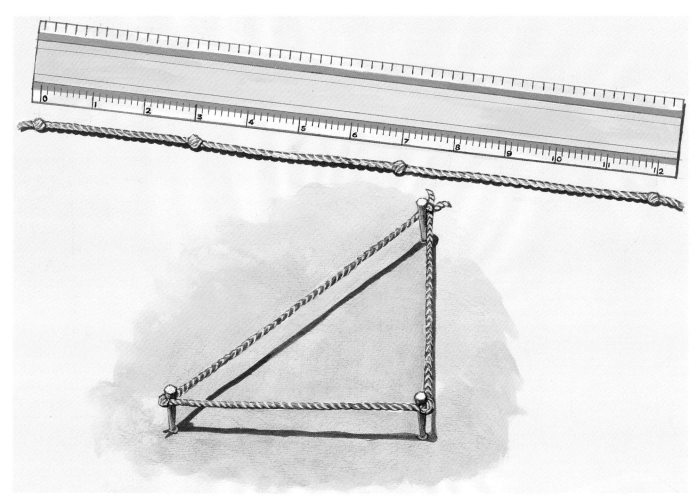

How to make a right angle with a piece of knotted string

How would you go about calculating the number of days in a year? It isn't as simple as it sounds – you can't just count because you don't know where to stop. The cleverest of the Egyptians worked it out by noting the position of the star Sirius in the sky and waiting until it came back again to that same position.

When the floods went down, a new problem appeared – where exactly was each peasant's farm? You couldn't mark the boundaries in the dry season, for such markers would have been swept away by the rising river waters.

It was left to those who could do the proper calculations to give each farming family the same amount of land as before. Another kind of calculation had to be made when civilisation really began: the designing of large public and royal buildings such as temples, granaries, palaces and tombs. It's surprising how hard it is to lay out the corner of a building so that it forms a right angle. You can't use the corner of a book or anything like it, as there wasn't, at that time, anything like it at all.

We don't know how, when or by whom the problem was solved but a method was hit upon. All we can do is guess that the river valley people used the string and pegs method.

If you make sure that the string is stretched and the three pegs positioned so that the tight cord between them measures three, four and five units (inches, footlengths – whatever you like) thus forming a triangle, you get an almost exact right angle.

All these sorts of tasks needed brain, rather than muscle power and they also required some method of recording, or writing things down. Ways of doing this varied from place to place and we'll look at how it was done later.

The men who could count, calculate, and set down their results for others to read had an edge over their neighbours. If they could work out how many men should be told off to dig a ditch, where it should run, what food each gang would need and how many bags of corn each peasant should be taxed to pay for everything, they would be looked up to as leaders – not only wise men but magicians. They were the first priests, rulers and kings.

Chapter 2   Sumer

The first settlers

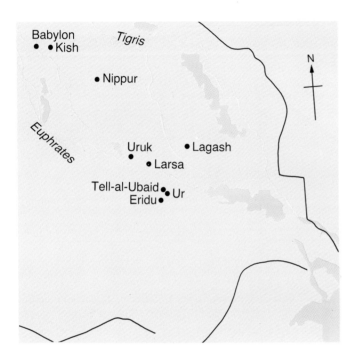

This is 'The Land Between the Rivers'. 'Mesopotamia' is what the Greeks called it. Iraq is its modern name. It – or parts of it – has had all kinds of names throughout thousands of years – Sumer, Shinar, Chaldea, Akkad, Assyria, and Babylonia are some of them.

Sumer is the name given to the earliest settled part – the area just inland from where the rivers Tigris and Euphrates empty their waters into the Persian Gulf.

Sumer can't have been a very attractive place for colonists and yet it was almost certainly here that civilisation first appeared in the world.

The rivers didn't always flood at exactly the same time each year. The floods were therefore not predictable – neither as to the time they could be expected nor as to the height of the water. It was quite a common happening for the flood to be so great that when it went down again the river had changed course.

There was little in the way of local building stone, so the first huts the people had were probably small round ones made of plaited and thatched reeds. As long as none of the peasant's family or animals had drowned in the flood, his hut could be quickly rebuilt and the outcome was not the disaster it might have been.

Modern Marsh Arab huts

Mesopotamian dairy scene

22

There were plenty of reeds and cane brakes but very few trees. There was desert land which needed irrigation and marshes which had to be drained. Above all there was the cruelly high summer temperature which often topped 100° fahrenheit.

Why then was the area settled at all? We can't give hard and fast reasons but we think it may have been on account of population pressure. In the mountain and hill valleys to the north and east of Sumer, people were running short of enough good farmland to feed all the extra children there were in the tribe. At least some of the families had to move on or go short of food for the rest of their lives.

We can imagine them packing up all they owned and strapping their bundles on to the backs of the donkeys they had tamed. The cattle, sheep and goats would be herded along the tracks and kept on the right path by the children helped by their dogs.

The travellers would have to live on the grain they took with them, at the same time saving enough barley and wheat seeds to sow once they got down to the river lowlands. They must also have carried dates both to eat and to plant for fresh date palm groves when they arrived in their new homeland.

The first sowing of seed was quite likely done as a ceremony with prayers to the gods of harvest, river, and weather.

Rainfall was too low to ensure the growth of the crops without some help, so every member of the family had to carry pots of water to the rows of plants in the fields. Everyone in this case meant the peasant, his wives and children, his brothers and their wives and children and even his own parents if they were not too old and feeble. They also had to join together to dig permanent irrigation ditches. By the time all the round, reed huts had been put up, there were the beginnings of a small village.

One huge advantage of being a farmer was that you had plenty of time to do other things while you were waiting for the grain to ripen. A man who hunted for a living found that it was a full time occupation and that he had very little leisure for anything else.

Pottery could be made to replace any that had been broken on the journey south. More elaborate and beautiful work could be done than was possible in a non-farming community. All kinds of storage jars, beakers, plates and dishes were fired in open, brush-wood furnaces and decorated with patterns in black, brown, red and cream.

We don't know what the people called themselves and we have no idea of the language they spoke. All we know is that, with the exception of scattered towns such as Jericho, they were laying the foundations for the oldest civilisation on earth.

Halaf pottery sherds

In the last section we mentioned the fact that the first settlers of Sumer had taken dates to plant in their new homeland. The date palm, according to ancient writings, had over 300 different uses. It's difficult to see how that figure was arrived at – the actual total is probably much lower. Let's see what this settler thinks about his date trees.

The peasant smiles, wipes the sweat from his brow with the back of his hand and invites us to sit down in his 'orchard'. As we settle our backs against a sturdy tree trunk, he smiles even more broadly.

'You see, he says, 'you've found out one of its advantages straight away. Without the broad leaves of the palm, there would be no shade at all in this land – and that would be hard to bear, for in summer it gets as hot as an oven. If it wasn't for the very fertile soil, I don't think anyone would actually choose to live here.'

He hands us some dates to nibble. 'Here is another of the tree's gifts – its fruit. Do you know that you could live off dates plus a bit of the fresh fronds at the top of the palm? Not that you'd want to; it'd get pretty boring, having the same thing for every meal. But you could if you had to.

'Then again, you can press the dates and squeeze out the juice. It makes a nice, refreshing drink. Or if you wanted to you could leave it to ferment and turn it into wine. That's nice too, but you shouldn't have too much, particularly if you've got to work afterwards. It's better to take some in the cool of the evening. It's not much fun hoeing a field with a dry mouth and a splitting headache, which is what you get if you drink too much of it.

'Now then, if you leave the wine in the open air for some time, it goes sour but you can still use it. You sprinkle it on your young palm leaf salad. We just call it "sour wine" – do you know what I mean?'

'Yes,' we say, 'our word is vinegar and that means "sour wine" too.'

The peasant nods approvingly and goes on with his list of good things the date palm gives him.

'You can collect the dry stones, or fruit pips, until you have two or three large bags full of them. You pile them into a heap and light a fire at one side of it. When it's going well, you cover up the fire with wet earth or clay, just leaving a little hole here and there. After a few hours the stones aren't burnt, they're cooked and you've got (for just a few hours' work) a half bag of charcoal. Marvellous stuff for cooking.

'Now, what else? Well, you can always make a string or rope from the fibre. You can pick a leaf and use it as a hat or a sunshade. You can take the main rib out of a leaf and make some kinds of furniture. You tie several of them together in whatever pattern you like. Of course there's better furniture to be had from the trunk itself. When the tree is old and past its best years of fruit bearing, it's chopped down and turned into tables, chairs, boats or even firewood.

'You could make moulds for mud bricks, or fish and wild fowl traps, or you could—'

'Thank you very much, 'we say,' you've given us quite a lot to think about.

Date cluster on a tree

Dates

Nam-sha learns to read and write

'Oh, no,' says Nam-sha, when we ask him, 'not everybody learns to read and write – only the ones the gods pick. There aren't very many scribes and you have to work hard to become one. The course lasts about twelve years. A boy is roughly eight years old when he begins but he's a man of twenty when he finishes.

'I've been doing it for four years now but my teachers keep telling me that I still don't know very much. I suppose that's true: the only things I can read are very simple tablets.'

'Tablets?'

'Yes, that's what we write on – tablets of soft, damp clay. We use reeds to make the marks. Like this,' he says, picking up a flat lump of clay.

'If you try to draw what you want to say – a picture of a hand, a tree, a foot perhaps, it gets harder to pull the reed through the surface and bits of clay twist up in front like the bow wave of a boat on the river Tigris. So we don't just draw, we use the end of the pen to stab little marks like this:

Babylonian clay tablets

It still looks like the picture of the thing you wanted to put down but over the years it gradually gets altered. We start, say, with a man's head: Done in 'print marks', it probably looked like this: Then it got turned on its side: Finally, it wound up as: You can't recognise it straight away now, not unless you know what it is.'

'Does this mean you have to learn a new sign for every new word?'

'Not quite but pretty nearly. There are tens of thousands of words in our language and it's fine if you can draw the word you need, such as 'palm tree' or 'house' but how do you draw 'fright' or 'greed'? Oh, I know you could sketch a person who is frightened or greedy but that's hard to do just with these stab marks.'

'How do you manage then?'

'Well, one sign often does duty for several words; a foot might mean 'foot' or 'kick' or 'stand' or 'measure'. On the other hand, there are over thirty different signs for 'sheep'. You can also have signs standing for parts of words and that helps a lot.'

'Oh, yes, I know – you could draw for 'bee, leaf' (belief) which would be hard to draw otherwise.'

'That's the idea,' says Nam-sha, 'Are you scribes too?'

We look a little bit embarrassed. 'Well,' we say, hesitating a little, 'we *can* read and write but only in our own language, not yours'.

'Does it take a long time to read in your foreign tongue?' asks Nam-sha.

'No,' we say, 'not nearly as long as it does in the Land of the Two Rivers. You see, we have only 26 signs to learn – one for each sound. Well, almost like that. We call our collection of signs an alphabet.'

'We don't have an alphabet,' says Nam-sha, 'I don't think it would work.'

'How did writing start?' we want to know.

'No one is sure. I asked my teachers and they said it was given to Man by the gods. But I think it started with the temples rather than the gods.'

'How so?'

'Well, in the beginning, those who ran the big farms and large estates (which mostly belonged to the temples anyway) had to have some way of helping their memory.

'If you have to remember what amounts of fish, meat and grain you produced last year and how much had to be collected from each peasant and how much given to each servant and workman – it just gets too much. It's so much easier to draw a picture of an ear of grain or an ox head and to add strokes to show how much of a thing. Then you could put a different sign for each man who paid taxes or was paid wages. It sounds complicated but it isn't. Those doing the note taking probably wrote on slabs of stone to start with but clay is easier to find, it's cheaper and there's a lot more of it.'

Nam-sha is right. The Land of the Two Rivers is built of clay. Of course, the clay tablets might have lost their picture words after twenty or thirty centuries but luckily for us some survived. Important tablets were sometimes baked deliberately to preserve them. Quite a few burnt in accidental temple and palace fires. Thus the words were fixed for ever.

Clay bricks and buildings

Making mud bricks

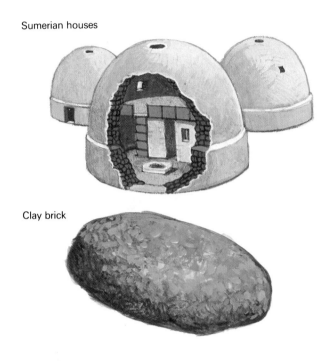

Sumerian houses

Clay brick

Gradually, as scientists have dug into the mounds of ruins in Sumer and elsewhere in the valley of the Two Rivers, enough clay tablets have been found to rough out a sketchy outline of Sumerian history.

No one king ruled over the entire area. On the contrary, in early times, each city was independent of the others. The local king or priest/king ruled an area around his own stronghold.

At the beginning of written history, about 5,000 years ago, Sumer was governed in this way but as the centuries passed, other peoples overran the area. There were the Akkadians and they in their turn were conquered by the Amorites or Babylonians. The conquest of the latter by the Assyrians takes us to only a few centuries before the Christian era. The last people to subdue the area before the time of Christ were the Persians.

Buildings changed with the years and so did the bricks from which they were made. Originally, settlers may simply have used handfuls of wet clay to make a crude wall, keeping the mounds of mud from toppling over by one of two methods. The peasant might outline his house's shape with lumps of clay which he then allowed to dry in the hot sun. Further handfuls were placed on top and heat hardened in their turn.

This was a very slow method if you had to wait hours for each course to dry out. A simpler way was to use timber shuttering and ram or stamp the clay down between the boards.

Later still, bricks were invented. The first Sumerian bricks were very oddly shaped. The worker took a double handful of clay and rolled it roughly into a shape like a small marrow. Then he slightly flattened top, bottom and sides. After this, workers took square wooden frames which they filled with a clay, sand and straw mixture. Then the frame was lifted off and the whole process was repeated. Long rows of bricks were allowed to harden in the sun; only if they were to be used in a place where they needed to be waterproof were they baked in a kiln or brick oven. It wasn't until civilisation was well established that bricks were made absolutely square with flat, even faces.

The colour of the bricks was determined by the colour of the clay from which they were made, varying through yellow, brown, red, grey or even black. If this was thought to be a bit dull, lines of coloured clay cones were pressed into wet clay walls in patterns.

The bricks were stuck together with wet mud or bitumen, a tar-like substance which will not let water through. Bitumen occurs naturally in parts of the Middle East, oozing up from the ground.

In earliest times, the only buildings made of brick were public ones – temples, palaces, or granaries. The temple was a shrine to a local or more widely worshipped deity.

Quite often the people did not start a new temple elsewhere when their present one was destroyed or it wore out. They filled in the empty spaces with brick rubble or clay and then built a new temple on top of it. Thus as the years went by, the temple mound grew larger, taller, wider and longer with the remains of a dozen or perhaps even twenty earlier temples buried inside it.

Some of the largest of these are known as 'ziggurats'. They are faintly similar in size and shape to the pyramids of Egypt but were never used as burial places. Moreover, the wide, flat terraces were often planted with flowers, bushes and even trees. From this custom comes the story of one of the seven wonders of the world, 'The Hanging Gardens of Babylon'. It must have been very pleasant for the priests who served the god to be able to sit out in the shade of some large tree in a land famous for its searingly hot summers. It can't have been much fun for the gardeners, though. They had to haul up the water needed by the vegetation. It's surprising the vast number of gallons required each day by even a modest sized tree.

If a building isn't kept in good repair, it gradually crumbles. This true of almost any building, even stone ones, given enough time. For those made of mud brick, the process was quicker. Once the repairs stopped, the passing years saw the ziggurat collapse on itself like a weak blancmange or jelly. Weeds grew on the crumbling brick. What had been a proud temple now looked like a low hill standing in the desert.

The modern Arabs that live there call such a hill a 'tell'. It took a great deal of digging in the 19th century to prove that these hummocky tells were really the remains of a great civilisation.

Ziggurat in ruins at Uruk

Rebuilt ziggurat

CHAPTER 2

Gods and heroes

It is sometimes difficult to say who was a god and who was a hero in the Land of the Two Rivers. Because facts are rather scarce for the very early periods, a number of beings could have been either or even both at once.

The Sumerians had very many gods. Some, such as En-lil or Marduk, were worshipped, at one time or another, all over the area. Others were venerated in only one town or village – for example, the worshippers of Shara were to be found at Umma alone.

Every single place had its patron god, and there were heavenly beings who looked after all parts of

Gudea

The Goddess of Earth

earthly life. Ashnan was in charge of the barley fields, Shumu-qan looked after cattle, and the goddess Gula protected mothers-to-be.

The countrywide gods included An, chief of the gods, the moon god Nanna and his child, the sun god, Utu. There was Ninurta who protected warriors, Pasag, who did the same for travellers, Inanna, the goddess of love and Dumuzi, her husband. Enki was the god of life-giving waters.

It was thought that the land of Sumer belonged to the gods, and the priests carried out their wishes. Everyone was expected to sing hymns, say prayers, make sacrifices and bring offerings to the local temple. This might be a wayside shrine, an altar at the corner of a city street, or it could even be one of the gigantic ziggurats mentioned on the previous page.

Gods could be annoyed at what you did and punish you, or they could be pleased and reward you. There were so many of these heavenly beings that the average Sumerian's life was totally hedged about with religion – or perhaps we should call it superstition.

Once a year, particularly in later times at places such as the city of Babylon, the new year festival (called Akitu) was held. It celebrated the sacred marriage of the gods plus the anniversary, both of the creation of the world and also the present king's reign.

There were many creation myths. Some resembled those told in the Old Testament of the Bible. Perhaps the most striking resemblence between the religions of Sumer and that of the ancient Hebrews is the story of the heroic god-king, Gilgamesh.

Gilgamesh was the fifth king of Uruk, an early Sumerian city. Saddened by the death of a friend, he learned of a holy man named Ut-napishtim who, rumour had it, would never die. Gilgamesh resolved to find out his secret.

Gilgamesh is often described as a cross between Hercules and Ulysses, a bearded strong man, brave as a lion who would fight any man (or wild animal) and win.

After many adventures, Gilgamesh finally met Ut-napishtim and begged for his secret. The latter told him this story.

'Mankind had become so sinful, that the gods, especially En-lil, made up their minds to destroy human beings utterly, by means of a great flood. But Ea, one of the gods, secretly took pity on us. One night as I lay half awake, a voice spoke to me through the thin wall of my reed hut.

'The voice advised me to tear down the hut, forget my possessions and build a ship big enough to take not only me, my wife and family and all my workmen and their families but also examples of every living thing. I did all I was bidden. When I had finished the ship, I loaded it up with gold and silver and sat down to wait.

'It wasn't long before the clouds piled up in the sky and the first raindrops began to fall. The human beings and animals came aboard and I closed all the doors and windows. The worst storm ever known then broke and my ship was soon afloat. It rained as hard as you can imagine for six days and nights.

'On the seventh day the rain eased off, so I opened a window. We were alone on an empty sea but before long we settled gently on a half submerged rock. I found out later that it was the top of what had been Mount Nisir.

'I sent out a dove but she came back. A week later I sent out a swallow but she also returned. Another seven days passed before I released a raven which did not come back to us. This meant that the waters were going down, so we landed on the island mountain top and burned a sacrificial offering of sweet cane, myrtle and cedar.

'The gods smelled the smoke and came to look. En-lil was angry that he had been disobeyed and he blamed Ea for warning me. But Ea spoke so warmly of mankind that En-lil's heart was melted. He blessed me and gave my wife and me the gift of everlasting life.'

Then was Gilgamesh sad; for immortality was not a secret to be learned but a gift of the gods.

Houses and everyday life

At the dawn of Sumer's history, families moving to the south of the country often lived in houses made of bundles of reeds. Naturally, none of these has survived but we have a fair idea of what they looked like from clay tablet pictures and descriptions. Even today, some of the people who inhabit parts of the marshy south still live in similar huts. (see page 22).

Farther north on a tributary of the River Tigris, archaeologists have dug out a village called Jarmo. The houses there were made of rammed clay. Bricks had not been invented at that time, some eight or nine thousand years ago. Later on in Jarmo, stone foundations were laid before the walls were set up. Roofs were thatched with reeds and plastered with clay.

Each house had several rooms, none of which was more than about six feet in length. In some, a hole had been scooped out in the floor and lined with clay. These were the first direct evidence of a cooking device mentioned on page 27. The cook dropped hot stones into the hole after filling it with water, thus boiling whatever food was also put in.

Possibly only about 150 people lived there but Jarmo is one of the earliest villages known to be dependent on farming rather than hunting.

Jarmo

Among the crops they grew were kinds of wheat and barley, peas and lentils. The only farm animal was the goat: if the villagers wanted the meat of pigs, sheep or cattle, they still had to hunt them. It seems from the enormous number of snail shells that these creatures must have been on the menu too.

Even after the invention of writing some 5,000 years ago and the development of cities such as Ur, Eridu, Lagash and Uruk, the bulk of the population still earned their living from animal and crop farming. Barley, wheat and millet were staple crops, the grain being used for porridge, bread or beer. Peas and lentils were grown as were onions and garlic, leeks and melons, cucumbers and lettuce, watercress and spices. Sesame was planted for the oil it yielded – oil which must have been used for cooking and lighting.

Among the fruits the Sumerians enjoyed were apples, peaches, cherries, plums and (of course) the very useful date. Apart from bread, fruit, vegetables and some meat, Sumerians seem to have eaten a lot of cheese. In addition, the rivers and sea abounded with fish and there were always birds such as ducks and geese to be snared.

About 4,000 years ago, the houses took on a pattern that was to survive in the Middle East right to the present day. Let us visit the ancient town of Ur in 2,000 B.C., probably at the same time and place that Abraham was born. Here is a man named Ruk-shin who will take us to see what his house is like.

He beckons us away from the granaries, huge temples and public buildings to a narrow street running southward. In fact, all the streets are narrow – so much so that carts could not get through them. Even a laden donkey would cause us to press ourselves against the windowless walls.

'Just along here,' our guide says, 'I must go to the market to buy a jug for my wife.' We walk down another narrow street which widens out into a small square. The shops are mostly one, two or three roomed buildings with storerooms or workplaces at the back. On the street side goods are spread out for sale on stalls both inside and outside the shop. Awnings of woven reeds give welcome shade to most of the businesses.

Street scene

Cooking

A colourful scene meets our eyes in the square. Amid the salesmen crying their wares of food, clothes, spices, and earthenware there are street musicians, entertainers, jugglers and acrobats. There are pedlars, water sellers, writers of letters for those who can't do it for themselves – and even a story teller with a small audience hanging on his every word.

Ruk-shin has got his jug and leads us on to his house. 'In here,' he says, opening a small wooden door for us. We step through and immediately notice how much cooler it is in the interior courtyard. We wash the street dust off of our feet and pour the water away down a central drain which also helps carry flood water away when the river rises. Ruk-shin made sure that the lower brick courses of his house were kiln fired and thus waterproofed. Higher up where the floods cannot reach, sun-dried bricks will do.

The lime-washed walls rise to a narrow gallery supported on wooden beams. This divides the house in two – the upper part for the family's private rooms and the lower for the kitchen, work and storerooms and the room for entertaining guests. This latter is a long, narrow room with seating all the way round three sides. It is very like what is seen in a modern Arab house. There are a couple of small tables and many cushions and rugs.

Also on the ground floor is a courtyard partly roofed over. Here are Ruk-shin's household gods. The statuettes in the little chapel are the family's 'guardian angels'. The chapel is not only a place of worship, it is a burial vault too. There is a tomb below the brick floor where Ruk-shin's dead ancestors lie. Many years before, the dead had been buried in separate cemeteries, well away from town but this is no longer the custom and the ancestors are nearby where the family can pray to them and involve them in the life of Ruk-shin and his relations.

We say goodbye to our guide at his door and make our way down the street. We notice that although most of the houses seem to show a modest prosperity, there are poor families living in half ruined houses, or even in lean-to shacks.

Conquerors and kings

Babylonian soldier

Sargon's head

Here's a soldier we can ask about the great rulers in his part of Mesopotamia. He agrees to talk to us but has never heard the word 'Mesopotamia'. We have to explain that although we call the area 'Iraq', the earlier name comes from Greek words meaning 'Middle of the Rivers'. The name isn't earlier to the soldier: it is Greek and he has never heard of the Greeks or their language. For him they don't yet exist and his description of the valleys of the Tigris and Euphrates are the words 'Sumer' for the south and 'Akkad' for the central region.

By our reckoning it is 1740 B.C. but of course our soldier hasn't heard of Christ either so he calls the year the 52nd of the reign of Hammurabi.

'Who was the greatest conqueror?' we ask.

'I suppose that must be Hammurabi, our present king. Mind you, the first great conqueror in the world ruled in Akkad more than 500 years ago.'

'Who was that?'

'He was called Sargon. No one knows much about his early life. We think he was the son of a shepherd up river – near where the tributary Khabur joins the Euphrates. He got a job in the local king's palace and rose to be cup bearer to the king of Kish. What happened next is a mystery: the next thing we know is that he's become king himself.

'Shortly after that, he reorganised the army. Before his time, a king had only a few full time soldiers but Sargon reckoned to be able to muster 5,000 fully armed professional fighting men whenever he wanted to. When he planned an attack on a neighbouring kingdom, he made army service compulsory for hundreds of thousands of young men.

'A king's normal bodyguard had uniform helmets and spears and attacked behind lines of shields. In fact the whole army had tended to advance in that sort of formation. A phalanx, they called it.

'Sargon made many alterations to battle tactics. He broke up the phalanx and armed the infantry with bows and battle axes. Then he had some battle wagons made – little four wheeled carts drawn by four onagers, or wild asses. Each one had a driver and a warrior wielding a battle axe and hurling spears from a large sheaf. They were neither manoeuvrable nor fast enough to deserve the name 'chariot' but they were good for medium and close range fighting.

'Sargon used his new army to carve out a larger kingdom for himself by conquering neighbouring kings. Then he moved south and struck at the Sumerian cities of the plains. When he captured Uruk he had the walls smashed and took its king, Lugalzagesi a prisoner in chains. Then he attacked north westward towards the Great Sea* and the mountains of Lebanon and Turkey.

'Eastward, he beat the Elamites and the men of Assur—'

'I think we call that Assyria.'

'He forced open trade routes to every nation round about and even down to the coast of Africa. It's said he carried out his conquests because of a need to get stone, gold, silver, copper, tin and even timber but that's only half the story. I believe he conquered because he was made that way – some men are.

'He reigned 56 years and boasted that his empire would last for a thousand. But his descendants let it fall to pieces and the last of his line died out less than two centuries later.'

'What about Hammurabi?

'Our present king? Oh, yes, there's a lot of similarities between Sargon and him. He didn't come from a humble family of course – his father was already king of Babylon. Our city wasn't as big, as important or as beautiful as it is now: after all, his kingdom was only a strip of land about 40 miles up river and the same distance down, with a width of no more than 20 miles. All around us were larger and more powerful kingdoms.

'Hammurabi prepared the army for five years before trying his strength. Then he struck in three directions at once – up river, down river and eastward across the Tigris towards the mountains.

'All was successful and the next twenty years were spent in making an empire out of his conquests. But in the 29th year of his reign, we were attacked by a huge army made up of most of the enemies we had fought against. Praise to the Gods! We won an enormous victory. The following year, the priests who told fortunes from the livers of animals told him that the signs were favourable, so we attacked – again in all directions. Again we were successful and by about 14 years ago, we Babylonians owned the whole area from the gulf up to Assyria. Now Hammurabi can call himself "King of the four quarters of the world."'

*The Mediterranean

Battle scene

Law givers

The stele of Hammurabi from the Louvre, Paris

Our soldier is still willing to talk to us about Babylon so we ask about the system of laws his king has set down. 'Come with me,' he says and we walk some distance until we come into the courtyard of a temple where there is a round stone pillar, or stele, about eight feet high. It is covered with hundreds of lines of Babylonian writing, or cuneiform, and has a picture carved in the stone of Hammurabi praying to Marduk, the chief god and god of the sun and of justice.

'You see,' says our informant, 'you know now what a great military man Hammurabi is. What you don't know is what a good king he is too. He runs the empire

very well and has made our city of Babylon stronger and more beautiful than it has ever been.

'He has also set out the laws which we must all obey. They were written on clay tablets at first. Now they are carved into pillars of black stone and are set up in temple courtyards for everyone to see all over the land.'

'But can everyone read these laws?'

'No, they cannot. I can't read myself but I have been told what they are.'

'Could you tell us, then? We can't read Babylonian either.'

'Certainly. As much as I can remember. To start with, you've seen this picture of our king? Underneath that, there are a few sentences about who he is, what the laws are and how everyone must obey them. Then it explains how justice must be done. You know, punishment for someone telling lies at a trial, or the throwing out of a judge proved to have taken a bribe.

'You realise that all these laws haven't been invented by Hammurabi? Many are what you would call common law – that is to say, a law may be written down but it's only something that has always been done, written or not. In any case, Hammurabi wasn't the first ruler to lay out a complete set of laws; other kings have done the same thing, I'm told – for example, Ur-nammu, ruler of Sumer and Akkad nearly four centuries ago. Then there was Lipit-Ishtar, who lived about two hundred years ago – and many others.

'There are 282 laws all told. The biggest section deals with family problems – you know, marriage and the duties of husbands and wives, desertion, adoption, inheritance, divorce and so on.

'The next group is to do with land. That is to say, laws dealing with trespass, rent, land use and the rights and responsibilities of landlords and tenants.

'The third group is about business and trade – matters such as what people owe, what to do with someone who runs off with something they've been trusted with, rates of interest and things like that.

'Then there's the criminal law – how to keep crime down, punishments for theft, robbery and attacks on the person.'

'Ah! "muggings"! So you have them too?'

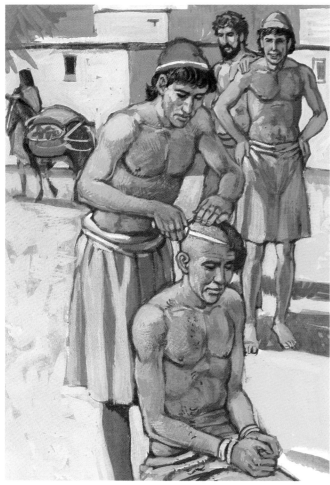

'I don't know if you'd include this in the list of mutilations but if you tell lies about someone's wife you could have half your hair cut off.'

'You must be joking!'

'I'm a soldier. I wouldn't joke about things like that. In fact there are other laws that probably sound just as strange to you. If it can be proved that you've hit your elder brother, disowned your parents, or kicked your mother, you can be made a slave.

'Mind you, not all the laws are like this: there are rules about business, lots of them – you know, rates of pay, the rate for hiring a cart or a boat and all sorts of other everyday things.'

'A great man, your Hammurabi.'

'Well, we think so.'

Hammurabi

'Of course we do. And the single biggest change the king has brought in here is the severer penalties for this kind of crime. In the old days, most gentlemen could settle a matter like this by paying a fine. Well, we've still got fines but there are all sorts of punishments nowadays. The death penalty operates for housebreaking, being a brigand or a witch, kidnapping, receiving stolen property and even telling lies in some kinds of court cases.'

'How are death sentences carried out?'

'Oh, they might be tied up and thrown in the river, or killed with a sharp implement, or even burned.'

'That sounds pretty horrible.'

'Some might say it was better to be dead than mutilated.'

'Mutilated?'

'Oh, yes. If you put someone's eye out, you get your own eye put out. If you break someone's arm or leg, the same thing happens to you. Actually this could happen even if you meant no harm. For instance, if you were a doctor and you operated on someone carelessly and they lost an eye or a limb – well you know what would happen: you could lose your own eye or have a hand cut off.

The royal tombs at Ur

Archaeologists learn a lot from ancient graves, particularly when it was thought a dead person would need his earthly possessions in the afterlife and they were buried with him. For this reason, Sir Leonard Woolley was delighted to have come across what have come to be known as 'The Royal Tombs at Ur'. Ur, you may remember was the birth-place of Abraham.

From 1926 onward Sir Leonard dug a number of two month seasons, during which he turned up some 450 graves. One has become famous as 'The Death Pit of Ur', a description given it by Woolley himself.

When the earth had been carefully removed from the large, oblong hole, a gruesome sight was revealed. One corner of the grave had a sizable limestone-walled tomb built into it but on the floor of the pit were 74 human skeletons. Some of them had jewellery scattered about the bones – for example, silver and gold hair ribbons and many semi-precious stones.

There were other interesting finds, including the remains of what turned out to be harps and a statue of a ram caught in a thicket, reminiscent of the Bible story about Abraham and Isaac.

To begin with, the archaeologists were puzzled. It wasn't easy to reconstruct the events leading up to the funeral just from the remains of bodies and objects which had lain underground for well over 4,000 years. Sir Leonard Woolley himself gave this version of what might have happened.

'The royal funeral in the limestone tomb was completed when the workmen filled in the doorway with bricks and stone and added a top coat of plaster.

'In the opposite corner of the pit, an earth ramp leads down from the ground surface. Moving slowly downwards, a solemn procession walks along the ramp, lower and lower into the grave. These are the human sacrifices – members of the royal court, both men and women – servants, courtiers, soldiers and grooms. Each one is dressed in his or her best garments, the women with headdresses of precious metal foil, plus carnelian and lapis lazuli jewels. One woman must have overslept and is a little late for the ceremony, for at her side (possibly in a long rotted pocket) was a roll of silver foil which ought to have been in her hair. (When *we* say 'silver foil' we mean a thin sheet of silver coloured metal of a cheap kind: in the death pit it was real silver).

'Then come the musicians with their harps and cymbals followed by the ass- and ox-drawn chariots, the animals being led by the grooms of the royal stables. All of them take up their proper places on the floor of the tomb and a guard of soldiers forms up at the entrance.

'As the mournful music of the harpists sounds through the grave, each man and woman fills a little stone or metal cup he or she has brought, from a bowl of liquid in the centre of the grave bottom. This is a container of poison.

'Then everyone lies down and readies themselves for death.

'Probably the animals were then slaughtered and the earth shovelled into the hole until it was level ground once more. It's quite likely that the place was marked by the setting up of a small memorial chapel at the very top.

'It's strange to find so many human sacrifices. Although the practice isn't unknown from elsewhere, it is pretty rare.'

Cylinder seal and impression

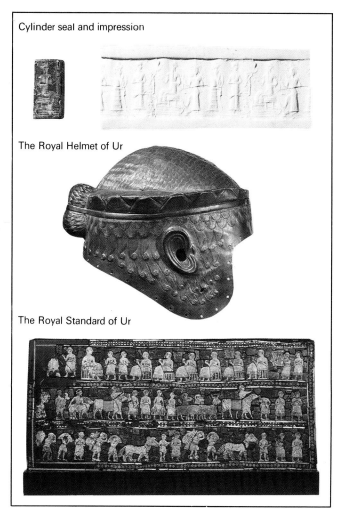

The Royal Helmet of Ur

The Royal Standard of Ur

Woolley found all sorts of interesting things in other graves, for example, some beautifully fluted gold beakers, helmets, swords and daggers, necklaces and headdresses. A number of cylinder seals have also come to light but in spite of the vast number of graves, the names of only four rulers have been identified – two kings and two queens.

The body of a prince, Mes-kalam-shar was found with his head in a helmet of high quality gold. The helmet had once contained a padded cap held in place by means of a lace passed through small holes in the rim. The skull was well enough preserved to show that the prince had been left handed.

The picture above is often known as a 'royal standard' and shows the king at a civilian banquet. A second panel shows him among his soldiers on the right, accompanied by chariots with solid wheels drawn by asses. The standard is made of lapis lazuli and mother of pearl embedded in asphalt on a wooden base. Archaeologists call it a 'standard' but no one really knows what it is. However, it does give us a useful insight into the life of a king of Ur, possibly 5,000 years ago.

Babylon

The Land Of the two Rivers had been first settled in a civilised way far to the south of the region – in an area called Sumer. This had been overrun by the Akkadians, their neighbours to the north west. Then Babylon rose supreme over all other cities, particularly under Hammurabi. After his time a new power appeared – again to the northwest and up river from the Persian Gulf. This new power was based on the city of Assur.

The inhabitants of Assur are known to us as Assyrians. The Assyrians carved out an empire including Babylon. Their might lasted for centuries but had waned by about 600 B.C.

Once again Babylon became a great and powerful city. Under its kings, Nabopalassar (626–605 B.C.) and his son, the better known Nebuchadrezzar (604–561 B.C.), Babylon was to reach its greatest glory and to become for the last time, 'the mistress of the world'. The whole region came to be called 'Babylonia'.

41

Science in Babylon

If you grow vegetables in your garden, how do you know when to plant the seeds? 'That's easy,' you say, 'just look on the packet.' But suppose there are no packets and that the only food you are going to eat is that which you've grown yourself. It comes down to knowing when the seasons start and finish and to the exact length of the year. On p. 21 we saw how ancient peoples worked out an answer to the question, 'How long is a year?'

If you live in a sunny country as they did you could put a stick in the ground and measure its shadow several times every day until you get the shortest measurement of all. This will be at twelve noon on midsummer day. Then you can count the days until the shadow is as short as that again.

The Babylonians found that their first count, although not very accurate, was a very handy number.

The figure was 360 which will divide exactly by 2, 3, 4, 5, 6, 8, 9, 10, 12, 15, 18, 20, 24, 30, 36, 40, 45, 60, 72, 90, 120 and 180. How convenient this was for anyone trying to design a calendar and what a wide choice of unit time lengths. Why do we have twelve months in the year or seven days in the week? Why 60 seconds in the minute and the same number of minutes in an hour? Why, for that matter, are there 360 degrees in a circle? No one knows the answer to these questions – all we are sure of is that the wise men of the twin valleys first decided these matters.

Of course, all this was very fine until someone spoilt things by discovering that there weren't in fact 360 days in the year. It didn't take long in Babylonia to see what was wrong: if you based your farming life on a calendar of twelve thirty-day months, you'd be five days out at the return of the next midsummer and in less than 40 years, you'd be celebrating the longest summer day on the shortest winter one!

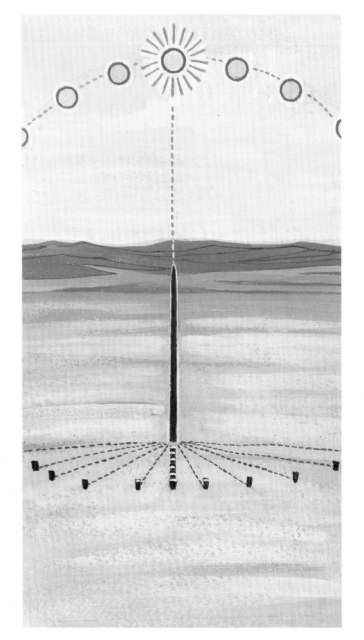

Finding noon on Midsummer Day

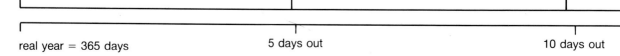

Babylonian year
Real year

(5 years Babylonian time scale) = 360 days

real year = 365 days   5 days out   10 days out

It says a great deal for the wise men that they eventually got it about right. They studied more than the movements of the earth round the sun. They also kept records of the moon's phases so carefully over many years that they were able to predict eclipses.

The fact that they were good at astronomy is even more remarkable because there were no telescopes in those days. All their observations were made with no artificial aids at all. Their best chance was to go to the top terraces of the local ziggurat and stare up at the night sky.

In this way they were able to group the stars in what to them were recognizable pictures of people, things and animals. These constellations, as they are called, formed a zodiac, or complete band round the heavens.

The wise men then attempted to predict the future from the movements of the heavenly bodies. They identified Mars, which they called Nergal, after their god of the lower world. The war god, Ninurta was what we know as Saturn. They also understood the apparent movements of Mercury, Venus and Jupiter, which were named respectively, Nabû, Ishtar and Marduk.

Science, religion and superstition went hand in hand. Observations of the stars and planets were good and accurate. Less scientific were their attempts to tell fortunes from their movement. Even more questionable, though just as popular, was the casting of horoscopes from the livers of animals.

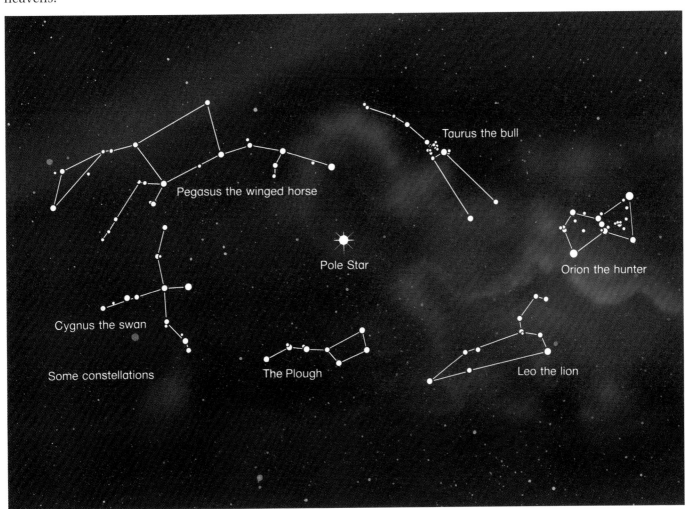

How some modern astrologers imagine the constellations

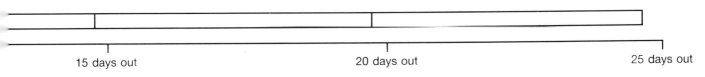

15 days out   20 days out   25 days out

Reading the wedge-shaped writing

We saw on pp. 26–27 a little of how ancient Mesopotamian languages were set down in clay tablets. What we didn't find out is how people of our own time can read what was written over 5,000 years ago.

At some time in the past, the knowledge of reading and writing these ancient languages was lost. This was why, when travellers from the middle ages onward brought back stories of ruins and inscriptions from Mesopotamia, the little wedge signs were often dismissed as mere decoration. It wasn't until after 1700 that a few Europeans began to suspect that they were, in fact, some unknown language.

The men who became interested were German, English, French and Danish. Carsten Niebuhr, an engineer officer in the Danish army, copied Persian inscriptions and published them in 1765. He was the first person to decide (correctly) that they should be read from left to right and that there was more than one script involved.

Friedrich Münter, another Dane, noticed that one group of signs:

Sumerian clay tablet

kept on turning up and he assumed it probably stood for 'king'. Georg Grotefend, a German, agreed and added another group which frequently went with the first one. This, he guessed meant 'son of'. With 'king' and 'son of the king', it became possible to say that the groups following stood for names. In this way, he managed to decipher 'Darius' and his son 'Xerxes', the names of two Persian kings, familiar to us from the pages of Greek history.

This was the only success he had and it was left to others to increase the number of signs that could be read – partly from the lists of conquered nations which also appeared in the inscriptions.

The most adventurous of the decoders was an Englishman named Henry Rawlinson. He learned Latin and Greek at school and added Arabic, Persian and Hindustani later. As an employee of the East India Company he was sent to Persia where he became very interested in the carved wedges. He was told of a large inscription some twenty miles away at Behistun.

Rawlinson

Unfortunately, the carvings were 300 feet up a sheer cliff. To get close, Rawlinson had to climb down a rope or be lowered in a kind of bosun's chair. He had a ladder lowered but the ledge it was to stand on was so narrow, he couldn't set it at a safe angle. Nothing daunted he climbed it and balanced on the top rung, at the same time copying the carved marks.

At one point he tried to cross to another part of the monument and the only way he could bridge the chasm was by wedging his ladder over the gap thus:

Halfway across, he suddenly felt the lower upright and half the rungs fall away from under his feet and he had to scramble back to safety, but he managed to record two of the inscriptions entirely. The third, apparently in old Babylonian, seemed to be totally out of reach. Then a young Kurdish boy volunteered to swarm upwards and sideways over a rockface which seemed to have neither foot nor fingerhold.

Now owning copies of all the writings, Rawlinson quickly made out the names of Persian kings and also some syllable signs from the names of Persia's enemies. Finally he was able to read, 'I am Darius, the great king, king of kings, king of Persia—' etc. Then follows his ancestry and an account of those of his forbears. At the end is carved, 'You who pass by in the future will see this inscription which I ordered to be made. Leave my monument as it is: destroy nothing: efface nothing. As long as Man shall last on earth, keep it intact.'

That was in old Persian but the Babylonian part was not nearly so easy. To start with, there were far too many different signs for it to be in an alphabet. The royal names could be identified and some sounds obtained but at that point (for the time being) Rawlinson could get no further. Then in 1850, the Rev. Hincks discovered that a single sign could be pronounced in perhaps half a dozen ways. Furthermore, it could stand for a word, a part of a word or even act as a pointer to show what kind of a word was coming next.

If we had the same thing in English, for example, we might draw ⬭ for the word 'mat', or we could use it with other signs to make words such as 'material', 'mathematics', 'automatic', which have nothing to do with the original meaning. On top of this, the sign would also appear in front of every word which belonged to the same class, for example, carpet, floor, wood blocks, concrete, lino, tiles and so on.

It made things very difficult, but gradually, the stone carvings and clay tablets gave up their secrets and we can now read most of anything written in the many languages of the Land of the Two Rivers.

45

Chapter 3   Egypt

Before the pyramids

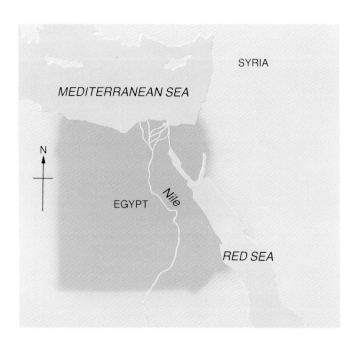

Experts on ancient Egypt are known as Egyptologists. Let's ask one of them to tell us what the land was like before the pharaohs appeared on the scene.

'It's very difficult,' he begins, 'to say anything very definite – for all sorts of reasons. You see, we're talking about a period before writing was invented, so everything has to be found out from whatever the people left behind them.

'There's even a snag to digging up Egypt's long gone past. Lower or northern Egypt around the Nile Delta was where many prehistoric peoples lived. The trouble is that farming, flooding, irrigation and the buildings of later inhabitants have destroyed the traces of the earliest tribes. The only thing to do is to dig at sites a long way up the river where remains haven't been obliterated. Then we can use what we find to make guesses about the rest of the country.'

'What were those early tribes called?'

'I'm afraid I don't know. I can't see any way that we'll ever know. Remember that there was no writing then. All we can do is to label the various peoples with the names of the places where their remains were first found. For example, the Tasians from Deir Tasa, or the Badarians from El Badari.

'The various groups most likely came from outside Egypt, attracted no doubt by the rich farmlands of the valley. There are of course some even earlier peoples but of these there are only skimpy remains plus a few skeletons. Some years ago an old stone age cemetery was unearthed about 150 miles north of the Aswan dam. There were nearly sixty men, women and children and a good half of them had died by violence. but as I say we know little or nothing of their lives, which probably came to an end some 12,000 years ago. Strangely enough, we have sickles and grinders showing Man as a farmer which are at least 3,000 years older than that.

'Perhaps it was wild grain that attracted people to the valley in the first place. We know that Man reaped natural seeds long before he hit on the idea of growing them deliberately. There must have been more vegetation in those days – the valley was wetter and there were many small feeder streams. Today they are just wadis – dry water courses.

'We think that the tribes who lived there found that they could grow more food than they could eat. This led to a big increase in population and then once more there were shortages. More land had to be put under the plough. The ancient Egyptians began to drain marshes and bring life giving water to dry areas.

'The ditch could serve both purposes. In wet regions, water would seep out of the surrounding earth into the furrow. The latter could also lead water from the river to the parched fields. It could be used both for drainage and irrigation.

'At a time just before Egypt became a kingdom, the farmers had tamed the goat, sheep, pig and cow. They grew their food, raised their animals and lived in little round reed huts. They had clay pottery and from the pictures they painted on it we know what they looked like.

'They were slimly built people, of medium height with brown skins and black or dark brown wavy hair. They mostly wore kilts of animal hides, although they did sometimes weave clothing from linen thread. They could make baskets and knew how to store their extra food in mat-lined grain pits. They wore beads and bracelets made of ivory and sea shells. They even painted their eyelids with green paint – whether for beauty's sake or to protect their sight from the sun, we don't know.'

'You said something about Egypt becoming a kingdom.'

'Yes. All the extensive irrigation and drainage work meant lots of people working but not growing food. There had to be someone to run things and that's when overseers and local headmen arose. Gradually more and more small areas joined together. It must have been an advantage for the areas which combined. It's not just a question of being able to do a common task quicker or better. I'm sure you can imagine circumstances where a certain piece of work could be done by a whole population but not at all by one person. Think of dragging a hundred ton stone to strengthen a river bank, for example.

'Anyway, the process went on and on, until about 3,200 B.C., the whole valley, both Upper and Lower Egypt, was united by a man called variously Narmer, or Menes. He was the first pharaoh.'

Menes (Narmer) palette from Hierakonpolis

Pre-pyramid Egyptian village

47

The discovery of metal

At the time when Menes was becoming the first pharaoh of the first dynasty, or family, many Egyptians were still using stone tools and implements. Many, but not all. For some time before this, unknown people had discovered the first metal.

This was copper. There were at that time places where lumps of it could be picked up. You may imagine a stone age man trying to strike flakes off it as he could do with a nodule of flint. The copper merely took a dent. It wasn't long before Man learnt how to hammer out his copper lump to form rings, pins and bracelets. Then he discovered the art of making edged tools such as axes, knives and daggers.

These discoveries were not necessarily made in Egypt at all and in any case there wasn't a great deal of metallic copper lying about, so it was a lucky day when someone hit on a method of making metal from a copper ore. This is copper combined with some other mineral, for example, oxygen, sulphur or carbon.

The coppersmith had to heat lumps of the ore in heat-resistant pots over an extremely hot fire. An ordinary bonfire isn't really hot enough so a charcoal oven was probably used and its temperature raised with bellows. If you can shoot a jet of fresh oxygen-laden air into your fire, it glows brighter and reaches a higher temperature.

Early bronze objects

The Egyptians used a kind of foot bellows, consisting of a pair of animal-skin bags whose mouths led into pottery funnels. These conducted air to the fire. The smith's assistant stood with a foot on each bag. There might be as many as four helpers doing the same thing. A helper lifted one foot and at the same time pulled up the middle of the bag with a leather thong. Then he pushed his foot down to blow air into the tube, at the same time lifting his other leg – a sort of marking time.

The copper ore in the pot melted and the metal could be poured out like a liquid. The smith then treated the solidified puddle in the same way as he dealt with natural metal lumps.

Then someone thought it would save time if the molten metal could be poured straight into a shape, made perhaps from stone or clay. A lump of limestone with hollows scraped out could produce, say, several knife blades at one melting. From there it was a short step to an upright mould with its top end open. This could be used for a variety of more complicated shapes.

The search for copper ores went on. As soon as they were found, methods discovered from flint mining were put into operation. More often than not, the ores were not pure, having various minerals mixed with them – tin, antimony or arsenic were among these impurities. When they were present and became part of the smelting process, a new metal was produced. We call it bronze.

It was a little harder than copper or tin on their own but it flowed more easily into the moulds. The bronze-smith, as we must now call him, began to mix the two ores deliberately, altering the amounts of each that were used until he got the metal he wanted. There was very little tin in Egypt, so it either had to be bought abroad, or the Egyptians had to do without, using arsenic instead.

One metal that was plentiful in Egypt was gold. Prospectors panned for it in river gravels and eventually it was dug from underground mines.

Surprisingly, iron was also known in the Nile valley – and from a time almost as early as copper, bronze or gold. It wasn't mined though – it occurred as lumps of meteorite which had crashed from outer space and there wasn't much of it.

One trouble was that although copper melts at just over 1,000° centigrade, iron won't do so until it's half as hot again. Early Man couldn't produce temperatures like these and it wasn't in fact until the later middle ages that furnaces were made to generate so much heat.

All the Eygptian craftsman could do if he got the rare chance to work on a chunk of heavenly iron was to heat it as much as possible and then hammer out the impurities. Amid showers of sparks, repeated blows gradually turned the iron ore into a metal. Bronze remained the most important metal for the next two thousand years.

Building temples and pyramids

If there is one thing that seems like a trade mark to the modern Egyptian tourist it is the pyramid. Pyramids have filled travellers with wonder from the earliest times. They seem such a colossal waste of time, energy and wealth. Where did the riches to pay for them come from? We've already seen how peasants in the valley could easily grow three times as much food as they needed. The surplus could be traded abroad for the things Egypt lacked but there was still a lot left over. it was this extra wealth that fed the armies of non-farmers who were used to carry out all kinds of grand schemes.

Menes and the pharaohs who followed him were able to spend this wealth as they wished. However, it was four centuries after the reign of Menes before the first pyramid was built.

For many years the cult of the dead had been growing. Egyptians firmly believed in an after life, particularly for their dead king who was expected to plead to the gods for the well-being of his people. Gods, naturally, they thought, would pay little heed to a man with few possessions and would only deal with someone of their own social class. So the custom arose of burying the dead ruler with all his favourite treasures.

In earlier times, the dead (even common people) were buried in the ground; sometimes flat stones were set around the body and on top of it to prevent it being dug up by wild animals. This developed into a low rectangular stone building called a mastaba.

These got larger and more elaborate as the years went by until in the reign of the pharaoh Djoser (about 2750 B.C.) the first pyramid was built. It was designed as the king's tomb by one of ancient Egypt's most outstanding men, the minister of state, Imhotep.

Imhotep, had many talents: as well as being in charge of the court's religion, he was also an author, a wise man, an astronomer, a doctor and above all, a very great architect.

It may not be so, but it seems as though Imhotep had laid out an enormous mastaba and had then placed a slightly smaller one on top. He was to do this a further three times, finally winding up with a wonder of the age, over 200 feet high. Inside the pyramid was a maze of corridors joining rooms and the whole building was surrounded by a wall about ten metres high and almost two kilometres long.

Djoser

Imhotep

A step pyramid

The pyramid of Cheops

From then on, most pharaohs and many other important persons had pyramids built to house their dead bodies and as rich a selection of precious goods as could be afforded. Probably the most important pyramid was that of the pharaoh Cheops. It was built about 2650 B.C. and is the largest of all – in fact, almost certainly the biggest single building in the world, if one excepts the Great Wall of China.

Its size is really remarkable. Each of its four sides measures 750 feet and its height is a mighty 474 feet. Do you know what this is?

Yes, you've guessed – it's a map showing 8 football pitches side by side. This huge area would be only just large enough to take the base of the Great Pyramid.

The stone with which this enormous tomb is constructed was quarried on the spot but the shining white limestone cladding was ferried across the river. All told, more than two million blocks were cut and moved. The largest stones weighed about 15 tonnes, although the average was only two tonnes. If you were to cut up each stone into rods three inches square and put them end to end, there would be enough of them to reach from the earth to the moon!

No one knows what kinds nor how many men worked on the Great Pyramid. In ancient times, Greek visitors were told that it had taken 100,000 slaves ten years but this is probably an exaggeration – it's likely that there were few slaves among the work force.

Another mystery is the method they used to haul the massive stones into position. We think that they were split in the quarry, roughly squared and then pulled away on sledges or wooden rollers.

The first layer was positioned from the centre outwards until the marked out square was full, making allowance of course for all the galleries, stairs, passages and tomb chambers. Then a ramp of stones, clay, mud bricks and sand was led to the top of the first course of blocks, up which the stones for the second course were hauled. As each layer was put in place, the ramp was lengthened and made higher. Some authorities say that the ramp may have wound round the half finished building. The last few stones were set in position and the outer skin of dazzling white limestone was added.

Some of Egypt's most striking temples were also built with the aid of ramps. An oblong of bedrock was cleared and levelled before the position of the columns was marked. These were prefabricated in drum-shaped pieces. The first drums were manoeuvered into line and the spaces between and all round them filled in with hard-packed sand and dirt. Then ramps were made and the next layer of stone column drums moved in. When the pillars were complete they were joined at the top with spans of roofing stone. When all was over, the packing earth and ramps were dug away.

The inside of a pyramid, showing internal passages, staircases and burial room

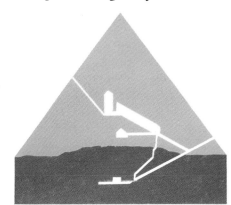

CHAPTER 3

The oldest ship in the world

Have you ever noticed the rather pleasant smell that comes from a newly sharpened pencil? If you have, the pencil was probably made from a cedar tree. How long do you think the wood might go on pouring out this scent – a week, a month, a year? Kamal el-Mallakh from the Egyptian Antiquities Service could still detect the special cedar smell from timber which had been buried for forty-five centuries.

How did this come about? Shortly after the end of the Second World War, the Egyptian government decided to tidy up some of the pyramids near Cairo.

At Giza, just across the Nile from Egypt's capital, stands a group of pyramids among which is that of Cheops, the largest of them all. Archaeologists working on nearby tombs had dumped unwanted soil at the base of the Great Pyramid.

The workmen slowly cleared the dirt and sand from the north, east and west sides without finding anything exciting. Then they began to shift the spoil from the south side. Although the heap was 65 feet high, they couldn't just bulldoze it away for fear of destroying something of interest.

However, nothing turned up and they finally came to a line of smooth limestone slabs almost 15 feet wide and nearly two feet thick. One stone stood up slightly higher than the others and Mallakh recognised the hieroglyphic: ⬚ It read 'Djedefre'. He knew that this king was the son of Cheops and suspected that these stones might cover a boat pit. Several of these were already known but all that had ever been found in them were a few scraps of wood and some decayed strands of rope to show that there had once been a vessel buried there.

At about midday on the 26th May 1954, the workmen managed to finish chipping a hole through the stones. The sun was so hot and bright that Mallakh could see nothing but blackness, so he used a small mirror to reflect sunlight into the pit and peered down. Was it a boat? He held his breath. The beam caught and held the sight he had hardly dared hope for – the blade of a long rowing oar. It was then that Mallakh became aware of the faint but unmistakable scent of cedar wood.

A piece of the planking was taken to the British Museum chemical laboratories and proved to be not

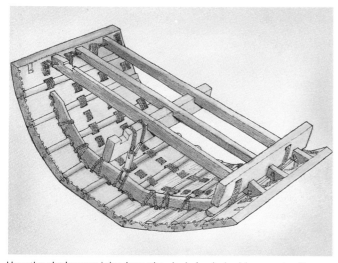

How the planks were joined together, by being lashed (or sewn) with rope

The burial ship in pieces, as it was found

only cedar wood of the right age but surprisingly well preserved. The sealing of the pit with stones and wet mortar had prevented the timber from drying out and turning to dust.

A shed was built over the boat grave and the stones removed by cranes. This took two months.

Hadj Ahmed Youssef Moustafa, in charge of the restoration, faced many problems. The ship was in pieces and had to be assembled like a 3D jigsaw puzzle. Each piece had to be drawn and photographed before it was moved and treated with chemicals to prevent decay. There was, of course, no picture or instruction booklet to help him, so Moustafa had scale models made of each piece – all 1224 of them. The planking turned out to be 'sewn' together with rope, of which there were great lengths. The rope went into a hole on the wide part of the plank and out through the edge, so that no rope could be seen on the outside.

A special museum was built on the site and Moustafa made five different reconstructions before he was satisfied. The finished vessel is over 142 feet long, nearly 20 feet across as its widest part and would displace about 45 tonnes. From beginning to end, the project took fourteen years.

The royal ship of Cheops was probably used to take his body from Memphis to Giza. Although there were five pairs of oars between 20 and 30 feet long, it is quite likely that the vessel was towed down the River Nile before being taken to pieces and buried.

It remains to this day the oldest, largest and best preserved vessel from the ancient world.

Cleopatra's needle

Most people have seen or at least heard of Cleopatra's needle on London's Victoria Embankment, alongside the River Thames. The word 'needle' may give you the wrong idea if you've never even seen a photograph of it. Another word is 'obelisk' and this means a tall column whose four sides gradually taper to the top where a small pyramid finishes it off. The Egyptians put up many of these columns – as signs, memorials or monuments.

If 'needle' is not too happy a word, then 'Cleopatra' is even more ill-chosen. The Thameside column has little, if anything, to do with the famous queen. It was, in fact, erected on the orders of Thotmes III* many centuries before Cleopatra's time. Originally at Heliopolis, it was moved to Alexandria during the reign of the Roman emperor, Augustus. The move occurred at about 12 B.C., when the obelisk was already almost fifteen centuries old.

Cleopatra's needle, London

In 1819 A.D., the Viceroy of Egypt presented the thing to the British people. A special vessel to contain it was built. After a series of misfortunes, including its near loss crossing the Bay of Biscay in a storm, it finally arrived on the Thames. It was not set up in its present position until 1878. Under the base, the Victorians buried a British railway timetable, a copy of *The Times* and some current coins.

The 'needle' is covered with carved Egyptian writing as are the other obelisks in Rome, Paris, Istanbul and New York. The American one is the twin of ours but the others are from different places and of different ages. The Romans began the custom by taking several obelisks back home with them – just like tourists collecting souvenirs. Of course, they had the same problem as the original owners whenever they wanted to set one up again. At least the Victorian British had steam engines to help them – but how did the Pharaoh's men manage? Let's ask one.

'I wouldn't say it was easy but there aren't any really unsolvable problems. To start with, you need very many people to help – sometimes only a handful of men, sometimes thousands.

*Thotmes is only one of several English versions of the name: others include: Thotmose, Thothmes; Tutmose, Tuthmosis, Tutmoss, etc.

'Only the best stone will do. We get much of ours from Syene. It is a hard, pink granite. We make sure that the piece we are going to work on is free from flaws or cracks. We wash it down thoroughly and then inspect it. It's easier to break out if it's on the edge of a low lip of rock in the quarry. The shape is outlined with paint made of animal fat and ground charcoal. Then metal chisels make holes along a line. When the holes are deep enough, large wooden wedges are driven in and surrounded by low clay walls. Water is poured in, the wood swells and, if we are lucky, the stone splits along the line we want and we can topple it sideways onto rollers. It's much harder if we have to dig all the way down through solid granite with chisels and stone hammers – a long and tiring job.

'At last the obelisk is free and ready to be worked on. The stone masons can get it smooth and polish the sides until they shine but it needs the special skills of the scribe/stone carver to add the writing. The finishing touch is the capping of the top pyramid part with metal, often gold.

'With levers, rollers, ropes and thousands of workers, we slowly move the huge mass down to the water's edge. It's far easier, when you've got to move a thing this size, to use a boat.

'When we get to journey's end we have to unload by doing in reverse what we did to load up at the quarry. Then we manoeuvre the obelisk to its final position. It's quite tricky getting it to stand up. Gangs of men are ordered to make a hill with a height just over half that of the pillar. It has to have a steep slope one side, opposite a gentle gradient.

'Then with hundreds of men on ropes, levers and rollers, we nudge the thing up the slope and hope we've worked it out so accurately that the obelisk tips up onto its base and stands upright in the right place.'

We thank him and think about the muscle power needed to shift these enormous masses of stone. The smaller of the obelisks were not much higher than a tall man but some of the larger ones were so big, it's hard to imagine them being moved at all. Perhaps the biggest are to be found, not standing proudly erect but still in the quarry where they were left thousands of years ago. Although an average height might be about 70 feet, the one still lying at Aswan weighs well over a thousand tonnes.

How the obelisk is made to stand upright

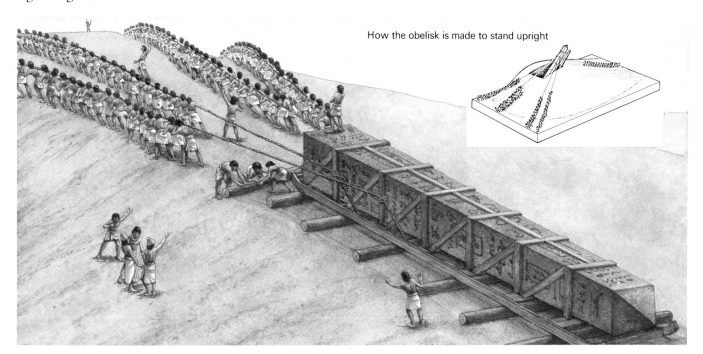

Mummies and tombs

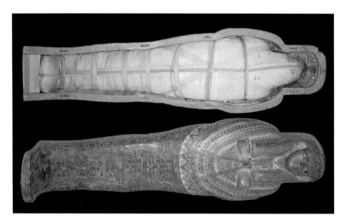

A mummy

Perhaps we could ask our Egyptologist about this. 'What is a mummy?' we say.

He laughs. 'It's not a children's word for mother,' he says, 'It's actually an Arabic word meaning 'wax'. Arabs were the first people in modern times to find the preserved dead bodies of ancient Egyptians. Some of the earliest had been crudely dipped in pitch. The first Egyptians believed that you couldn't go to heaven if you didn't have a body to go in. They also thought that each one of them had a spirit 'double', or 'ka'. After death the ka could leave the corpse and consume the food and drink left for it in the tomb. But should the body be destroyed, then that was the end of the ka and the end of immortality.

Papyrus picture of 'Ka' from the *Egyptian Book of the Dead*

'We think that the idea of deliberately trying to preserve the dead body occurred to the people after it had happened accidentally. In the British Museum is the corpse of a peasant who died and was found over 5,000 years later in good condition, thanks to the hot sand which had blown across and covered it.

The preserved Egyptian peasant from the British Museum

'At the time of the first pharaohs, priests tried at least to keep the shape of the corpse by binding the trunk, head, limbs (even the separate fingers) with gum-soaked bandages. When the gum dried the linen strips still showed the outline of the body no matter what had happened to the flesh inside.

'Eventually the priests worked out the best ways of embalming. The dead person was brought to them and they began by removing the inner organs. To put it crudely, it was a bit like gutting a fish before smoking or drying it! Except for the heart, the organs were put in canopic jars. These were made of pottery and usually had a sculptured human head on top. The brain was hooked out by way of the nostrils and the body was then ready for the treatment. It was laid in a wooden box and covered with natron crystals.'

'What's natron?'

'A chemical often found at the edges of lakes. Its proper name is hydrated carbonate of soda and it can soak up 75% of the water a human body is composed of. The process took ten weeks, at the end of which the shrinking was practically complete.

'The skull was packed with natron and plaster, then artificial eyes of black stone were set in place. The heart

very wealthy family, such as that of a pharaoh, would provide the costliest funeral of all with an outer stone container, or sarcophagus.

'A pharaoh's body, bound for burial in a pyramid was probably carried along the Nile on a specially built boat and delivered to the outbuildings for the embalming. It was then taken along a covered causeway to the building where almost the last ceremonies were held. Eventually the bearers moved the royal coffin to its final resting place in the heart of the pyramid.'

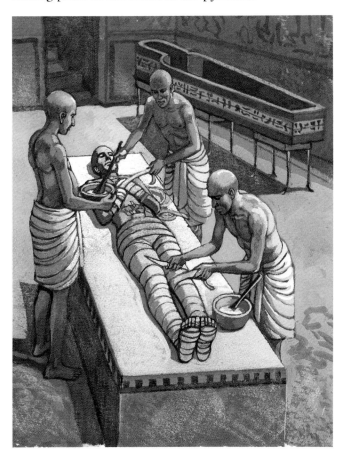

The Egyptologist sighs but goes on. 'Unfortunately, all the pyramids were robbed of their precious contents within a very few years of the burial. The tomb builders did all in their power to fool the thieves. They made false doors, staircases and corridors. They would put a blocking stone at the end of a passageway and plaster it in. The idea was that the thieves would break through only to find solid rock behind, whilst the real way forward was via a trapdoor in the ceiling.

'As I say, every pyramid and all but two of the rock tombs were stripped of their treasures.'

We thank him and move off. The two rock tombs we later learn are those of Tutankhamen and Queen Hetepheres, the mother of Cheops, builder of the Great Pyramid. We'll find out later how they were found.

was put back and held in position with wads of linen rags. At each stage the priests chanted prayers and spells and added lucky charms to the corpse. The wealthier the dead person, the richer were the jewels laid on the body which was ready for bandaging after being rubbed with ointments.

'The linen strips were soaked in a solution of natron and the swathing began. Occasionally, a prayer for the dead written on papyrus paper would be bound in. Sometimes the prayer was inked straight onto the linen. These were supposed to ward off evil spirits.

'Only the very rich could afford all the rites and processes in the early days but gradually things became cheaper and thus more common. A poor person's funeral might make use of a nearly plain wooden box for the corpse with just a line or two of prayer painted on the lid. Those who could afford better would have several coffins, one inside the other, each elaborately painted with sacred verses, the name of the departed and representations of the various gods. Now and then, an imaginary map of the land of the dead was painted on the bottom of the coffin. The inner coffin was shaped roughly to the same outline as the finished mummy. A

Akhenaten and religion

Osiris

We see a family coming from a temple, dedicated to the god Osiris. We ask the father about religion.

'We Egyptians are very religious,' he says, 'We believe in many gods and goddesses and make magic a part of our everyday lives.'

'Magic?' we ask, disbelievingly.

'Certainly,' he says, 'all the religions I know have magic in them or superstition, I suppose you might call it – you know, things that defy logic. Take this story of Osiris, one of our greatest gods.

'He started as a simple earth god. He is credited with inventing farming and wine making. The shepherd's crook and the farmer's corn flail, carried by all pharaohs, are his signs. In this story, his brother Seth was jealous of him and persuaded him by a trick to step into a wooden box. Seth shut the lid and locked it, then threw the chest into the Nile, where Osiris drowned. The magic is that he came back to life. In fact, another version of the story has Osiris's body being hacked to pieces and his wife finding the parts in different regions of Egypt and sewing them together again. We think the drowning and coming-to-life story really stands for the life-giving Nile floods which make the growing of crops possible.'

'But the two stories can't both be true.'

'Why not? It's quite possible for us to believe things that disagree with each other. For example, we have a goddess with two names – Bastet and Sekhmet. Bastet is a friendly cat which the women like to make a fuss of. But under her second name she has the head of a lioness on a human body and is shown as a lover of killing, slaughter, butchery and cannibalism.'

'Hmm, yes. What about an after life?'

'Do you know about mummies?' We nod and he goes on. 'Well, after he has passed on, the dead soul is shown into the hall of judgment by the jackal-headed god, Anubis. His heart is weighed in the scales against the feather of truth, whilst the ibis-headed god, Thoth writes down the verdict. A demon, called the 'heart-eater', who is a cross between lion, hippopotamus and crocodile, waits eagerly to be fed if there is a guilty verdict. While the weighing is going on, the dead soul

Anubis and the weighing of the soul

has to deny committing all kinds of lifetime crimes before the 42 gods on the jury. If they say 'not guilty', he is led by Horus to Osiris, the latter's father. Osiris sits on a throne in a pavilion at one end of the hall, attended by his wife, Isis and her sister, Nephthys. It is here the soul is told the verdict. The reward for his innocence is everlasting life.'

'This is for the pharaoh only?'

'It used to be but nowadays everyone wants to go to heaven so even quite poor people put food and drink in the tomb for the loved one's journey to the west. If you can afford a proper coffin in a tomb we paint a door on the side of the coffin, so that your soul can get to the food.'

'If a painted door will do instead of a real one, why bother with embalming a dead body? Can't you just pretend it isn't rotting?'

Our friend smiles and shrugs. 'There are too many gods to please,' he says, 'I've mentioned some of them but there are hundreds more. Once, not so long ago, there was a pharaoh who tried to change all that. He was annoyed that the priests of the different temples seemed to be getting more wealthy and powerful than the king.'

'Who was this ruler?'

'Amenophis. He came to the throne when his elder brother died young. His father had the same name, the third pharaoh to be so called. For a while he was known as Amenophis IV but after five or six years he changed his name to Akhenaten. He forbade the worship of all gods other than Aten, the sole god and embodiment of the golden sun. He built himself a new capital city and allowed artists to produce natural works of art. From then on, they could show people as they were and not as tradition said they should be shown. One example is this bust of Nefertiti, Akhenaten's beautiful wife.

'He ordered the closing of all "non Aten" temples and the chiselling off the names of other gods from carved inscriptions. So busy was he with these matters that he ignored military dangers and managed to lose most of the empire beyond our borders. I suppose he was intelligent – he had an enormous head but he was a most odd-looking fellow.

'There was much discontent here at home – his religious ideas never caught on with the common people. After he died, his half brother ruled for a few months but then Akhenaten's son-in-law came to the throne. He was only nine years old and had been known as Tut-ankh-aten in his father-in-law's time. He had to change his name to Tutankhamen. He died when he was only eighteen. He isn't very important and I don't suppose you've ever heard of him.'

Ahkenaten

Nefertiti

Tutankhamen's tomb

We've seen how the pyramid developed from the mastaba, but pyramids fell out of fashion because they were so easy to rob. The next development was the tomb cut into the rocky cliffs lining the Valley of the Kings. In spite of this, no one in modern times has ever found a royal grave completely untouched and un-robbed. As we can now account for most of ancient Egyptian royal burials, the chances are that we never will. The nearest we ever came to finding one was in the case of Tutankhamen. We ought to ask the Egyptologist who actually found the tomb to tell us about it.

'My name is Howard Carter,' he says, 'I was employed by Lord Carnarvon to look for any new tombs we might find in the Valley of the Kings. The silly thing is that a man named Ayrton, who was here before me, actually turned up some old vases marked with Tutankhamen's name. He didn't think much of them and sent them to New York's Metropolitan Museum where they were put away and forgotten. If only someone had told us of the discovery, we wouldn't have spent so long looking in the wrong place.

'In 1922, after many years of digging, my employer told me that this was to be the last year he could afford in Egypt. We went back to a little triangle of land where there were the remains of some very ancient workmen's huts. We knocked them down and found underneath many tons of rubble from the tomb of Rameses VI in the cliff above. It seemed unlikely that anything was there but the area had to be searched.

'On the morning of November 4th, I was struck by the silence. Usually the workmen were constantly chatting, laughing, shouting – now, there was nothing. I went to where the first trench was being cut: a workman's spade had struck rock. It proved to be the top step of a stone staircase going down into the rock. It took us three days to uncover as far as the twelfth step. When we did I saw the plastered up top of a possible doorway. I was sure we were on to something important. There was a seal on the doorway from the ancient Royal Cemetery Commission but nothing to tell us whose last resting place it was.

The first view inside the tomb

Entering the sealed chamber

  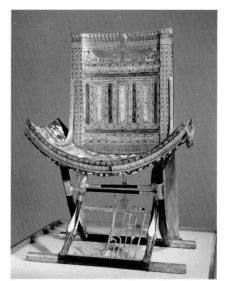

Objects found in Tutankhamen's tomb

'I had the steps filled in again and sent a telegram to his lordship, telling him what had happened. He got here in only eighteen days and we opened up the staircase once more – right down to the bottom of the door. A seal of Tutankhamen was found – but worryingly, it showed signs of having been fixed more than once. I thought to myself, 'Have the thieves beaten us to it once again?'

'I made a hole in the door but all I could see was rubble. We removed the door and the rubbish behind it and found a second door along a short passageway. Again there were signs of breaking and resealing. My heart sank.

'I made a hole in the top left hand corner of the door and put a candle into the gap. A gust of hot, dry air from inside made the flame flicker. Then the guttering stopped, the flame steadied and I could see inside. What met my gaze was a room full of things – couches, chariot wheels, boxes, animal models, jumbled furniture, chests – and everywhere the glint of gold.

'Very carefully we removed the door and began to check on what we'd found. There were so many things to draw, photograph and measure, that it was three months before we'd cleared the room. It was obvious that although thieves had been in the antechamber and had forced open some of the caskets, they must have been interrupted, for the contents had been hastily bundled back again. There didn't seem to be anything missing.

'We removed a third doorway – the one to the burial chamber – on February 17th 1923. A wall of gold was revealed. It was part of a gilt wooden screen. There were four of these shrines, one inside the other, surrounding an enormous sandstone sarcophagus. Inside was a nest of three coffins – two of gilded wood and one of gold.

Within the last lay the king's mummy with a gold face mask and gold protectors for the fingers and toes. Scattered about the corpse and covered by the linen bandages were dozens of jewels and lucky charms.

'There were two other small rooms to investigate and a tremendous number of items to list, including a chariot, couches inlaid with gold and ivory, chairs, tables, storage chests, games, clothing, gloves, a throne with the young ruler and his queen pictured on the back rest. Many of the caskets were ornamented with hunting or battle scenes.

'The whole effect was overwhelming and made huge newspaper headlines all over the world. Any one object would have been reward enough for a year's digging.

'One thought keeps coming back to me. If they could bury this unimportant king with so much splendour (and in haste, too) whatever must the tomb of a well established pharaoh have looked like? Unfortunately, we'll never know – all the tombs were robbed – and in the lifetime of those mourners who were at the funeral. What a pity!'

Tutankhamen's death mask

Tutankhamen's scarab and scarab bracelet

The lost toy cupboard

In March 1920, an Egyptologist decided to make a plan of a previously explored tomb west of Thebes. He had cleared out most of the rubble, when a workman drew his attention to a crack in the floor down which some of the swept up dust was disappearing. Puzzled, he had the stone removed and found himself gazing down into yet another tomb.

It hadn't belonged to a famous pharaoh but to a royal civil servant named Meketre. What made it interesting were the wooden models which the room contained. It was as if a child had put his toys away for the last time and never returned to play with them

again. This toy cupboard, however, had been closed and forgotten for 4,000 years!

In reality, these were models intended to assist the departed soul in heaven – but they have given us a marvellous picture of the life style enjoyed by a wealthy man who lived a time that was farther in the past to Jesus Christ than He is to us today.

These are not great works of art and they have no hieroglyphic inscriptions accompanying them, yet they tell us a great deal about upper class daily life in ancient Egypt.

Yacht

House and garden

Brewery and bakery

63

Everyday life

We've seen how farming was done in the great river valleys, including that of the Nile. More than 90% of the population spent most of their time farming. Wheat for bread and barley for beer have been mentioned but many other things were grown.

Among the vegetables produced were onions, radishes, peas and beans, leeks, garlic, cucumbers and lettuces. In his orchard, the well-to-do Egyptian might grow gourds, melons, figs, dates and grapes. The last two, as well as being fruits, were also used to make wine.

Although donkeys and cows worked on Egyptian farms, they also (together with ewes) gave milk, both for drinking and making into cheese. Sheep provided wool and both they and the cows and bulls were butchered for their meat. Poor farmers tended to keep goats rather than cattle or sheep and they and their families sometimes ate pork although the priests said that pig meat was forbidden, as it was an unclean animal.

Other sources of meat were geese, ducks, cranes and wild waterfowl. The eggs of these birds were eagerly looked for as well. Rich people, such as the pharaoh and his courtiers might enjoy the flesh of gazelles or antelopes which they had hunted and killed in the dried up watercourses on the fringes of the desert.

Like pork, certain kinds of fish were held to be sacred in some places but this didn't stop peasants adding them to a diet that might have been rather monotonous otherwise.

Other things were grown that were not mostly (or not at all) intended for food, for example, flax for linen or linseed oil. Oils were also extracted from olives and from the castor oil plant. They were used as a fuel for lighting lamps or even as suntan oils!

In a tomb belonging to an upper class lady of second dynasty times, an actual meal was laid out on plates for the departed to feed on. Even after several thousand years it was still possible to identify the items on the menu. These included fish, pigeon stew, kidneys, quail, barley porridge, ribs of beef, bread rolls, small round cakes, some cherry-like fruit, plus stewed figs and finishing with cheese, wine and beer. Not the sort of thing enjoyed by peasants but a typical spread at a well-to-do dinner party.

The giver of such a feast, in common with most Egyptians, washes completely, morning and evening. He sits on a stool in a stone floored bathroom and cleans himself with soda, after which a servant pours water over him. He oils his skin and dabs on perfume. He shaves with a bronze razor, then wraps a linen kilt around his middle and slips on his sandals. Then he pulls on his wig and he is ready. Many people wear wigs, some because they are going grey or bald, others because it's the fashion. One of his bald friends has been advised to rub the top of his head with an ointment made from the fat of snakes, hippos and crocodiles.

Poor peasants couldn't afford an elaborate toilet and had to be content with a bucket of water outside the door if they wanted a bath. Young children wore few, if any clothes, so they could swim and bathe whenever they wanted, merely by diving in the nearest pond.

Beauty aids for the Egyptian woman included green and black eye paint, haematite powder or red ochre for lips and cheeks, perfume and pots of face cream. She did her hair with a bone or ivory comb and held her tresses in place with pins of the same materials. She wore a long sheath dress which went under her arms and just about reached down to her ankles. Spinners of linen yarn managed to get it so fine that the finished cloth was more like silk and almost transparent.

Jewellery of all kinds was worn by men and women. There were necklaces, anklets and bangles of ivory, copper or gold and rings set with semi-precious stones. Lucky charms such as the scarab beetle in precious metal were also worn. Both sexes were fond of elaborately jewelled necklets and all kinds of beads, particularly those of blue lapis lazuli.

Poor peasants no longer lived in reed lean-tos but in huts of mud brick. These were small and rectangular with flat roofs. In cold weather, the peasant slept under a blanket but if it was hot he tended to stretch out on the roof to catch whatever cool breezes there were. In one room the housewife ground the grain into flour which she then turned into dough and baked her bread in a clay oven in one corner. For fuel, she burned straw, the dried roots of papyrus plants, date stone charcoal, or even animal droppings.

The houses of rich people were more elaborate, even though still made of sun-dried mud bricks: only temples, tombs and monuments were completed in stone. For this reason, very few houses survive, although tomb paintings and models give us some idea of what they were like.

A typical rich man's dwelling was enclosed within a high wall. Also enclosed was a tree shaded pool surrounded by flowers and ornamental bushes. The house itself might be two stories high with the rooms opening into a central courtyard. The walls were plastered and painted. The ceiling was held up by brightly coloured wooden pillars, shaped to look like large bundles of reeds.

There was very little furniture. People sat on the mat-strewn floor or on cushions scattered along a mud brick ledge. There were a few chests and boxes in which to keep clothes and valuables and that was all, apart from some small, low, round tables which were big enough only for one or two diners each. The tables could also be used for board games – a bit like ludo or draughts. There were no dice but they did have 'dice sticks' which could be thrown to give random numbers.

The disappearing queen

In 1925 at Giza, near the Great Pyramid, a photographer who was working for an American group was just setting up his tripod when he noticed a discoloured patch of stone near his feet. The deputy director of the group ordered the men to dig it up.

Below was a staircase in the rock, rather like the one leading to Tutankhamen's tomb. This one, however, led to a deep, vertical shaft filled with blocks of limestone. The workmen began to lift them out. At a depth of thirty feet there was no sign of anything interesting. Then suddenly, a niche in the side of the shaft came to light. It contained some beer jars and the remains of beef joints – all that was left of some ancient sacrifice. From then on they found more and more fragments of pottery.

When they had gone down eighty feet, they reached a double layer of carefully laid stones, which they took away, revealing the edge of a ceiling over a rock-cut room. By now it was late afternoon and the light was fading. One of the wall blocks was removed and the archaeologists could just make out the vague outlines of a stone coffin and the occasional glint of gold.

The following morning they fixed up an ingenious arrangement of mirrors, so that a ray of sunlight could be shone down into the grave.

On one side of the room stood a coffin of alabaster. Across it and all over the floor there was a tremendous jumble of bits of gold, broken pottery and masses of pieces that couldn't be identified immediately. There was scarcely room to stand in the narrow room without doing damage.

Each piece within reach had to be measured, drawn and photographed before being fitted onto a master plan. The room took two years to clear, fragment by fragment. As soon as the first scraps reached the top of the shaft, a team on the surface began to try and put together the pieces of a giant 3D jigsaw. It was extremely difficult for they had little idea of what the finished articles would look like. As they went on it became obvious from the hieroglyphic inscriptions that this was a royal tomb of Hetepheres, wife of the pharaoh Sneferu and mother of Cheops, builder of the Great Pyramid.

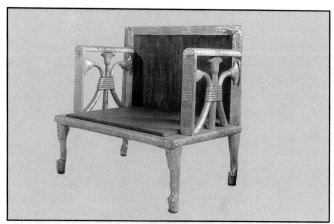

Objects found at Giza

So well was the rescue work done that the team was able to say what sizes and shapes the pieces of wood had once been from the remaining gold sheathings and inlays. When they had finished reconstructing, the items of furniture were shown to have been: one bed in ebony and sheathed in gold (beaten gold glued to a coating of plaster) with an ebony footboard inlaid with faience and carnelian. For a pillow there was a decorated ebony head rest. There was a box containing bracelets and trinkets and a chest for holding canopy curtains. Others held gold vessels and gold toilet accessories. There was a carrying chair and two armchairs. Above all, there was, when all the pieces had been fitted together, a huge, gold-covered wooden framework over which went the curtains designed to screen the furniture.

What the archaeologists couldn't understand was why the queen had been buried so secretly and in less than royal splendour, considering that she was a pharaoh's wife. They soon had another question to answer, for when the coffin was opened, it was found (apart from some stains) to be totally empty. Where was the body? Why were there all the trappings of a royal funeral if there were no corpse? What had happened?

Then another discovery was made. Inside a sealed recess in the wall they found a container with four compartments, in which were the internal organs of the queen. These, by the way, were the earliest surviving evidence of the practice of embalming. So, Hetepheres had been in the coffin once. But why was it now empty?

After a good deal of thought, the excavators themselves put forward a theory. Of course, it could never be proved but it seemed to fit the facts.

Hetepheres as the wife of Sneferu had probably been buried royally and properly near her husband's pyramid, some miles away. When her son Cheops was on the throne, robbers had broken into her grave, taken the mummy outside to remove all the gold and jewellery hidden under the linen bandages. Leaving the body to be scavenged by desert jackals, the thieves were on their way back to continue plundering the tomb when they were disturbed. They either fled or were arrested.

The officials dared not tell the pharaoh the whole story but got his permission (on some pretext or other) to rebury the grave furniture and coffin at a better protected site near the Great Pyramid, hoping that he'd never find out that his mother's body was missing. They would have breathed easier if they'd known it was to be 4,500 years before the theft was discovered. They'd also have been more than surprised to learn that even after that enormous length of time there was still some embalming fluid left in the canopic container!

Grave robbers at work

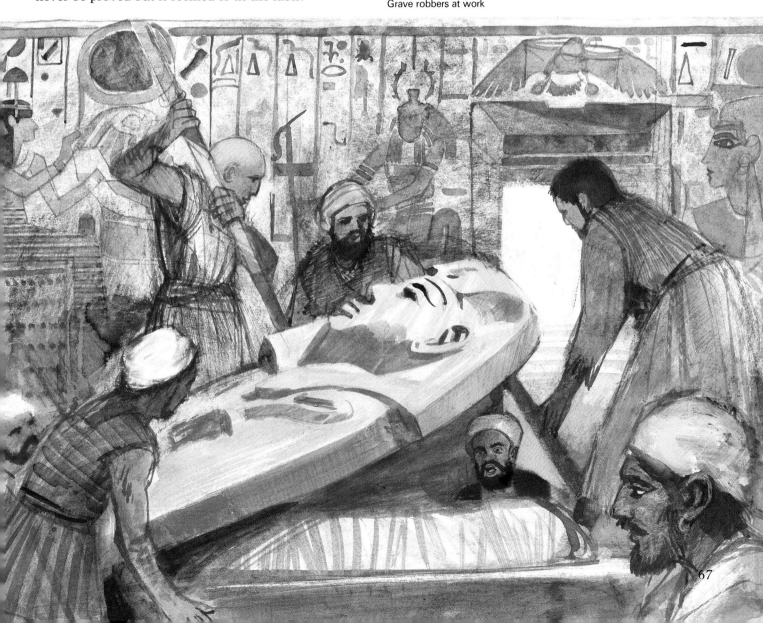

67

Paper, ink, hieroglyphics

A boy learning to be a scribe in ancient Egypt had to go to a special school – probably one attached to a temple and run by priests. If it was nearby he would be a day boy; if not he would have to live away from home.

It took many years to learn all the signs – there were several hundred of them. Some signs were alphabetic (like our own letters), some were pictures of the thing the scribe wished to mention and others stood for the sound of the word or part of the word. In addition, you often had to put in a 'class indicator' sign. This came after a word and showed which group it belonged to. Thus it could be that the word was written in letters, drawn in a picture, split into parts for the sound of its syllables and followed by a symbol showing what type of word it was. All very complicated. English is not so good as Egyptian for this kind of writing but if we used the same methods for 'caterpillar', we might wind up with: CTPLR

This is supposing that the sign -Ọ- means the class of creepy crawly insects and similar creatures. You will have noticed that the alphabetic version uses no vowels. If we did this in our language, you wouldn't know whether 'BT' stood for 'bat', 'bet', 'bit', 'but', 'boot', 'boat', 'bought', 'beat', 'bout', or 'bait' without some other indication.

As though that were not difficult enough, Egyptian scribes sometimes wrote from left to right, sometimes from right to left and, occasionally from top to bottom. No wonder the scientists took so long to crack the code. In addition they were faced, not only with an unknown way of writing but also an unknown language.

Their first break-through came with the discovery of an inscribed stone at Rosetta on the Nile Delta. The inscription was in both Greek and hieroglyphics (or 'sacred carvings', as these signs are known). They guessed that the names of pharaohs which they could read in the Greek part were the same as the groups of signs surrounded by a thin line. Assuming that one name was 'PTOLEMY' and another 'CLEOPATRA', it became possible to suppose that the first letter of 'Ptolemy' should be the fifth sign of 'Cleopatra' and so

The Rosetta stone

on. It was. Similarly, the sign of 'L' was also in the right place as were those for the other letters which appeared in both names.

All this is very much simplified. It's wasn't as easy as all that and took decades before much ancient Egyptian could be read.

A boy learner was given pieces to copy and he used anything that could be written on – a slab of stone, a broken pot or a plaster covered board – just so long as they could be wiped clean and reused.

Writing fluid was not really ink but more like our water colour paints. Red and black were the popular colours, made from powdered red ochre and lamp black. The powder was mixed with gum and water into a thick paste which was poured into little round pans to harden, whilst a 'pen' was made of a twig or reed, chewed into a frayed condition and then sharpened.

Paper was used for important documents. It was made from the papyrus plant. Nowadays this grows only on the banks of the upper Nile but thousands of years ago it was common along all of the river. It was cut in bundles and sent to the paper maker.

He chopped the stalks into one foot lengths, peeled off the bark and cut the inner pith into long thin slices. Some of these were laid side by side on a flat surface and others placed across them at right angles. Then the paper maker pounded them with a wooden mallet until they stuck together.

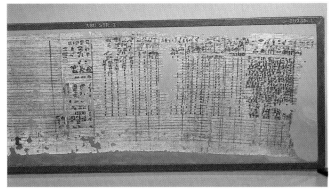
Temple accounts

The resulting sheets were either hung up to dry and trimmed to shape, or hammered and pasted edge to edge with others to make a long strip. The longest we know of is the so-called Harris Papyrus, which is 135 feet long.

The first papyrus seems to date back to the earliest days or writing – that is to say, some 5,000 years ago – and is a humble set of temple accounts. However, as time went on, scribes ventured into the realms of verse, drama, story telling and history. The latter has proved very valuable to us in the modern world, for we now know more about ancient Egypt than any similar civilisation which never developed writing.

Making papyrus

It's just barely possible that the idea of writing was copied by the Egyptians from the scribes in Meso-potamia. If this is true, then they took nothing but the idea: the two systems are not alike. Hieroglyphics were purely a product of the Nile valley.

Practising writing

69

Chapter 4   Other early civilisations

The Indus valley

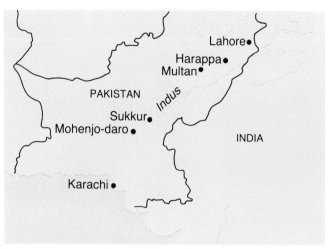

No one in Europe knew about the ancient civilisation of the Indian sub-continent until the 19th century but those who lived in the land of the two rivers 4,000 years ago knew about places such as Harappa and Mohenjo-daro. These cities in the valley of the river Indus in modern Pakistan were trading with the people of Mesopotamia 2,000 years before Christ.

Harappa in our times was no more than a massive hill of ruins when it was reported to be of interest in about 1820. Many seal stones kept turning up. These had carved pictures of animals and signs in some unknown script. Some of them were published and brought to the attention of scholars.

Seal stone

The ruins didn't look very promising, as nearby towns and villages had used them as a free quarry for centuries. Even the British company that had built the Karachi to Lahore railway in 1856 had removed tons of 'hard core' for the permanent way. It wasn't until January, 1921 that Indian archaeologists began the first scientific investigations.

The discovery of the second site of the same civilisation came by chance. In 1922, another Indian scientist was working on an early Buddhist monastery, when it became obvious that its foundations were much older than the rest of the building. The ruins were called Mohenjo-daro (the Place of Death) and were excavated by Marshall and Mackay during the 1920s. Some other sites of the same type were also found.

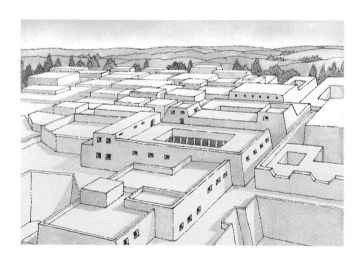

Soon, the outlines of large, well designed towns began to emerge. The houses and other buildings were made of kiln-dried, rather than mud brick, which seemed to point to a somewhat rainier climate than the modern one. The Indus was more like the rivers of Mesopotamia than the Nile. It flooded once a year, bringing down the fertile silt but it was much less easy to forecast, both as to time and amount of water. Occasionally the river rose high and violently and even changed course.

However, the region would grow crops such as wheat, barley, rice and even cotton and there were

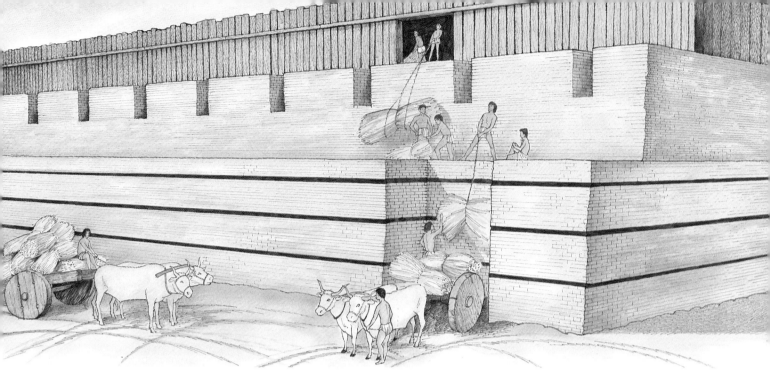

Reconstruction of granary at Mohenjo-daro

plenty of animals to hunt or to tame. There are drawings or carvings of tigers, elephants, water buffaloes, crocodiles and rhinoceroses.

In addition, animals such as the horse, camel, sheep, goat, cow and donkey were tamed – probably long before the people lived in towns. In fact, the towns were most likely founded about 2,500 B.C., when the villages had already been in existence for a thousand years. The Indus valley civilisation is something of a mystery, as it did not apparently develop from the kind of life that went before it on the river plain. No one knows for certain how it arose, but at about 2000 B.C., the whole of north west India was sprinkled with towns, all seemingly laid out by the same designers.

There were well built two storey houses enclosing wells, private bathrooms and lavatories, with earthenware pipes to carry the waste out to neat, brick-lined drains, all equipped with inspection holes at regular intervals. There doesn't seem to have been a single grand temple but at Mohenjo-daro a large bath for some sort of religious bathing was discovered.

Another prominent feature was the citadel with high walls and towers. Many Indus valley towns show extensive remains of huge granaries. At Mohenjo-daro, the unloading bay for the carts was identified. Grain seems to have been brought to the store by boat at Harappa.

So far, not much in the way of art has turned up although there were some quite good statues and figurines. The best work is seen on the stone seals carved with animals that have been appearing for over a century,

These animal pictures are accompanied by signs in an unknown script. It's strange that the three most important ancient civilisations should each have produced its own special way of writing. The cuneiform of Mesopotamia and the hieroglyphics of Egypt finally gave up their secrets and we can now read what the ancient people wrote.

Unfortunately, the Indus valley inscriptions are too short and too scarce for much progress to be made. There are no long rock-cut inscriptions, nor lengths of papyrus. The pieces we have may be nothing more than proper names – we just don't know. And, of course, the biggest barrier to breaking the code is that we haven't the faintest idea of what language the people spoke. So, even if we were lucky enough to find a sort of Indian Rosetta stone, it wouldn't be much good to us.

The life of the cities seems to have come to an end some time between 1750 and 1500 B.C. We don't know why but there are several possibilities. Did the soil become less fertile? Were trees and other natural resources exhausted? Was the soil washed away by floods? Was there a revolution against a too severe government? Were they invaded?

It's true that the houses had begun to decay and ones which were little more than hovels were built on top of the remains. As the decay went on, the cities were slowly turning into slums. In the upper layers of Mohenjo-daro, the archaeologists found several skeletons showing signs of a violent death.

In extent, the Indus valley civilisation was far larger and more uniform than that of either Mesopotamia or Egypt: it didn't start until they had been going for a thousand years and it finished when they still had about another thousand years to run.

China

Most people who are interested in history seem to know something about China in prehistoric times. They've heard of Peking Man who lived half a million years ago and is the first human being known to have used fire. They may also have heard of the discovery of old stone age tools together with the remains of modern man, dating back to 30,000 B.C. Not so many know of China's middle stone age, traces of which have turned up in the northern frontier region, in the south and south west, as well as on the island of Taiwan.

We find new stone age settlements appearing in the north and north west, dating from about 4,000 B.C. Here, along the river valleys, the soil was particularly well suited to the primitive farming that was done. The name 'Yang-shao' is applied to these people, who still probably relied more on hunting and fishing than they did on growing things. Their houses had low walls on a round or rectangular pattern, topped off with a roof of thatch and clay which may have reached the ground all round the dwelling. They knew nothing of metal and had only flint tools and weapons.

It seems that the various farming peoples who lived along the valleys of Chinese rivers existed very much as the dwellers in ancient Egypt and Mesopotamia must have done and had many of the same problems to solve.

The discovery of bronze goes back to about 1600 B.C. which also roughly marks the beginning of the first historical period. It is known as the Shang. A kind of picture writing, not very different from its modern forms seems to have developed at about the same time.

The rule of the Shang kings lasted about 500 years until they were conquered by a people known as the Chou. The area they controlled gradually increased to include a good deal of what we think of as modern China. Their capital was at first at or near Hsi-an.

Among the features of their civilisation were 1. The beginnings of social classes 2. Burials with rich grave goods and human sacrifice 3. War chariots 4. Growth of towns. The use of bronze and a system of writing have already been mentioned. The rule of the Chou collapsed into civil wars until 246 B.C. when the self-styled first Emperor of China, Ch'in-Shih-huang-ti, came to power.

He laid the foundations of a united China in language, religion, systems of weights and measures and government, many of which have lasted until modern times. He was responsible for ordering his general, Meng T'ien to build the Great Wall.

The Great Wall of China

According to the historian of the court, one of the emperor's first acts was to start planning his own tomb. Three quarters of a million labourers were assembled to dig it out. The burial chamber was to be filled with miniature buildings, precious stones, storage jars, small scale rivers (to be imitated with mercury), models of the heavens and the earth. Whale oil lamps were to give illumination and crossbows were fixed and cocked to fire automatically at tomb robbers.

When the emperor died, the second emperor ordered all his father's womenfolk to be buried with him. Then someone suggested that the skilled workmen knew too much about the tomb they had constructed, so orders were given that they too should be shut up alive in the grave. As far as we know, robbers don't seem to have done much damage and in 1985, excavators have found the walls surrounding the burial chamber. They also found a high level of mercury in the soil – perhaps the remains of the model rivers?

Less than a mile and a half away, one of the greatest tomb discoveries ever made came to light in March 1974. It was in that year that the local people decided to sink wells to improve their water supply. The diggers suddenly came across a life-sized pottery figure which looked as though it had been there for some time. According to the museum authorities who were then called in, it had.

It was the first one of some 7,000 buried soldier-statues which had lain in the earth since the funeral of Ch'in-Shih-huang-ti, although they were not mentioned in the history.

By digging here and there, archaeologists established that the original pit was almost 700 feet long and nearly 200 feet wide. It had eleven parallel corridors packed with life-sized model soldiers – each corridor with over 600 men except the two narrower outside ones. In six of the passages were chariots drawn by four horses. Men were arranged in long lines, three abreast, across the short sides. There were ramps leading up to the surface at each end. Even six years after the first discovery, no more than 2% of the 'grave' has been dug up.

A second pit turned up in May, 1976 with another 1400 statues, mostly cavalry and charioteers. A month later, the archaeologists found the army's headquarters staff in a third grave. A fourth pit was empty, although, like the others, it had brick pavements and wooden roofs.

The labour represented by these 7,000 soldier figures was enormous. To start with, they were not pressed from moulds – no two are exactly alike and even the faces are different. Most of the arms are real weapons; some of the swords were still razor sharp. Each statue had been carefully painted in one of several colour combinations, for example, black shoes, blue trousers and green cloaks. The armour, which consisted of many little metal plates, was painted black with white rivets.

In the nearby museum are specimen warriors and a restored chariot. The locals think that other pits may yet be found. Even if they are not, this private army for a dead emperor must rank with the great archaeological discoveries of all time.

The Emperor's warriors and horses at Xi-an

The Hittites

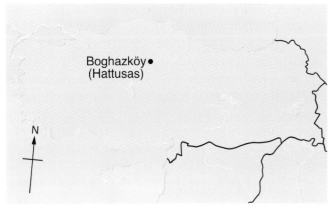

Turkey

Pass at Boghazköy

Just over a hundred years ago, the name 'Hittite' was almost unknown, apart from one or two references in the Bible. Then, in 1880, an Englishman named Sayce said that in his opinion, a number of rock carvings in modern Turkey and further south were the visible remains of a long forgotten empire – that of the Hittites. He was proved right. In 1906 a large number of clay tablets was unearthed at a place called Boghazköy.

The tablets were mostly in the wedge-shaped signs of Mesopotamia and some could be read without too much difficulty. Others, although looking like straight-forward cuneiform, turned out to be in an unknown language. There were also inscriptions in a kind of picture writing. It took many years before it became possible to decipher the picture writing. The decipherers were helped when some stone pillars with messages carved on them were found at Karatepe. There were two languages, Hittite and Phoenician, the latter being already known. The columns were rather like the Rosetta stone in Egypt, giving the decoders more new symbols and their meanings. It had long been suspected that Hittite might belong to the same group of languages as the ancestors of most modern European ones – including English. Now the scholars could make out 'WÄDAR' and 'EZZATENI' and translate them as 'water' and 'eat'.

They also found out that the place where the first tablets were found was in fact called Hattusas at about 1600 B.C. and was the capital of the ancient empire of the Hittites. Much else came to light.

Hattusas had a fortified citadel and massive surrounding walls over two miles long. The Hittites claimed that it was one of the cities taken by their half legendary kings, Pithanas, and his son, Anittas. A few other conquered towns can be identified – enough to show that at its greatest extent, the whole of Anatolia (mostly modern Turkey) had been overrun with Syria, the western coast of Turkey, much of the Holy Land, Cyprus and a good deal of northern Mesopotamia.

One Hittite king made a surprise attack down the Euphrates in 1595 B.C. and captured Babylon. Another, Suppiluliumash, was such a great conqueror that the widow of Tutankhamen wrote him an official letter asking that one of his sons to be sent to Egypt to marry her.

Ordinary Hittites were of medium height, thickset and with bony noses. They wore felt boots and short, belted kilts. Some were bearded and others clean shaven. They grew barley and wheat and raised sheep and goats.

Like most ancient peoples, they worshipped numerous gods, the chief of which was Teshup, a sort of middle eastern Thor, for he is shown as holding a hammer and a flash of lightning. Like Thor, he was the god of the storm. His wife was the goddess of the sun.

One of the secrets of Hittite military success was their use of iron for weapons. Before 1400 B.C., it was known that some red minerals (e.g. iron oxide) would reduce to metal at temperatures not much above those for producing molten copper from blue and green ores. But iron will only flow like copper or lead in much hotter fires, a process which was not to be invented for nearly another 3000 years.

The Hittite method was repeated heatings and hammerings to drive out the rock impurities. If you were lucky and had a little natural carbon in your iron ore, you got a very good metal from which to make swords. The knowledge of how to do this wasn't available to the rest of the world until the collapse of the Hittite empire in about 1200 B.C.

Just before this happened, Muwatallis, the Hittite king, claimed a great battle victory against the Egyptians. Rameses II, the Egyptian leader, also claimed to have won, as his numerous monuments bear witness. The battle was probably a draw. It was the last great engagement of the Hittite army with its light, spoke-wheeled and horse-drawn chariots. Great movements of peoples in the middle east only a lifetime later led to the disappearance of the Hittite empire.

Some of the old provincial city states survived for a few more centuries, for example Carchemish, Malatya and Karatepe. It was probably one of these small shadowy Hittite kingdoms to which the Bible refers in the story of Abraham.

Five hundred years after the destruction of the capital, Hatussas, the last traces of the Hittites disappeared from history.

Hittites

Walls at Hattusas

The Hebrews

Man working on Dead Sea Scrolls

In a laboratory in Israel a man is carefully cutting into pieces an ancient looking roll of thin copper plate. We would like to know what he is doing. He tells us.

'This is one of the Dead Sea scrolls,' he says. 'There are many of them, some written on linen – all more than 1900 years old. They are mostly religious texts – parts of what you would call "The Old Testament," he adds with a smile.

'The Bible tells the story of the Jewish people, the Children of Israel, as we call ourselves. It's strange that a people so small in numbers and so beset with enemies has survived. Our first ancestors lived long ago – as far in the past to the writers of these scrolls as the writers are to us.'

'That must be about 4000 years?'

'Something like that, yes. One of our earliest heroes was named Abraham. He is supposed to have been born in Sumer at a place called Ur. We were a nomadic people, keeping goats and sheep and always shifting

about. We travelled slowly and over the centuries we gradually moved up the Euphrates and into Canaan, our promised land. Some of us crossed the desert into pharaoh's empire and many of us did well in Egypt. This must have been roughly about 1700 B.C. and things might have gone on like this for a very long time. But then a pharaoh (who may have been Rameses II) made life so hard for us that, after a series of adventures, we escaped from Egypt altogether.

'Under our leader, Moses, we once more became wandering shepherds with tents of woven goat's hair. We spent forty years in the Sinai desert and began to forget our covenant with God until Moses showed us the holy laws he had received from the Lord on Mount Sinai.'

'The ten commandments?'

'That's right. These rules kept us together – that and the fact that we had only one god to worship. Mind you, Akhenaten tried to bring in a religion with only one deity. He might have been more sympathetic towards us had we stayed. However –' he shrugs.

'We left Egypt in about 1280 B.C. and started the conquest of Canaan forty years later. Moses was dead by then and Joshua had taken his place. You may know the story of how Joshua's trumpeters marched round the first enemy city they came to, blowing their rams-horn trumpets. The walls of Jericho definitely fell, as the Bible tells us but archaeologists have found traces of an earthquake, which God probably used to carry out his will.

'Anyway, in fifteen years the tribes of Israel had settled all over Canaan, or Palestine as it was sometimes known – from the Philistines who also lived there. You've heard of David and Goliath? Samson and Delilah? Well, both Delilah and Goliath were Philistines.

'David came to the throne about 1012 B.C., succeeding Saul, our first king. Then there was Solomon, our most magnificent ruler. He had hundreds of wives and thousands of slaves. He had many gorgeous palaces made and it was he who ordered the building of the Temple in Jerusalem.

'Sargon II of Assyria captured Samaria in 721 B.C. and carried its people off into slavery. He had an inscription made. It's still in existence and gives the exact number of Jewish prisoners – 27,280! Even this wasn't the biggest disaster. Nebuchadrezzar and his Babylonian armies conquered Jerusalem itself in 587 B.C. They smashed the temple on the hill of Zion and marched hundreds of thousands of captives off to Mesopotamia. There they stayed for nearly fifty years until Babylon itself was taken by the Persians under King Cyrus and they were freed. But you can read most of this in your own Bible.'

'Tell us more about the Dead Sea scrolls.'

'They were found in a cave near the Dead Sea by a young Arab boy. He'd gone into the cave to look for a stray goat when he found these rolls of manuscript in pottery jars. They were brought to the attention of the authorities and we're now carefully unrolling and studying them.

'They seem to have been owned by a community of monks called Essenes. The remains of their monastery are still to be seen at the foot of the nearby cliffs.

'One of these copper rolls tells an incredible story. Whilst most of them are the oldest versions of books in the Bible yet known, this one tells where the monks hid their valuables – treasures given by friends and supporters and any possessions the monks themselves had once owned. The total of gold and silver tucked away is stated to be an unbelievable 160 tons! I'm afraid none of it has ever been found. If it ever was there, it's gone now.

'Of course, far more valuable than that are the religions. The middle east, you know, has produced three of the great world religions: Judaism, Christianity and Islam. Don't forget that your Christ was a Jew.'

Reconstruction of the monastery of the Essenes

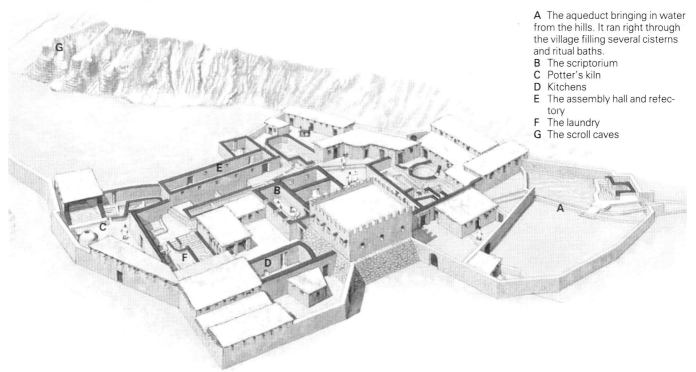

A The aqueduct bringing in water from the hills. It ran right through the village filling several cisterns and ritual baths.
B The scriptorium
C Potter's kiln
D Kitchens
E The assembly hall and refectory
F The laundry
G The scroll caves

CHAPTER 4

The Assyrians

Assyria

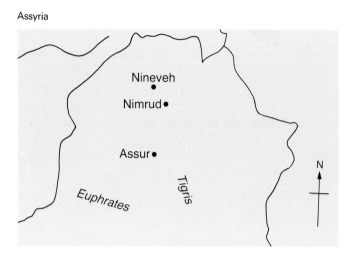

The Assyrians were a hard, war-like people. They began to emerge as a world power by about 1350 B.C. There was a period of chaos after the Hittite empire collapsed but by 1115 B.C., when Tiglath-Pileser I became king, Assyria was a mighty country once more, with flourishing trade protected by a strong army. When Assyria and Egypt exchanged ambassadors, the pharaoh sent the Assyrians an interesting present – a live crocodile.

By the mid tenth century B.C. no one could withstand the Assyrian armies and the land itself was like a huge military camp. Every man had to be able to use weapons, a store of which was kept in the citadels of the chief cities. If he were rich, he had to supply his own arms – a bow and arrows, a nail-studded club, a spear, an axe or even a horse-drawn chariot. The cavalry rode both horses and camels.

There was an efficient corps of spies who reported regularly to the king, so he knew where and when to attack. He could then order his men to fight a battle or besiege a city, an art at which they were experts.

The army made a fortified camp near the town they were attacking and the engineers set about assembling their assault machines – scaling ladders, battering rams, armoured carts and assault towers. It was an Assyrian idea to make such machines so that they could be taken to pieces for crossing rivers or difficult, mountain country. Even the chariots might be carried as parts on pack animals. One piece of Assyrian art shows their soldiers swimming a river in full kit but staying afloat by means of air-filled leather bags. Without them they would have drowned for they wore heavy leather boots and chain mail. When the men had got over the walls or smashed holes in them with battering rams they quickly disposed of the enemy, some prisoners being impaled or beheaded. Loot was then loaded onto captured baggage wagons and the town burnt to the ground. High officials who had been spared were made to march barefoot back to Assyria, often with the severed heads of their leaders slung round their necks.

Assurnasirpal was a great conqueror. He extended Assyria's boundaries in all directions, campaigning down the river valleys and to the Mediterranean coasts. He used the spoils of war to build several palaces, including an enormous one at the modern Nimrud. The throne room alone was over 7,000 square feet in area and had to be approached through a gate flanked by the typically Assyrian statues of bulls with human heads, each with a carefully curled beard. The statues weighed thirty or forty tons apiece and were probably ferried along the Tigris to the palace in the very large coracles that were common in those days.

It was under Assurnasirpal that Assyria gained a thoroughly deserved reputation for ruthlessness and cruelty. It was his successors who pushed the empire to its greatest limits. Tiglath-Pileser, Sargon II, Sennacherib and Esarhaddon between them besieged Jerusalem, captured Babylon, drove out the pharaoh and occupied Egypt.

Esarhaddon's son, Assurbanipal, attacked Thebes and tried to destroy its colossal temples. He carried off two large Eyptian obelisks to his palace at Nineveh. It seemed that the Assyrian empire would last for ever but Assurbanipal was becoming more interested in his vast library at Nineveh than in the army. There were more than 20,000 clay tablets copied from all over the empire. (These, by the way, were later to provide archaeologists with a valuable key to life in Mesopotamia.) The king liked nothing so much as to browse among his 'books' and then discuss them with scholars. He reigned from 669 to 626 B.C., but even in his lifetime, the empire had begun to show cracks.

In 652 B.C. his brother led a revolt of neighbouring nations which was crushed within four years. It was Assyria's last successful campaign. A year after his death, Assurbanipal's sons quarrelled over who should be the next king. While they argued, Babylon rose in rebellion once more. Under their leader, Nabopolassar, father of Nebuchadrezzar, the Babylonians joined forces with the Medes and threw off Assyrian rule. They did more – their victorious soldiers chased the defeated enemy back to Nineveh, which they captured in 612 B.C. So much treasure was looted, the amounts were uncountable and the Assyrian capital was left in heaps of smoking ruins.

Dust drifted over the dead ashes and even the sites of the Assyrian palaces were forgotten, until they were dug up again in the nineteenth century. Among the finds at Assur, an earlier capital, was a fine piece of low relief sculpture, showing a charming family scene. Assurbanipal and his wife are eating an outdoor meal at a table surrounded by grape vines. Servants bring food and cool them with fans. This picture of domestic bliss is shattered in characteristic Assyrian fashion – in the background there is a severed human head hanging from one of the trees!

The Persians

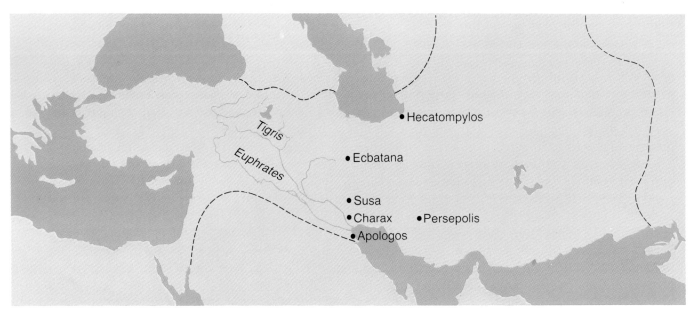

The Persian Empire

The Persian empire was the largest the world had seen. It was also one of the shortest lived. It burst upon the scene in about 550 B.C., filling the space left by the collapse of the Assyrian empire. Under its emperors, Cyrus, Cambyses, Darius and Xerxes, it was extended from eastern Europe through the Asian middle east to the banks of the Indus in modern Pakistan and south to the ancient kingdoms of Babylonia and Egypt. But in just over two centuries it was all over. What had happened?

Cyrus beat the king of the Medes in battle and took him prisoner. This was important for it was the Medes who had taken over what was left of the Assyrian empire. Cyrus then began to look westward towards Greece and the rest of Europe. Only Lydia stood in his way. Croesus, king of Lydia, was believed by his contemporaries to be the richest king who had ever lived. He had made the mistake of consulting the oracle at Delphi to decide whether to make war on Persia or not. The oracle told him that if he went to war he would 'destroy a great empire'. Gleefully, Croesus made his preparations, unaware that the oracle's pronouncements could nearly always be given more than one meaning. Croesus went to war. He did, indeed, 'destroy a great empire'. Unfortunately, it was his own!

Cyrus used the wealth from the Lydian gold mines to set up a military expedition to Babylon. He and his men attacked at night. So as to make full use of the surprise, he had previously ordered his engineers to divert the river which protected one wall. Thus, he and his infantry were able to creep along a dry river bed and attack where they were not expected.

The conquests of Cyrus were not held down with Assyrian cruelty and force – the beaten peoples were often allowed to keep their own religions and languages, even their own rulers, provided that tribute was sent regularly.

Cambyses was not so kind as his father Cyrus but in his short seven year reign, he enlarged the empire by beating Phoenicia, Egypt and the island of Cyprus. The next ruler was his son, Darius, who further expanded the boundaries towards Southern Russia, India & Northern Greece. He landed a large army at Marathon with the object of conquering Greece. This is the origin of the 'Marathon' run, for a Greek was sent at his fastest pace to warn the Spartans. The Persians were soundly defeated by a small Athenian army and Darius never got another chance. Shortly after starting the building of the great Persian capital at Persepolis in 486 B.C., he died.

Other Persian building achievements included a good network of fine roads, one of which ran for over 1500 miles. It was said that messengers using relays of horses could travel from one end of the empire to the other in just under a fortnight – extremely fast for those days.

One of the first decisions of King Xerxes was to do what his father Darius had been unable to do – to conquer Greece. He built up a large army and fleet and tried out a brand new idea. A bridge of boats was constructed by his Phoenician allies running from Asia to Europe across the Hellespont. The boats were anchored and tied side by side. Planks were laid from vessel to vessel. Then the army began to cross: it took a week of night and day operations to get them all over.

Eventually they captured Athens in 480 B.C. However, the remaining Greeks engaged the Persian fleet – all one thousand of them – at the battle of Salamis. Although the Greek ships were outnumbered by more than three to one, they outmanoeuvred the Persians and routed them. Xerxes withdrew from the Greek campaigns and spent the rest of his life adding to the beautiful city of Persepolis.

'Persepolis' is actually a Greek word meaning 'City of the Persians,' and was probably applied during the time of Alexander the Great.

Alexander crossed into Asia and defeated the last Persian emperor, Darius III at the battle of Gaugamela which means 'camel field'. The Persian ruler fled from the battle but was stabbed to death by one of his own men.

Alexander was usually generous towards his defeated enemies and never allowed his men to sack a town they had taken. In the case of Persepolis, he seems to have had a change of mind. Either that, or a terrible accident resulted in a disastrous fire, during which Persepolis was burnt to the ground. Only a few columns and sculptured stones standing at the head of splendid staircases serve to remind us of the largest empire of those times.

The Phoenicians

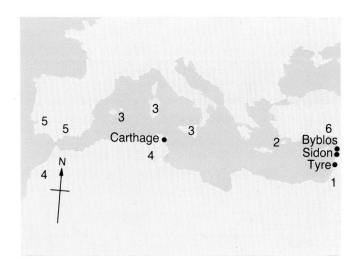

Unlike the majority of the ancient peoples we have looked at so far, the Phoenicians were not really warlike, nor did they have what anyone could call an empire. They lived in a coastal strip of what is now northern Israel and Lebanon and their chief cities were Tyre, Sidon and Byblos. The area was no more than 200 miles long and as little as fifteen miles across.

Because it was a poor region, the Phoenicians turned their attention away from the land and became Mediterranean sailors. After the Minoans, they were the great traders and seafarers of the ancient world.

Trireme

Their ships were biremes and triremes, driven by a rectangular sail on a single mainmast, provided the wind was right, and by banks of oars if it wasn't. They bought cheaply in one place and sold dear in another but always took most cargo space for their own products.

They were excellent craftsmen in copper, silver and gold jewellery; they carved ivory and turned pottery. They were fine woodworkers and knew how to decorate their other wares with coloured glass. They exported a purple dye got from a local shellfish which became the colour of authority and power. In Rome, only the emperor could wear, or even afford to wear, purple robes.

The Phoenicians had cut down and sold overseas huge quantities of building timber, particularly the cedar trees which grew in abundance on the hillsides. As early as 2700 B.C. they had sent wood to Egypt to be used in the royal funeral ship (see pp. 52–53). Solomon's great Temple at Jerusalem was partly constructed from the cedars of Lebanon.

They ventured farther and farther afield until they had trading posts or colonies all round the Mediterranean, for example: 1. the southern coast of Palestine   2. the islands of Rhodes and Cyprus   3. Sicily, Sardinia and the Balearic islands   4. almost half the north African coast including the Atlantic shore of what is now Morocco   5. southern Spain and Portugal   6. south east Turkey. There is a tradition that they visited Cornwall or the Scilly islands in search of tin but there is little evidence for this. Cadiz in Spain was founded in the 12th century B.C. At about 800 B.C.,

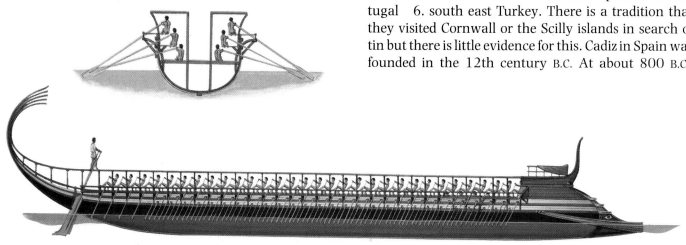

Carthage began as a colony (near modern day Tunis) and grew to be the largest and most important Phoenician city of all.

Signs of their religious life can be seen in the temples of their homeland. In Byblos, for example, a temple contained a double row of gold capped obelisks. We also know the names of some of their gods. They worshipped Baal and Astarte as the chief god and his consort: Teshub and Tanith were revered, particularly in Carthage and Baal Amon, their African god, apparently insisted that children were sacrificed to him.

From illustrations of the time we know that the ordinary Phoenician wore a white ankle length tunic with swathes of purple edged cloth wound round the body on top of the tunic, or a short kilt with a long overall like garment as outer wear. The men had beards but 'moustaches only' were rare: they wore their hair long, bunched at the back and kept in place with a narrow head band.

One of their legends says that Phoenician ships started from the Gulf of Suez, sailed south right round Africa, up the west coast and back home through the Pillars of Hercules (Straits of Gibraltar) and into the Mediterranean. They claimed to have observed the Tyrian Cynosure (Pole Star) getting lower in the sky each night until it disappeared completely – evidence enough, surely, that the sailors had indeed gone right round Africa.

But perhaps their chief claim to fame was the invention of the first successful alphabet. There had been alphabets before – even the Egyptians wrote the names of their pharaohs in a sort of alphabet. But it was the clever Phoenicians who took picture writing and

Phoenician traders

made from it a system for every day, where one sign always stood for one sound. From henceforth, all a learner had to do was to master two or three dozen symbols, in place of the several thousand that had to be committed to memory before.

They took this invention to their colonies and trading areas, whence it passed to the Greeks and Romans, and through them to the rest of the world. From Syria it moved eastward and became the ancestor of modern Arabic script. No one is very sure how the symbols of hieroglyphics were changed into letters but perhaps the following is not far from the truth: , an ox head, alters to because it was quicker to write and then to , which is even quicker. Phoenicians wrote it and the Greeks and Romans changed its attitude to the more familiar A . If the Phoenicians had never done anything else, this would have been enough to put us in their debt and to secure their place in history.

Phoenician ivory carving

Chapter 5   Pre iron age Britain

The first farmers

On pp. 12–13 we saw how hunting tribes gradually changed into farming tribes. The important word is 'gradually'. The gathering of wild plant products had always been done but what was happening here was that these products were slowly becoming a larger and larger part of the tribe's diet, until, thousands of years ago Man learned how to grow the plants to order, where and when he wanted them.

The discovery of plant and animal farming was made in western Asia, where the ancestors of domestic crops and beasts had once been wild. Several thousand years went by between the discovery of farming and the arrival of the first farmers in Britain. The reason for the delay isn't hard to find. No farmer in the middle east ever said to himself, 'Let's go and farm in Britain.' Of course not. People planted seeds and if the harvest was good they stayed in the same place, perhaps for decades, or until the plant foods in the soil were all used up. When that happened, the harvest would no longer feed everyone, so they moved on to a new spot and began again.

As populations got larger, it became harder to find fresh areas suitable for growing food. Families moved bit by bit into south east Europe and along its southern coasts to Greece, Italy, Spain and France. They also inched their way up the valleys of the great rivers such as the Danube. It took centuries for the new ideas to spread.

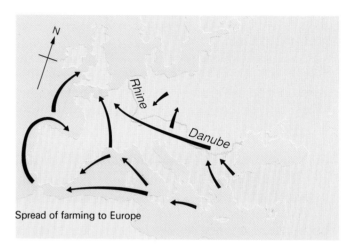

Spread of farming to Europe

Finally, by about three or four thousand years B.C. or perhaps even a little earlier, the first farmers arrived in Britain. They probably came from France and crossed the Channel at its narrowest place. The Channel was not nearly so wide in those days for the winter storms had not yet washed away so much of the cliffs on both sides.

The likeliest craft for the crossing were wooden framed boats covered with waterproofed animal skins. These would have taken the human beings with their bags of seed corn and also a few young animals with which they could start stock farming.

Britain must have been forested or marshy nearly all over, so they had to choose places not so thickly wooded. Then they began to cut down trees and burn the undergrowth. Oxen could be used to haul out the stumps. They planted their seeds and pastured their cattle on the plentiful grass. As well as cattle, they had sheep, goats, pigs and pet dogs. They grew wheat, barley and possibly flax. The latter was almost certainly for its oily seeds as the ideas of spinning and weaving linen, or wool for that matter, were still to come and our pioneers made do with clothing of soft leather and furs.

Cutting down trees needed keen edged implements – not the clumsy hand axes of the old stone age but smooth, sharp chopping tools, either home-made of local flint or got in exchange for food products. These 'foreign' axes could have come from as far away as Land's End, Wales or Langdale Pike in the Lake District, where there were clans which did little else but manufacture tools and weapons of stone.

As to the earliest farmers – very few traces of their houses have yet been found. For a long time it was thought they had lived in what are called 'causewayed cattle camps' such as the ones at Windmill Hill in Wiltshire, or Yeoveney near Staines in Middlesex. However, we now know that these earthwork circles were used for the autumn round-up of cattle. Grass doesn't grow in the winter so the beasts had to be collected together and most of them slaughtered before the cold weather was really under way. The earliest definite new stone age house remains have been found at Carn Brea in Cornwall and the cattle camps can't ever have been permanent homes.

Another change in the landscape made by the new stone age farmers was the building of large mounds of earth to house the dead. In the early days, the corpse or corpses were put inside a wooden structure which was then heaped over with soil. Later, they learned to make 'long barrows', as they are known, from 'trilithons' of stone.

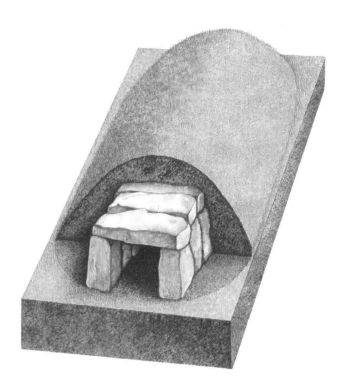

Now, when the earth was piled up, the stone didn't collapse as wood eventually did. The grave could be sealed by rolling a boulder across the end of the stone-built passage and opened every time there was a new funeral.

We don't know what language they spoke or what they called themselves but they were the first people in Britain to farm, the first to use proper pottery and the first to wield really smooth stone tools and weapons.

West Kennett long barrow

Skara Brae

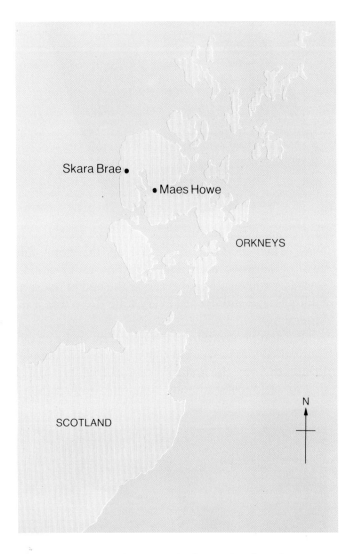

In the last spread we read about the first farmers in Britain. They arrived here before Egypt was united and before the building of the first pyramid. During the same period and at a time when Abraham was still hundreds of years in the future, a strange people built a strange village in the Orkney Isles to the north of Scotland.

Again, because they neither read nor wrote, we don't know who they were nor even the name they used for themselves as a group. Let's ask an archaeologist to tell us what is known about them.

'It's difficult,' he says, 'without any written records. We can only go on the actual things they left behind.

This is not an easy task. If you don't believe me, take a look around your own house or school. How much will still be in existence 5,000 years from now? (That's how old these remains are). Remember that glass and china may survive, plus some metal and stone but little else. What could a future archaeologist say about you, if all he had was a couple of tea cups, some shards of window glass, a bottle opener and a set of knives and forks?

'Anyway, let's begin at the beginning and see what we know and what we can guess. We must go back to a severe storm over the north of Scotland in the winter of 1850. The gale whipped up huge waves which crashed into Skara Brae on the coast of Mainland, the most important island of the Orkneys. Parts of the sand dunes collapsed, revealing what seemed to be a rubbish dump underneath. It was fifteen feet high and consisted mainly of ashes, although there were also some sea-shells, bits of horn, bone and half burnt wood.

'Eleven years later, the first proper dig was organised. It uncovered stone walled enclosures and passageways. In the next few years there were more digs. The pattern began to emerge of a small village. By 1867 four huts had been cleared and a number of stone implements recovered.

'Apart from some fairly aimless digging in 1913, nothing more was done until 1924, when the site was put under government protection. A lot of good that did!'

'Why do you say that?'

'Because a year later, another bad storm swept away some of the rubbish heap and part of the stone walling. They had to build sea defences to keep the site safe. While the building was going on, Gordon Childe made some important discoveries. Much of what we know we owe to him. It wasn't until 1973 though, that we got any reliable information about the date.

'There were nine stone built houses altogether. One was roofed in stone, the others had been thatched, perhaps with turf. The passages between them were paved and also roofed with stone slabs. The largest hut was about twenty feet square. Most of them were well furnished, with a hearth stone, wall cupboards, a stone table, bed spaces and even a sideboard or dresser.

Skara Brae as it is now (above) and as it was (below)

'The village seems to have been occupied on several different occasions. The earliest people must have lived here before the first pharaoh ruled in Egypt. From the rubbish we can tell that they ate mutton, lamb and beef, whereas the later squatters, if we can call them that, ate shellfish and wild deer meat. Were the first settlers wise men, perhaps? Did they come here from somewhere else in Europe? Did they bring a new religion with them? No one knows but maybe there's some truth in all these guesses. For not far away there are two stone circles of about the same age as the village. These 'henges', as they are called, are almost certainly temples, whatever else they may be. Perhaps our wise men preached a new religion and got the locals to put up the stone circles.

'It could be that they taught the natives how to build in stone. Skara Brae village is made and furnished entirely from stone slabs. Maes Howe, in the same neighbourhood, is a magnificent stone burial chamber. It's thirteen feet high inside and is constructed by laying stone courses one on the other until the roof line is reached. Then the slabs are pushed slightly inwards. This was done with each succeeding layer, piling earth up on the outside to stop them over-balancing and falling in. Finally the space left is small enough to be covered with a single roofing slab.

'Of course, we don't know if they were missionaries but it's an interesting idea.'

Silbury, Avebury and Stonehenge

Silbury

This artificial hillock looks a bit like one of the mottes the Normans used as bases for their castles, albeit an outsize one. It was never a base for anything as far as we know. It's a lot bigger than a castle mound and a lot older, dating back to well before 2000 B.C.

It was quite an eerie experience to walk down a tunnel dug by the Welsh School of Mining and to see chalky, earthen sides that no other human eyes had seen for over 4000 years. It seems terribly mysterious but at prehistoric ground level in the centre of the mound there is absolutely nothing – no burial, no monument – nothing

It is 130 feet high and covers $5\frac{1}{4}$ acres. The labour involved must have been enormous. It has been worked out that several million man hours would have been needed to build it. Considering that the toilers had no more than deer antler pickaxes, ox shoulder-blade shovels and perhaps leather bags for carting away the dirt, it's not surprising that it probably took several years to pile up from the surrounding ditch.

Avebury

There are something like 700 prehistoric stone circles in the British Isles: this is the largest. The huge ditch encloses $28\frac{1}{2}$ acres and is about 1400 feet in diameter. There is room inside for almost four Stonehenges in a straight line and the actual area is nearly 19 times as large as Stonehenge.

The ditch is half silted up and the outer bank overgrown with grass. Once the ditch was 30 feet deep and 40 feet wide at the top, with a bank of gleaming white chalk.

Around the inner edge of the ditch once stood nearly a hundred huge, rough sarsen blocks of stone. Only a few are left. There were four entrances, some with 'avenues' leading away from Avebury but these seem to have been added a good deal later.

Originally, there were two smaller stone circles inside the large one. These smaller circles are only just smaller than the one at Stonehenge. Few of the stones are still in position.

Stonehenge

The most important and impressive stone circle in Europe, probably in the world, was not erected all at once. In fact, the building was spread over at least a thousand years, from the late neolithic to the bronze age.

In the new stone age, the workmen made a bank and ditch around a circle measuring 380 feet across. Just outside the ring stood a single rough sarsen called the 'Heel Stone'. Inside the ditch a ring of 56 small holes was dug and almost immediately filled in again. Some of them contained the remains of human cremations. They are today marked with cement discs and are known as 'Aubrey Holes'.

At various dates, rings and horseshoe-shapes of dressed stones were put up, taken down and re-erected in other positions. Some of the stones came from only a short distance away but others were rafted and dragged on rollers from South Wales, well over a hundred miles away, even if you take a direct line. Again, the labour required to haul these massive slabs, some in excess of 30 tonnes, can well be imagined.

Today, although in ruins, Stonehenge has enough stones remaining for us to imagine the complete pattern. There were five 'trilithons' (Greek = 'three stones' – two uprights with a lintel across the top) arranged in the shape of a horseshoe at the centre. Then comes a circle of single standing bluestones, imported from Wales.

The outer ring is the most interesting. It consists of a circle of 13 feet high sarsens with lintel stones on top, once forming a continuous ring. The lintels are morticed and tenoned to the uprights and tongued and grooved to each other.

No one knows for sure how the building was done – perhaps the stones were levered up on a timber frame with long poles and ropes. No one knows why it was put up either, although all kinds of ideas have been suggested. Some people think it was a kind of observatory and it's true that certain stones are in line with important sun, moon or star positions. This could have enabled the wise men to calculate dates exactly – vital to people with no writing and therefore no calendar – and thus keep track of the seasons.

Bronze age barrows

'Barrow' comes from an old English word meaning 'hill'. In the latter part of the stone age, barrows were long and low, like the typical burial place at West Kennett, just south of Silbury. But in the bronze age, graves were almost always circular. Much of what we know of the bronze age in Britain comes from these round barrows.

It's a pity we don't know more than we do. Unfortunately, many of the barrows have disappeared in modern times – the result of intensive farming, mining, building, quarrying or gravel digging. Sometimes the barrows were deliberately destroyed.

In the late 18th and early 19th centuries, gentlemen interested in the past sent their servants to see what those strange humps were which showed above ground level in parts of the estate. They were not particularly interested in the bronze age as such, they merely wished to recover ancient or valuable articles. You can imagine a gentleman of those days sitting on a camp stool, sipping a glass of wine and watching his gardeners and footmen as they dug away three or four complete barrows in a couple of days.

There must have been many such burial mounds at one time: in the West Country alone, there are records of at least 6000.

Who built them and why? It seems that the first people to make round barrows are known only from the typical pottery which they made and used. We don't know what they called themselves, so we have called them 'The Beaker People'. They appear to have been the first people in Britain to cast copper and bronze weapons, tools and ornaments. Although metal working was known in the near east as early as about 6000 B.C., it wasn't until 4000 years later that it reached these islands.

Copper came first, then it was mixed with tin to make bronze. Bronze was used for daggers, swords, chisels, and jewellery. All the same, it remained expensive and flint continued in use for centuries afterwards.

In all, the bronze age in Britain lasted for about a thousand years. During that time burial customs altered. It's quite likely that the Beaker People, at least at first, buried their dead in the same long barrows that the new stone age tribes used. Then they began to make round barrows with the general rule that every corpse should have its own barrow.

After a while it became the custom to burn the dead, either where the funeral was to be or nearby. The ashes and bones were collected and put in a clay vessel over which the earth was piled and a ditch dug around it. Towards the end of the bronze age, about 1200 B.C., the burnt remains in their urn were just put in a hole in the ground which was then filled in.

The middle phase, that of the round barrow is the most interesting. There were several different types, called variously bowl, bell, disc, saucer or pond barrow, depending on the shape and size of the mound and ditch. They varied in size from the tiny forty footers up to, or even just over, 200 feet in diameter. It's sometimes possible to say whether a funeral was for a man or a woman from its shape and size.

We think that these graves were for the ruling classes – chieftains, their sons and other relations. As rulers, they would expect to have their earthly possessions with them in the after-life. The lucky

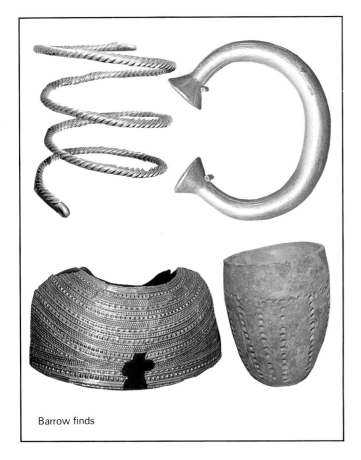

Barrow finds

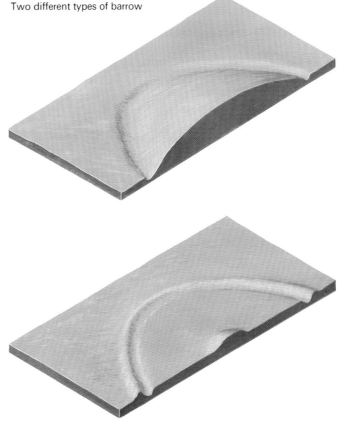

Two different types of barrow

Aerial photo showing Celtic field patterns

archaeologist thus had a chance to turn up finds in barrows that have been neither ploughed up nor robbed.

From such graves have come bronze knives, swords and daggers with gold and amber handles, earrings and cups of gold, beads of amber, jet, faience (possibly from Eygpt), shale and gold, battleaxes, the remains of clothing and shields, discs and squares of plate gold (used either as ornaments or as a display of wealth and power), a belt with a gold hook and eye fastening – even razors and trumpets have turned up.

Traces of square or rectangular fields can often be seen – in some instances carefully avoiding barrows, though we don't know very much about the *living* bronze age peoples, apart from their fields. The fields are marked on ordnance survey maps as 'Celtic Fields' or 'Strip Lynchets'. There are some faint traces of villages and single huts probably dating to the middle or late bronze age.

Some modern authorities believe that the owners of the fields and barrows may have been the ancestors of Celtic peoples such as the Welsh, driven westward by waves of iron using invaders, leaving behind them the chalk circles of their round barrows, dazzling white amid the short, green grass which was soon to cover them.

CHAPTER 5

The coming of the iron age

The Iron Age in Europe

Iron age

Iron was known thousands of years ago, even if very uncommon. It only came into general use with the Hittites between 1400 and 1200 B.C. Methods of smelting arrived in Greece about 1000 B.C. and into central Europe two or three centuries later. By about 600 B.C. iron working had started in Britain.

The Celts

If they were not here already, the people known as the Celts certainly came here with the beginning of the iron age. A loosely connected group of peoples, they occupied, at its greatest extent, a wide band of territory stretching across Europe from Ireland to Turkey. They were strong enough to attack Rome in 390 B.C. and Delphi in 278 B.C. but never disciplined enough to form a proper empire. Classical writers said they were quarrelsome and boastful with a childish love of personal finery. They were said to fight from two-horse, two-wheeled chariots and so scornful of death that they fought not only without armour but completely naked. They were brave and light-hearted, loved poetry and learning but were high-spirited and unstable.

Celtic war band

Salt mine

Hallstatt

The first site to show evidence of the earliest iron working in Europe was Hallstatt in Austria. In 1848, a large cemetery was discovered. The bodies were dated to about 650 B.C. and the graves were rich in iron swords and other weapons. The wealth of the nearby settlement had been built on huge deposits of salt – a vital substance for everyone. The Hallstatt peoples (probably Celts) spread across Austria, Switzerland, Southern Germany, France, Belgium and Britain. Their settlements in South East Britain are little different from late bronze age sites. We don't really know if the newcomers arrived in small peaceful bands or invaded under their chieftains.

Chariot burials

These are known in Britain but are more common on the continent of Europe. The dead person was laid by a wagon with rich grave goods. A wooden hut was built over the wagon or chariot and earth piled on top of it to make a barrow. The most famous is that of the 'Princess' at Vix, on the upper Seine in France. The body was that of a woman in her thirties and, apart from the normal grave goods such as flagons, plates, harness and chariot metalwork, there was a Greek cup and an enormous bronze cauldron decorated with beautifully sculpted figures. It stands over five feet tall and if filled with liquid, would hold almost 270 gallons. The title 'Princess' was given because of a gold head band or crown which was also found in the grave.

La Tène

This is the name of a place on Lake Neuchâtel in Switzerland, where, in the last century, more than fifty swords, some still in their scabbards, were discovered. They had beautiful patterns of twisting lines worked into their design. This style appeared on many objects from the later iron age, and was exported to Britain where it found expression, for example, on the backs of these metal objects.

Bronze objects with La Tène patterns

Lake villages

Occasionally, a tribe would feel safer if protected by water. A moat could be dug round the huts but it was easier to make artificial islands in a lake or swamp. This was done at Glastonbury in Somerset. The lake villagers lived by farming and also by fishing from dug-out canoes. They were good carpenters, potters and metal workers. They turned wooden items on pole lathes and had looms for weaving. Lake villages were also to be found in the margins of continental European lakes.

Names and coins

The Belgae, another people who invaded Britain, came here from about 75 B.C. onward. These were the first Britons to make their own coins – gold ones to start with, then silver and bronze. They are also the first people in our history to whom we can put names. These we know partly from the coins, partly from writers such as Julius Caesar. Thus we can point out the tribal areas of the Cantiaci, Silures, Iceni, Parisi, Trinovantes, Atrebates and Catuvellauni. We even know the names of some of their leaders, for example Tasciovanus and Cunobelinus (Shakespeare's Cymbeline) were kings of the Catuvellauni.

Early Celtic coins

Living places

Apart from hill forts and lake villages, many iron age people probably lived in large, round farmhouses, like the one that was excavated and then rebuilt at Little Woodbury. From posthole marks in the ground, it was possible to work out that the farmstead had consisted of a sizable, circular plan dwelling, several pens and huts for animals and storage plus a very large number of pits in which to keep the grain stores.

A reconstruction of Iron Age farm buildings

Hill forts

All over England, but particularly in the south east, iron age peoples built themselves hill forts for protection. The area enclosed by the defences might be as small as half an acre or as large as 200 acres. Some were little more than cattle enclosures, some were temporary hiding places in time of danger, others were lived in permanently. A common pattern was one or more ditches dug all round the top of a hill and the dirt piled up to make an embankment, behind which the defenders could shelter and from where they could bombard the enemy with sling stones.

Maiden Castle, Dorset

Part 2
The Greeks

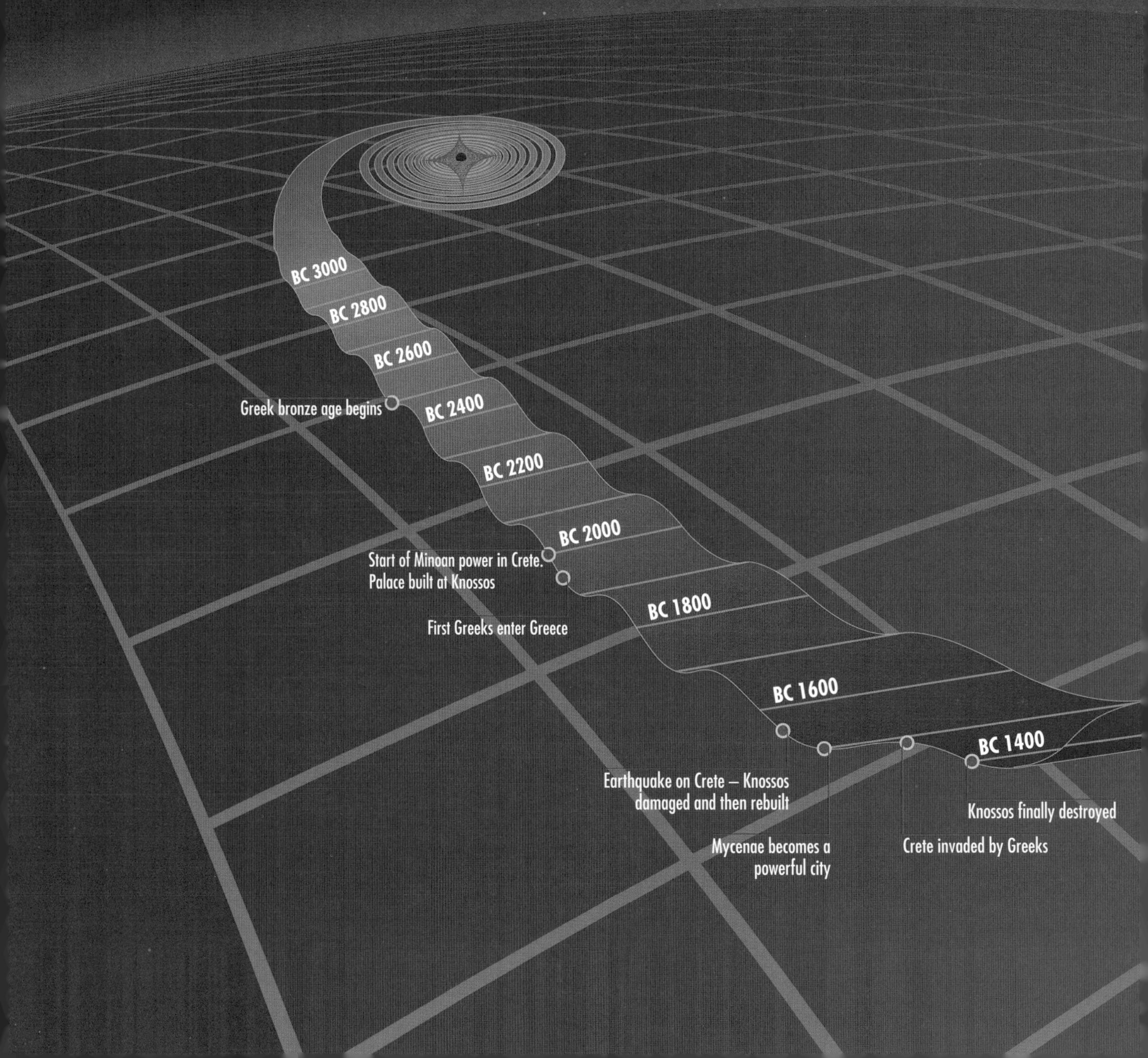

BC 3000

BC 2800

BC 2600

Greek bronze age begins

BC 2400

BC 2200

BC 2000

Start of Minoan power in Crete.
Palace built at Knossos

First Greeks enter Greece

BC 1800

BC 1600

BC 1400

Earthquake on Crete – Knossos
damaged and then rebuilt

Knossos finally destroyed

Mycenae becomes a
powerful city

Crete invaded by Greeks

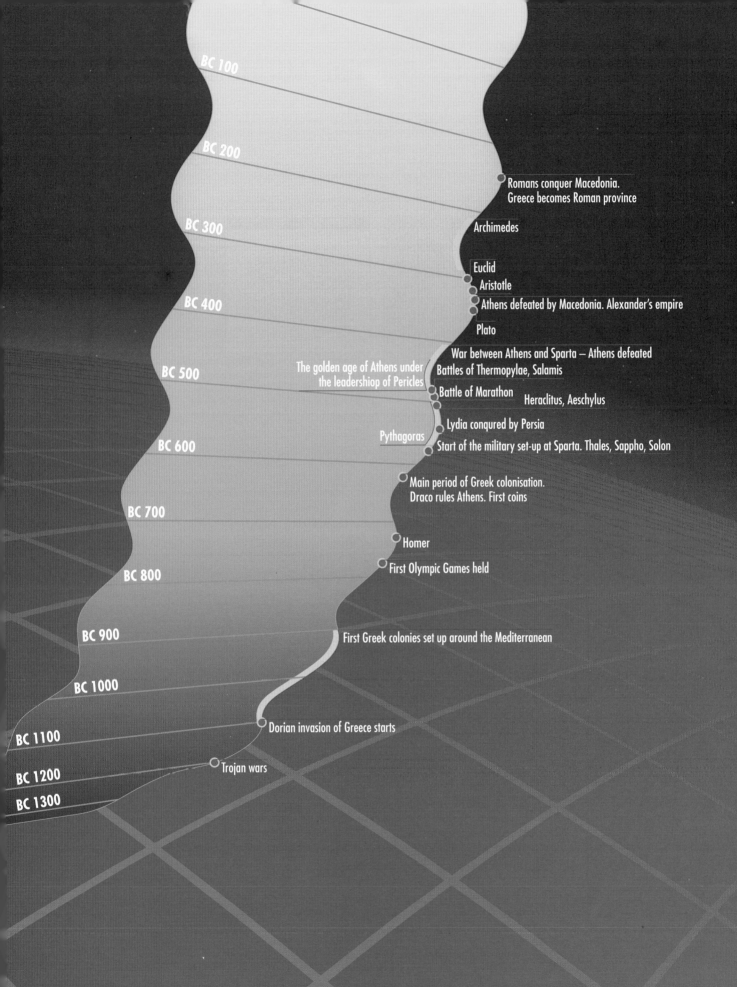

BC 100

BC 200

Romans conquer Macedonia.
Greece becomes Roman province

BC 300

Archimedes

Euclid

Aristotle

BC 400

Athens defeated by Macedonia. Alexander's empire

Plato

War between Athens and Sparta — Athens defeated

The golden age of Athens under
the leadershiop of Pericles

Battles of Thermopylae, Salamis

BC 500

Battle of Marathon

Heraclitus, Aeschylus

Lydia conqured by Persia

Pythagoras

Start of the military set-up at Sparta. Thales, Sappho, Solon

BC 600

Main period of Greek colonisation.
Draco rules Athens. First coins

BC 700

Homer

First Olympic Games held

BC 800

First Greek colonies set up around the Mediterranean

BC 900

BC 1000

BC 1100

Dorian invasion of Greece starts

BC 1200

Trojan wars

BC 1300

Chapter 6   The Minoans

The legend of the Minotaur

ONCE UPON A TIME, KING MINOS RULED OVER CRETE. RULERS OF NEARBY LANDS WERE AFRAID OF HIM.

GREECE

Crete

IN AN IMMENSE MAZE UNDER HIS PALACE, HE KEPT A MONSTER CALLED THE MINOTAUR—HALF MAN AND HALF BULL.

EVERY FEW YEARS, THE MINOTAUR WAS FED ON SEVEN YOUNG MEN AND SEVEN YOUNG WOMEN FROM ATHENS. IF THEY WERE NOT SENT, MINOS WOULD HAVE INVADED THEIR LAND.

ONE AT A TIME, THE YOUNG
PEOPLE WERE FORCED INTO
THE DARKNESS OF THE
UNDERGROUND MAZE WHERE
THE BULL-MAN COULD BE
HEARD ROARING.

YOUNG THESEUS PLEADED WITH
HIS FATHER, AEGEUS, KING OF
ATHENS, TO LET HIM TAKE THE
PLACE OF ONE OF THE VICTIMS.

THE KING AGREED, BUT WITH A HEAVY
HEART. 'IF YOU SURVIVE,' HE SAID,
'CHANGE THE SHIP'S BLACK SAILS FOR
WHITE ONES WHEN YOU COME HOME.
THEN I'LL KNOW WHAT'S HAPPENED
EVEN WHILE YOUR VESSEL IS
A GREAT WAY OFF!'

ARIADNE, THE DAUGHTER
OF MINOS, FELL IN LOVE
WITH THESEUS AND
SECRETLY GAVE HIM A
SWORD WITH WHICH TO
KILL THE MINOTAUR AND
ALSO A BALL OF WOOL SO
THAT HE WOULDN'T LOSE
HIS WAY IN THE MAZE.

AS SOON AS THESEUS WAS INSIDE THE MAZE, HE TIED ONE END OF THE WOOL TO A SPUR OF ROCK AND TOOK THE SWORD FROM WHERE IT WAS HIDDEN BENEATH HIS TUNIC.

THESEUS FOUND THE MINOTAUR BY ITS ROARING AND ATTACKED IT. THE MONSTER WAS SURPRISED AND ALARMED TO FIND THAT ITS NEXT 'MEAL' WAS ARMED. AFTER A TREMENDOUS FIGHT, THESEUS MANAGED TO KILL THE BEAST.

AAARGH!

THESEUS REWOUND THE WOOL AND THUS FOUND HIS WAY BACK TO THE OUTSIDE WORLD.

AS THE LOVERS FLED TOWARDS THE HARBOUR, IT SEEMED THAT THEY COULD STILL HEAR THE MONSTER ROARING. IN FACT, IT WAS AN EARTHQUAKE THAT SMASHED THE CRETAN KING'S PALACE AT KNOSSOS. THE FIRES THAT BURNT IT TO THE GROUND SIGNALLED THE END OF CRETE'S POWER.

THESEUS WAS SO DELIGHTED AT OVERCOMING THE MONSTER AND SO MUCH IN LOVE WITH THE PRINCESS THAT HE FORGOT ALL ABOUT CHANGING THE BLACK SAIL FOR A WHITE ONE.

AEGEUS, THE FATHER OF THESEUS, SAW THE SHIP IN THE DISTANCE AND NOTED THE BLACK SAIL. IN HIS MISERY HE KILLED HIMSELF BY JUMPING OFF THE CLIFF.

Sir Arthur Evans

The story on the last page is a legend – some would say a fairy story. However, many legends have some truthful parts. The question was, did this one contain any real history? No one knew until the early years of this century, when a man named Arthur Evans was responsible for the digging up of evidence for a totally new and hitherto unknown civilisation. The Minotaur legend could then be given an historical background.

Evans was born on July 8th, 1851 at Nash Mills in Hertfordshire. His father was a well known collector of ancient objects. Arthur was sent to Harrow and then to Oxford.

His adventures gave him material for the articles he wrote in the English newspapers. He was actually in England in 1878 and seized the chance of seeing the treasures dug up at Troy by Heinrich Schliemann. Coins and seals in an unknown language drew him to Crete in 1894 where he met a local archaeologist who had explored a little in the area of Knossos.

He spent several years digging there himself. To make sure there were no legal problems he bought the land. There was no longer any need to get permission for his excavations.

Sir Arthur Evans rebuilding the palace at Knossos

Sir Arthur Evans at Knossos

From his late teens onward, he was a keen traveller and loved nothing better than a tour of the less familiar parts of the world. He didn't mind hardships a bit if he could escape to places that were off the beaten track. In 1875 he was in what we now call Jugoslavia, when the native peoples revolted against their Turkish rulers.

What came to light was no less than a new European civilisation, able to take its place alongside those of Iraq and Egypt. In all, there were over 5½ acres of the ruins of a colossal palace with hundreds of rooms and apartments.

What Arthur Evans found you can read about on the following pages. His discoveries made him famous. He had already been appointed curator of the Ashmolean Museum at Oxford in 1884, a position he was to hold for a quarter of a century. He also became Extraordinary Professor of prehistoric archaeology at Oxford University in 1909, after retiring from the museum.

He had uncovered a 4000 year old civilisation and was one of the first to say that here was a corner of Europe with a written language dating back almost as far.

He was knighted in 1911 and died only three days after his 90th birthday in 1941. What he made of the Theseus legend you can see in the next few pages.

The palace at Knossos

Let's ask one of Sir Arthur Evans's men what it was like to dig up the palace at Knossos.

'It was a long time ago but probably one of the most important "digs" ever done,' he says. 'The remains of walls were only a short way down in the ground, and over the years we found a palace covering nearly six acres, surrounded by a somewhat larger town.

'The palace consisted of over a thousand rooms on at least five different levels ranged around a central courtyard.'

'What sorts of rooms?'

'All kinds, because the palace was used for varied activities. It was a house for a king, a court of justice, a suite of offices; it had reception, dressing, bed and dining rooms, a school, chapels, granaries, storerooms, studios, dungeons, annexes, workshops and many others. The most interesting, in my opinion were the bathrooms with their sunken baths but I suppose that the most important was the so-called throne room.

'The throne was made of stone and imitated the remains of a wooden one which we found in another part of the palace. On either side of it were long stone benches set against plastered walls. On the walls were painted plants and imaginary animals, reckoned to be griffins. That was the one thing about the palace that amazed everyone – the frescoes.'

'Frescoes?'

'Yes, the pictures painted on the plaster walls. You can tell from them what the Minoans looked like – medium sized, with long, dark hair and large, dark eyes. The common form of dress was a wrap-around kilt or loin cloth. Against that, we did find a statuette – of a priestess, I suppose she was, holding a snake in each hand. Now *she* was wearing a floor length skirt and a frontless blouse or jacket.'

'You said "Minoans": how do you know what they were called? Did they have a written language?'

'Yes, they had at least three, and only one of them has ever been deciphered. But we don't know what they called themselves. Evans got the terms "Minoans" from "Minos", the king in the legend.

'Another interesting word was "labrys" which means "double axe". This symbol turned up all over the

The throne room

Plan of the palace

place, in metal and in stone. It may have been a religious sign or a sort of royal trade mark. The word "labrys" is supposed to have given rise to the word "labyrinth".'

'That means "maze", doesn't it? Did you find any traces of the maze – you know, the Minotaur's lair?'

'I've a theory that the palace itself was the maze – the enormous number of rooms must have caused no end of confusion, especially to strangers. Can you imagine being given directions to a distant room? "Go along this corridor, turn right, second on the left, then turn right, down the stairs, take the third turn on the right through the little courtyard, up the stairs—". Wouldn't you tell everybody it was a maze?'

'The excavators thought it was more like a jigsaw puzzle than a maze – a lot of it had collapsed on itself. Sir Arthur had to reconstruct a good deal of what was found first before we could go any lower.

'I think what he rebuilt gives a marvellous idea of what the palace might have looked like. Notice, I only say, "*might* have looked like." Some people say he made it seem like a Victorian hotel and that he hadn't any real authority and not much evidence for what he did.'

'Do you think that?'

'Heavens, no. I believe his reconstructions were absolutely vital. No one could have any idea of what Knossos was about if he'd just left the ruins as he uncovered them.

A double axe

'Just a couple of other items. Some walls seem to have been designed to withstand earthquakes, one of which could account for the so-called bellowing of the Minotaur. Survivors of severe tremors often mention a continuous earsplitting roaring that they heard. And other walls show signs of the various burnings which destroyed the whole complex on more than one occasion. The last time was probably in 1375 B.C. The fire marks on the west facade of the new palace show that there was a southerly wind blowing at that time all those years ago.'

Earthquakes and fires caused the palace to collapse.

Daily life

The old Cretan road

The palace at Knossos had a great many places for storing farm produce – large pits, sometimes lined with lead, and rows of enormous clay jars. These were obviously used to contain the taxes from the peasants – paid in olives, olive-oil, wine and different kinds of cereals.

In common with other ancient civilisations, that of Crete depended on farming. The farmers had only a few horses but there were cattle, sheep, goats and pigs. Barley and wheat were grown, as were olives, grapes and almonds – in small, terraced fields. Ploughs and carts were drawn by oxen, probably under the control of slaves. Anyone could own a slave. If a slave were lucky, he might be taught his owner's trade.

Apart from ox wagons, goods could be carried on a pack donkey or a slave's back. There were tracks and paths all over Crete and even a few stone-surfaced or 'metalled' roads. One of them, near the palace itself, is reckoned to date from about 1500 B.C. and is thus the oldest metalled road yet discovered. Other forms of transport included going by boat along the coast and travelling (at least for palace officials and servants) in litters.

Farmers lived in little square, lime-washed houses in small towns or villages. Apart from Knossos, there were over a hundred other large and small towns. Sometimes an official had his office and living quarters at a distance from the palace and a village or town would grow up round it.

Houses for the well-to-do, particularly those near the palace, were made of sun-dried bricks on a burnt brick or stone foundation. Often, they were two or three storeys high. Lower floors were of stone, cobbles, cement or beaten earth, with sheepskin rugs to keep bare feet warm. Some outside walls were faced with square stones. There were the usual doors and windows (although earlier and poorer houses had neither: if you wanted to get out you climbed a ladder to the top of the wall, hauled the ladder up after you and used it to get down to the well drained and paved street. Someone still at home pulled the ladder back inside!).

Later doors were of wood and windows were divided into two or three with stone bars. The spaces were filled with oiled and stretched animal skin. Most houses had flat roofs for summer sleeping. Occasionally, there were storage cellars under the houses of merchants, of which there were quite a few in the ports, together with the houses of ship builders, chandlers and fishermen. Fishing boats must have been kept busy. Food from the sea was very popular if the pictures of various fish, octopuses and dolphins on Minoan pottery are anything to go by.

None of the towns seem to have been protected by

A merchant's house at Knossos

Octopus pot

Wall painting

walls – the Minoans relied on the fact that they were on an island so that their enemies would be dealt with by Minoan ships. They had a large fleet which traded widely all over the eastern Mediterranean.

Apart from the houses mentioned above, there were middle-sized dwellings occupied by gold and silver-smiths, weavers, carpenters, potters, basket makers and other craftsmen. As well as the two- and three-storied houses, there were villas with rooms round a central courtyard. Walls were often plastered on the inside and painted – red was a favourite colour. On these hung china plaques of fish or animals, rather like the flights of pottery ducks in some homes today.

The houses of the better off might have a dozen or fifteen rooms. Those with more than one floor had an outside staircase leading to the roof. Bathrooms were not unknown. The queen's bathroom in the palace had a terracotta bath which the servants had to fill from jugs of hot water. Afterwards, the used water was baled out and poured away down a drain in the same room. Richer Minoans had bathrooms of the same type.

Rainwater was used to flush the lavatory which often had a wooden seat. Water running off the roof was channelled into stone conduits which also carried waste away from all floors into a main drain. Heating in the cold weather might be provided by a portable metal brazier which burned charcoal.

Work was not the only way of spending your time. You could take part, or just watch or listen to a variety of pastimes including conversation, tumbling, wrestling and boxing, bull-leaping (see page 16), board games or dancing. Another interest must have been fashion but we only know how the people dressed from statuettes and wall paintings. The last named show women as white-skinned and men as brown. Whether this was like life or just the way they painted we don't know. It may suggest that women stayed indoors while men lived an outdoor life and were sunburnt.

Both men and women are incredibly wasp-waisted, the males with broad belts round their middles. Ladies wore their hair piled up high and kept in place with a bandeau. Both sexes were very fond of jewellery, wearing anklets, bracelets, necklaces and earrings of gold.

Religion

A goddess begging a favour of Zeus

It could be that a number of gods and goddesses whom we think of as purely Greek may have started off in Crete. For instance, Zeus (later taken over as Jupiter by the Romans) according to legend, spent his childhood on Crete. However, gods often took second place in the Minoan mind to goddesses. Cretans spent more time worshipping a mother goddess than almost any other ancient people – with the possible exception of the Maltese of those days.

On Malta there are many fine stone-built temples associated with statues of a mother figure. They are more than 5000 years old but we know very little of Maltese prehistoric religion or beliefs. Of course, we know little more of what Cretans believed; we can only put forward guesses based on the things they left behind.

To start with, there are no huge elaborate temples such as the ones in Egypt or Mesopotamia. Nor are there any gigantic statues of divinities. There were instead shrines of various kinds, many of which were adorned with the sacred bull's horns or the equally sacred double axe. The shrine might be in a palace

(there are several shrines at Knossos itself) alongside a track, in a cave or on top of a mountain.

In earlier civilisations, religion was entwined with warfare, sometimes accompanied with what seems like senseless cruelty to captives. Cretan art so far discovered shows no sign of glorifying fighting, military leaders, or even hunting, even though we do know that some hunting took place.

Mother goddess worshippers washed on entering her shrine or were annointed with oil – probably to wash away their sins before being shown into the holy presence. Occasionally, the priestess would blow a blast on a sea-shell horn to summon the goddess.

The worshipper then deposited the gifts or offerings he or she had brought. These might be food and wine or something more valuable – a necklace, a swordblade, a gold or pottery double axe or an armband. One shrine had two stone chests let into the floor, perhaps to hold the offerings.

A Minoan shrine

Cretan funeral rites

In one wall painting, women are shown praying and pouring wine as a libation to one of the pillars which held up the shrine roof. In another part of the palace at Knossos, towards the north west corner is an area flanked by two shallow flights of stairs at right angles to each other. We have no proof, but it may be that this was a theatre for religious dances. Some statuettes of dancers also show poppy heads and it's possible that the performers were drugged with opium. Possibly they didn't realise the terrible danger of taking this substance.

Burial customs, like most other religious matters on Crete, have to be guessed from very small pieces of evidence. We know that tombs shaped like old-fashioned beehives were being used as early as 2800 B.C. and that this particular type remained fashionable for almost a thousand years.

The dead bodies were laid above ground inside the building and decked in all their finery. The commonest kind of coffin was made of clay but one example was cut from limestone and coated with white plaster. Its four sides are painted with pictures almost certainly dealing with the funeral. On one long side, mourners are bringing a small boat and a pair of young bulls to be sacrificed. The dead person is shown as alive and accepting the offerings. Women pour wine into a special vase surmounted by double axes. A man in the background plays his lyre, a kind of harp. The second long side shows the sacrifice, with music provided by a double-pipe player. The short ends of the coffin show the dead person and the goddess in a chariot. One painted chariot is drawn by goats and the other by a pair of the imaginary animals called griffins.

Hardly any of the Minoan tombs have been found undamaged – many have been robbed and totally destroyed. However, not far from Knossos, at a place known as Arkhanes, a Minoan woman's body was discovered. It was dressed in a gold trimmed gown and was wearing a good deal of gold jewellery – rings, necklaces and a pair of tiny gold boxes lying on her chest.

One of the rings has a picture of a religious rite, showing the great goddess, in a similar costume to the dead lady, conducting a ceremony aimed at encouraging plants and farm crops to grow. There are some butterflies round her shrine and people dancing.

Bull leaping

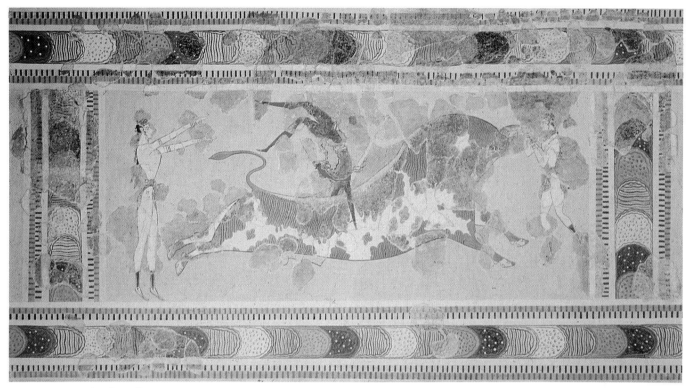

Fresco of bull-leaping from Knossos

Catching a wild bull, on the cup of Vapheio

One of the commonest souvenirs you can buy on Crete is a plaque, usually of baked clay, showing a youth holding the horns of a galloping bull and vaulting over its back. We know the bull was worshipped: even a stylised carving of its horns was looked on as sacred. The origin of this modern tourist's keepsake is to be found on seals and in a wall painting of the same kind of gymnastics.

It seems that bull leaping was either a religious or a popular performance rather like the 'games' that went on in Roman amphitheatres, or perhaps like bull-fighting in modern Spain, except that the bull was not killed.

The animals were apparently hunted and caught alive. There were many ways of trapping wild bulls. The two most popular seem to have been tripping the animals with ropes and tying them up, or driving them towards a large net stretched between two stout trees. Occasionally a cow was tied up nearby to act as a decoy. Someone had to wait until a suitable beast was entangled, jump on its back and wrestle it to the ground. Then the helpers would hobble its hoofs and take it off to an enclosure near the arena. Once there, it would be broken and trained.

Some modern experts believe that what is shown in the painting – the acrobat grasping the bull's horns and then turning a somersault over its back – is quite impossible. However, if the animal was tethered, tamed or even drugged, it might not have been.

This is not to say that there was no danger. The team of acrobats must have been at risk all the time – a false move, bad timing or a much too frisky animal and there was always the chance of one of the leapers being gored by a bull's horn. We mustn't exaggerate the danger; after all, performers on the high trapeze in a modern circus are in just as much peril but accidents are fortunately rare.

Rare or not, accidents did occur, even when the nearly naked leapers had trained intensively for months. Thus a steady stream of recruits was needed. Almost certainly this state of affairs gave rise to the part of the Theseus legend which spoke of seven Athenian boys (and the same number of girls) being sent to feed a bull-headed monster on Crete. Might this have been a half remembered attempt to describe the continuous tribute of young people to train as bull leapers for king Minos?

111

Michael Ventris and Linear 'B'

This is the famous Phaistos Disc. Phaistos (together with Mallia and Zakros) was one of the palaces on the island of Crete and was excavated by Italian archaeologists. The disc was dug up there. It is a little less than a foot across, made of clay and is stamped with 45 different characters.

Although it has been known for many years, its message is a complete mystery. No one has been able to decipher it. But that has not stopped both the expert and the not so expert from guessing its purpose. 'A set of mathematical tables', 'a peace treaty' and even 'a piece of music' were some of the suggestions.

Apart from the disc, other kinds of writing are known to date from the Minoan period. It took some time before any progress was made. The writings that survived were done on clay tablets which were often baked hard in accidental palace fires. Perhaps the Minoans also wrote on leaves, wood panels and other perishable surfaces.

The two most important methods of recording facts both had characters drawn with straight lines. Evans called them 'linear' because of these line-drawn 'let-

ters'. The two different systems were called 'Linear A' and 'Linear B'.

In 1936, Sir Arthur gave a lecture in London dealing with his discoveries in Minoan Crete. He showed slides of the various clay tablets and explained that the languages were unknown and had defied all attempts to translate them.

In the audience was a fourteen year old schoolboy named Michael Ventris. He was so interested that he vowed then and there that he would one day disentangle the meaning of the clay tablets. When he grew up he joined the Royal Air Force, for the Second World War had started just after his seventeenth birthday. When the war was over, he trained as an architect but he never lost his love or enthusiasm for the unknown tongues of ancient Crete.

He went to work on them, trying various different ways to break through. Some of his methods were those used to decipher enemy codes in wartime. One of the first things to do is count the number of 'letters' or signs to see how often each one is used. If the number is fairly low – somewhere between, say 12 and 50, the language is probably written with an alphabet, just as English is. If it runs into several hundred, it's probably a syllable system. This means that words are split into parts or syllables and each one has a separate sign. This is difficult to do in English but less so in some foreign and ancient tongues.

To make it more difficult, there were occasionally little drawings of the thing being written about and even crude attempts to spell the word. A further obstacle for Michael Ventris was that no one knew what language 'Linear B' was written in. The only thing the wise men were sure of was that it was about 600 years too early to be Greek. Ventris himself thought that it might be the language of the Etruscans, a people who flourished in Italy before the coming of the Romans.

After some incredibly complicated work on the clay tablets of Sir Arthur Evans, Michael found what he thought were place names and then – following a little drawing of a three legged support for a cooking pot – the signs for TI-RI-PO-DE (Tripod).

TI – RI – PO – DE

Using the signs discovered, he set them against similar signs on the tablets and began to realise that these were lists of stores, accounts of taxes and tribute paid, names and numbers of soldiers and similar matters. Furthermore, he was extremely surprised to find that the tablets were written in a kind of Greek – the one language everyone had dismissed as impossible.

Although some people still do not accept this solution even now, there has never been a better answer put forward. Ventris was tragically prevented from doing further work by a fatal car accident. He was only in his early thirties.

Perhaps you'd like to see what code breaking is like. Try your hand at this: 'BLLG BL CG GWKLL EISEIQ EV GWL WLCGW. TSLCUL HL GWLKL CVF FEVG HL SCGL. GWL VLYG GWKLL MLLQU MRSS ULL GWL LVF EP GWL BCGGLK.'

1 Count the different signs. If there are hundreds, it's probably a syllabic language: if only (say) 12–50 characters, it's alphabetic. (To make it easier this one's in English.)

2 Which letter occurs most often? (In English it's 'E'.)

3 Put 'E' wherever the most frequent letter sign comes.

4 Can you now guess which three signs are the word 'THE'? (It's the commonest '3-group' in English.)

5 When you are sure of (4), put 'T' and 'H' in their proper places. This should suggest some other words – for instance, there are several words which begin with the combination 'THE' – e.g. 'THERE', 'THEIR', 'THESE', 'THEN' etc.

6 By now you'll have enough letters to solve the code message.

A Minoan scribe

113

Atlantis

Plato

A Greek writer named Plato wrote a book called *Timaeus*, in which he describes how some priests of ancient Egyptian gods had told a Greek tourist called Solon a very curious story.

Until about 9000 years ago, he was told, there existed a huge island, which was rich and powerful and whose ships and soldiers had conquered all the lands around the Mediterranean. Only the Greek city of Athens had resisted them.

The people of this island had become so proud and conceited that the gods were offended and they sent tidal waves and earthquakes to punish them. In a single night, the island was overwhelmed and sank beneath the waters of the ocean.

Solon was told that the island was in the Atlantic beyond the Pillars of Hercules (the Straits of Gibraltar) and was known as 'Atlantis'. Modern scientists have been completely unable to find any evidence to support this remarkable legend and some have wondered if Plato didn't make the whole thing up.

Did Atlantis look like this?

Romantic novelists and writers of adventure stories took up the legend enthusiastically and produced endless tales of the miraculous Atlanteans. More serious thinkers began to wonder if there was, at least some truth in the story. Perhaps the timing or location of the disaster were wrong.

Then in the 1960s remains of a brilliant civilisation began to turn up on the island of Santorini, or Thera, to the north of Crete. Thera is almost a third of the way between Knossos and Athens on the Greek mainland.

From about 1967 onward, rain washing down had revealed traces of wall paintings very much like the ones in the palace at Knossos. Excavation confirmed that this indeed was a palace similar to that of king Minos on Crete.

There were also streets lined with houses of the same type as those found near Knossos, some as high as three stories. The archaeologists found rooms with giant storage jars and several plaster panels painted with scenes of everyday life.

One painting shows some beautifully graceful antelopes: another, a young fisherman with a string of fish in each hand. This is one of two boy boxers. They seem to be about ten or eleven years old and are wearing nothing but a waistband and what appears to be a boxing glove on the right hand only. A large part of this fresco is a restoration and if the modern artist is correct, it's very difficult to imagine what sort of boxing is being done. One suggestion is that each boy holds the other's hair with his left hand and hits with his right! This is not so unusual as might be supposed: not long ago in England, fighters stood still, toe to toe and took it in turn to hit each other.

From the kinds of soil covering the ruins of the palace and houses, archaeologists were able to say roughly when and how this rich and varied Minoan type civilisation had come to an end.

There had been a series of massive volcanic eruptions at about 1500 B.C. which had virtually blown away most of the island. The first eruption had blasted a hole in the side of the old crater, sea water had poured in onto the white hot lava and a titanic explosion was the result. This bang may have been the loudest ever heard. In the far east, a hundred years ago, an island called Krakatoa had exploded and the noise had been heard over a thousand miles away.

Scientists say that the disaster on Santorini was a good deal worse and the bang very much louder. There must have been huge tidal waves and it is tempting to think that the end of Minoan civilisation on Crete may have been the result of gigantic earthquakes and volcanic eruptions. These might have given rise to both the Plato story of Atlantis's destruction and also the legend of the Minotaur's death.

On the other hand, the truth (if we ever come to know it) may be nothing like the ideas given above!

Minoan fisherman, and boy boxers (below)

Chapter 7   The Mycenaeans

Homer

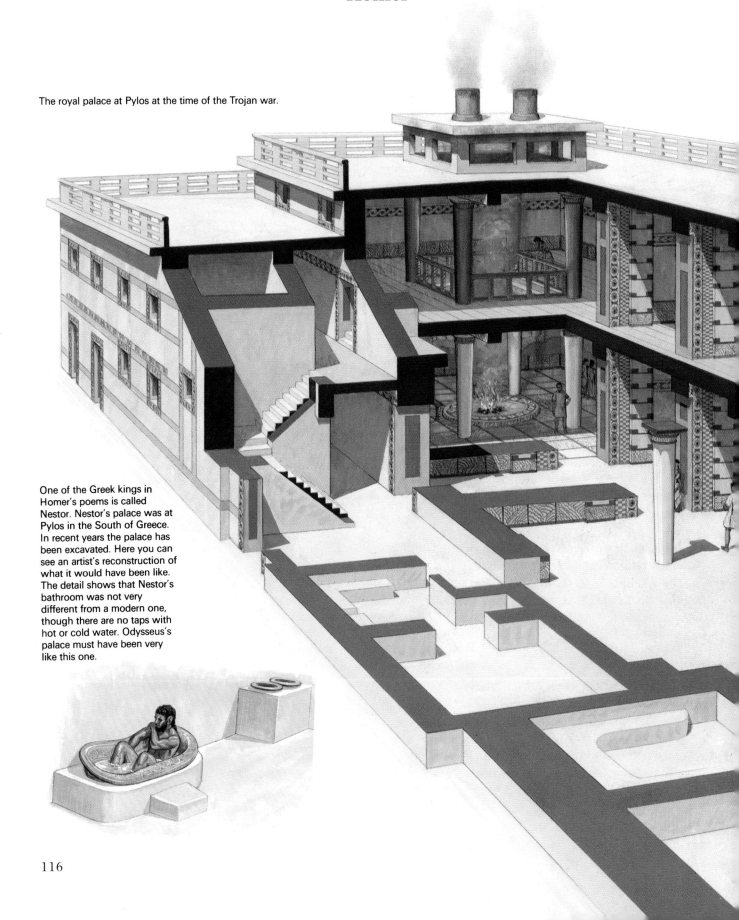

The royal palace at Pylos at the time of the Trojan war.

One of the Greek kings in Homer's poems is called Nestor. Nestor's palace was at Pylos in the South of Greece. In recent years the palace has been excavated. Here you can see an artist's reconstruction of what it would have been like. The detail shows that Nestor's bathroom was not very different from a modern one, though there are no taps with hot or cold water. Odysseus's palace must have been very like this one.

It is 730 years before the birth of Christ. We are waiting in the hall of one of the Greek kings. The meal is over – the last olive and sliver of cheese have been eaten – and boys are serving the wine. We ask our neighbour what kind of entertainment we are to be given. He replies, 'Why, it's Homer!'

We ought to be impressed but our friend can see that we've never heard of him, so he explains.

'Homer is blind, you know: he has to be led about everywhere. He was a slave many years ago but he became famous for his recitations. Whilst serving his master, he found he could repeat a poem of any length even if he'd only heard it once. He has friends who've written down the poems he's composed. Among the longer ones is a story about part of the Trojan war.'

There is a stir and Homer is led in by his attendants and settled down. His lyre is handed to him and he begins to tune it by tightening or loosening the pegs. He clears his throat, strikes a chord and starts to recite.

The poem is one of the longer ones of his own composition. At least the form of the thing is Homer's although the actual story has been passed on down the years for about five centuries before Homer's time. It is all about the adventures of Odysseus on his way back home to Greece after the siege of Troy. Now that it has been set down on paper, future generations will also be able to enjoy the Odyssey, as it is called.

Odysseus, or Ulysses, as the Romans knew him, set out from Asia to sail back to his queen in Ithaca, Greece. Unfortunately, he and his men were lured into one trap after another and many of them perished.

They were driven by storms to the land of the lotus eaters, where anyone who consumed the lotus forgot where he came from or even who he was. Then they were captured by a Cyclops, a one-eyed giant named Polyphemus who kept them prisoner in his cave, together with a flock of huge sheep. Odysseus had told the giant his name was 'Noman'. When the Greeks seized their chance to escape by putting out the giant's eye, Polyphemus shouted and roared until his neighbours came to ask what the trouble was. 'Noman has attacked me!' screamed the giant.

His neighbours then called back from the other side of the boulder which sealed the cave mouth, 'If no man is hurting you, it must be a nighmare. Go to sleep.' And they went away.

In the morning the giant tried to stop the Greeks getting away by riding out on his enormous sheep. As the animals passed through the rock opening, Polyphemus ran his hands over their backs. He could no longer see and wasn't aware that Odysseus and his crew were clinging to the wool of each sheep's belly.

Later, one of the gods gave Odysseus a goatskin bag, which he said contained favourable winds to blow them home. Some of the crew thought there must be treasure in the bag and undid it. Out rushed the angry winds and once more the ship was sent off course.

The crew escaped from the rock and whirlpool of Scylla and Charybdis and from the island of sirens, who would have entranced the sailors by their songs, had they not sealed their ears with beeswax. By a trick, the leader managed to free his men from a spell cast by a witch named Circe, which had turned them into pigs.

Finally the wanderer returned to his homeland of Ithaca in disguise. He found that his wife Penelope had been besieged by men wanting to marry her and thus become king, firmly believing that her husband must be dead. Penelope still thought he would return even after ten years of wanderings, so she said she would marry the man who could bend her husband's great war bow – knowing that it was unlikely that anyone could do so.

She was right. None succeeded until the lonely, dust-covered stranger not only managed to bend the bow, he also slew the pestering suitors with sharp arrows.

The notes of the lyre die away and we ask our friend about the other legend he mentioned – the siege of Troy.

'Come in a week's time,' he says, 'Homer will recite that story then.'

Odysseus slays the suitors

The Trojan War

Once again we sip our wine and listen to Homer as he tells us something of what happened when the Greeks fought the Trojans. Unfortunately, Homer doesn't deal with the whole story, so we have to ask our companion about the rest. From the two of them we can piece together most of the main events.

Troy, or Ilium, as the Greeks called it, was a city in the country that we modern people call Turkey. It stood on the Mediterranean coast, a short distance from the sea. Its king was an elderly man named Priam. He sent his son, Paris, as an ambassador to the court of Menelaus, king of Sparta.

Tragically for all concerned, Paris fell in love with Helen, the beautiful wife of Menelaus. He took her away secretly to his ship and sailed back to Troy.

Menelaus was beside himself with fury and called on his fellow Greek kings to rescue the lady and help him to his revenge on Paris. Those who heeded his call and turned up with ships and men were the aged Nestor, Diomedes, Odysseus and Menelaus's brother Agamemnon, king of Mycenae, who became the expedition leader, and Achilles, greatest of the heroes.

The fleet sailed across the seas and dropped anchor off the coast near Troy. The city was a formidable sight with its 25 feet high walls. The Greeks made camp and thought about the problem. All they could do was to encircle the city. Unluckily for the besiegers, there were countless sorties by Trojan heroes such as Hector, Paris and Aeneas. These drove off the enemy and raised the siege – even if only temporarily.

Often, the encounters took the form of single combat. Achilles, however, had quarrelled with Agamemnon and went off to sulk in his tent. His closest friend, Patroclus, borrowed his armour and took his place. Sad to say, he was slain by Hector, the Trojan commander.

Achilles drags Hector round the walls of Troy

Achilles then sought out the slayer and avenged his friend's death, only to die later himself, killed by a poisoned arrow fired by Paris. The arrow had struck Achilles in the heel, the only part of his body that was not magically protected.

Homer's recital finishes here so we have to get the rest of the story from our friend. He tells us that the siege dragged on for another ten years. Then the Greeks had a brilliant idea. They made a huge wooden statue of a horse and left it in front of the city. Then they set sail and their fleet headed out to sea.

The next morning, the astounded Trojans saw this enormous horse and a bay empty of Greeks. 'The enemy has gone!' they shouted, 'and they've left us a present.' Some wanted to bring the horse into the city but others were more cautious, saying, 'Beware of the Greeks when they bring gifts.'

However, there didn't seem to be any danger, so the horse was brought inside the walls and the Trojans began to celebrate the end of the war. By the evening,

most Trojans had drunk more than was good for them and a good many collapsed in a stupor, not knowing that they were about to lose the war. They were ignorant of the fact that some soldiers were concealed in the hollow body of the horse.

In the middle of the night, the Greek warriors unbolted a trap-door in the animal's body and shinned down ropes to the ground. From there they went around, unchallenged, opening the city gates.

The main Greek army, which had not gone home, but merely hidden in the next bay, swarmed in through the gateways. Nearly all the men and boys were slain. The women were taken back to Greece as slaves. Priam was dead and Troy utterly destroyed. Helen was returned to her husband, Menelaus, and the war was over.

We have imagined what it might have been like to listen to Homer speaking the lines of his famous poems, 'The Odyssey' and 'The Iliad'. But it is imagination, nothing more. In fact, no one knows exactly when Homer lived. We're not even sure if he was one man or several and many towns in the Mediterranean area have claimed to be his birthplace.

On the next page, in the story of Heinrich Schliemann, we'll try to see if *this* legend has any basis in fact.

The wooden horse is dragged towards Troy

Heinrich Schliemann

One man who was sure that Troy really existed and that the Trojan war had actually been fought was Heinrich Schliemann, a somewhat unlikely archaeologist, who spent a good part of his life making money.

He was born in 1822, the son of a poor clergyman in Germany. When he was seven, one of his Christmas presents was a book of Greek legends. At that time, Troy had vanished so utterly that no trace of it still existed and no one had the faintest idea where it had once been. Young Heinrich promised his father that one day he would find the site of Troy and prove it to the whole world.

He was brought up amid grinding poverty and was forced to find ill-paid work as a grocer's boy at the age of fourteen – not the background you'd expect for a great excavator. Ill health made him give up this job and then he became a cabin boy on a ship which was wrecked off the coast of Holland.

Heinrich Schliemann

An artist's impression of Troy

In Amsterdam he was employed in a merchant's office and began to learn foreign languages – Dutch, French, English, Spanish and several others, taking no more than six weeks over some of them. In 1846 he went to Russia for his firm and a few years later to America where he made a fortune buying and selling.

He travelled more and more extensively and had made so much money by the age of 41, he was able to retire from business and devote himself to archaeology. By the late 1800s he was convinced (from details in the Homeric poem) that Troy lay beneath the soil of a hill called Hissarlik, in modern Turkey.

Between 1870 and 1873 he excavated Hissarlik with over a hundred workmen. They toiled hard and removed mountains of soil. The finds consisted largely of pottery fragments – but pottery of a type not previously known. The diggers also found walls and even walls underneath the walls. Schliemann was forced to conclude that one city had been built right on top of another, and earlier, one.

Nowadays, we know that when a city was sacked or burnt down, the rebuilders often just levelled off the ruins before starting again. Schliemann uncovered the layers of no less than nine different occupation levels,

the earliest going back (we now know) to before 3000 B.C.

In those days (i.e. the 19th century), archaeology had scarcely begun as a science and Schliemann had little idea of the dates of the various layers. In the fire-scorched ruins of the second and third oldest cities, he found a tremendous hoard of valuable items. He immediately announced that he had found 'the treasure of king Priam'. In fact, the articles in question that he had found were a good thousand years earlier than the Troy of Homer's poem but Schliemann was dazzled by his boyhood dreams of finding the classical city.

The treasure consisted of thousands of different things – beakers, cups, plates, necklets and necklaces, bangles and bracelets. There were over 8000 gold rings.

Heinrich continued digging into the hill of Hissarlik on and off for the next few years. Other archaeologists came to help from time to time but many scientists were not convinced that this was indeed Homer's Troy. However, in our own time, most people are now sure that Schliemann really did find the ancient site of the Trojan war.

Remains of the Trojan walls

Schliemann at Mycenae

Schliemann mistakenly claimed this as Agamemnon's death mask.

We've already seen how Agamemnon became the leader in charge of the Greek army which attacked Troy. He was the king of Mycenae, which had been for some time the leading city of Greece. Thus it was natural for the 'King of Kings' to give orders to everyone else.

Unlike many other sites, Mycenae had always been visible to travellers throughout the ages. Ancient writers referred to it as a powerful and 'golden' city state. It is not, therefore, surprising that Schliemann should turn his attention to it. In 1874 he made his first survey, digging a number of holes and trenches. Nothing of great interest came to light but he discovered in some deep graves no less than five bodies.

The corpses were loaded down with gold. The faces were concealed beneath masks of gold and, buried with the dead, were weapons, cups, beakers and ornaments – all made of solid gold. Schliemann immediately jumped to a wrong conclusion, just as he had done at Troy. 'I have looked upon the face of Agamemnon', he said. However, these bodies were not of Agamemnon and his family; their funerals had taken place a good four centuries before the famous king of Mycenae was born.

Schliemann also turned up decorated daggers, bowls, plates, cups and beakers. Often the decoration took the form of illustrations of daily life, which in this case consisted largely of military and hunting scenes. Mycenaeans, it seemed, were far more warlike than the gentler Cretans.

Other archaeologists followed Schliemann's example and, over the years, a picture of the powerful and aggressive city state emerged. Outside the walls, graves even older than those first found were discovered. Again, the funerals were accompanied by many articles of silver and gold. Clay tablets were found in house foundations just outside this extremely strong fortress. The tablets were written in what we call 'Linear B' (see p. 112).

The main entrance is known as the 'Lion' gate because of the magnificent sculpture above the stone lintel. Apart from the size and strength of the city walls, attackers faced an even greater problem. Almost certainly unknown to would-be besiegers, the Mycenaeans had a secret water supply, within the defences, from an underground spring, just outside.

Then a number of 'tholos' tombs came to light. Each contained just one king and his immediate family together with the funeral offerings. The remarkable thing about these old-fashioned beehive shaped graves was their huge size. One tomb, known as the 'Treasury of Atreus' measured nearly 48 feet in diameter and one of the lintel stones over the doorway has been reckoned to weigh over 100 tons.

We know from written Greek history that Mycenae was the strongest and richest city in the whole of Greece. Its art and fashions, types of weapons and pottery were exported and copied all over the known world – to such an extent that it is possible to speak of other 'Mycenaean' cities in the Greek world.

It was Homer who used the word 'golden' to describe Mycenae: it was a fitting description. More gold has been found there than in all the other ancient Greek sites put together.

Mycenaean merchants exported wine, perfumes, manufactured metal goods plus clay pottery and they imported ores of both precious and base metals. They set up trading posts which developed into colonies in many places. Finally, the Mycenaeans (probably taking advantage of the chaos caused by the earthquakes and eruptions in the area) invaded Crete and captured Knossos. They ruled the island for more than two centuries.

Even if a Mycenaean man was a merchant, he would also have a farm of some kind on which he grew grain and fruit and raised sheep, goats, pigs and cattle.

At Mycenae, there were found, as well as the fortress, substantial foundations of houses belonging to the traders and to workmen.

All indications show that the city was powerful, rich and extremely well protected. It is therefore all the more surpising to find that the fortress of Mycenae was conquered by bands of wandering Greeks known as Dorians about eleven or twelve centuries before Christ.

The Lion Gate at Mycenae

123

Chapter 8   Early Greeks

Achaeans and Dorians

Armour of the period

With the end of the Trojan war, the rule of the Mycenaeans also came to an abrupt end. No one is sure why this happened: some say the climate began to change and much of Greece became a good deal drier. Earthquakes and disastrous fires have been blamed as well, but the most likely cause was a series of invasions.

The land of Greece probably had as many outsiders fighting their way in as anywhere else in Europe but the first group we can put a name to were the Achaeans. Homer in fact uses the term for all the Greeks who fought in the Trojan war, no matter from which city they came. Therefore from his point of view, the citizens of Mycenae and similar strongholds were also Achaeans.

The new invaders were known as Dorians because they were believed to come from a place called Doris in northern Greece. Their conquering of the Achaeans started apparently well before 1100 B.C. When it was over, the whole of Greek civilisation had taken several steps backward.

Strangely enough, their weapons, although crude, were better than the beautifully wrought swords and daggers of bronze the Achaeans used. The reason they were superior was that they were made of iron. Thus, the Dorians were the people who introduced iron-working to the land of Greece.

The words 'Greece' and 'Greeks', by the way, were not the names they gave themselves but Latin words, bestowed by Romans of a later generation. Greeks of the generation after Alexander the Great called themselves 'Hellenes' but it's very unlikely that those who lived at this early stage thought of themselves as 'Greeks' at all, nor of 'Greece' as a nation. The Dorians conquered places and settled there, regarding themselves merely as citizens of whichever city they lived in.

It seems that the newcomers spoke a kind of Greek, although they knew nothing of reading and writing. The Linear B script died out completely. When the 'dark ages', as some people call them, were over – about four centuries later – the Greeks had borrowed a proper alphabet from the Phoenicians with which to record their language.

The Dorian invasions were thorough, overrunning

most of the important towns. Athens seems to have been an exception. Either the northern conquerors never tried to capture it, or they did try and were unsuccessful. Their chief town in the newly won south was Sparta.

One result of the Dorian invasion of mainland Greece was that some Achaeans left in large numbers, searching for somewhere to live that was free of the hated Dorians. The islands around Greece provided the safety sought by such groups. Others migrated to the western coasts of what is now Turkey.

Two of these groups of Achaeans were known as Aeolians and Ionians. They founded Greek colonies in Asia Minor that lasted until just after the First World War, in this century.

By about 800 B.C. the dark ages were drawing to a close. The Greeks had a common language even though there were local dialects. The first written accounts of many popular myths and legends date from this time, although they may have been passed on by word of mouth for centuries before the Greek alphabet was invented.

At the same period, iron-working became much more common. The first Greek colony in the western Mediterranean was set up at Cumae in Italy. Trade was beginning to recover and there was a rebirth of culture, including art, literature and science. In short, the classical age of Greece was about to dawn – with a certain amount of tension between the two rival cities – Athens of the Achaeans and Sparta of the Dorians.

As a footnote, it is only fair to point out that some historians don't accept the story of Dorian invasions. They say that the differences between the various Greek settlements can be accounted for by the separate development resulting from the isolation of cities by ranges of mountainous country. We don't have sufficient evidence yet to be sure.

Battle scene

The emergence of cities

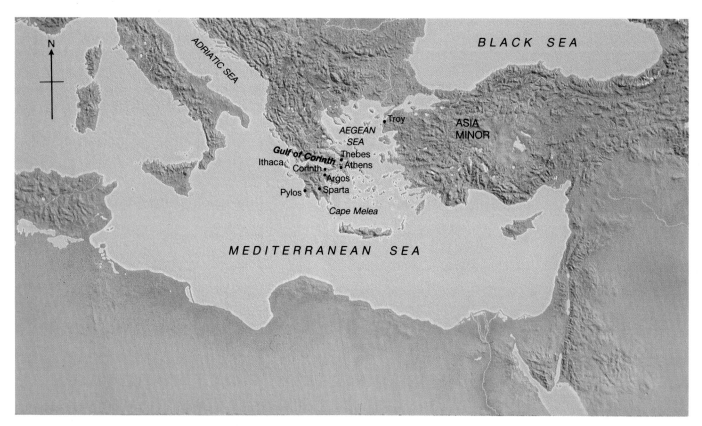

Ancient Greece never became a nation in the same way that France, Britain, or even modern Greece did. The reason was touched on at the end of the last page and can also be gathered from a glance at a map.

Greece is a stony, mountainous land, shaped rather like a hand with fingers stretched out into the Mediterranean sea. There were odd spots of fertile land but they were few and far between. They were separated from each other by arms of the sea or steep ridges of limestone mountains. The country was almost divided in half by the Gulf of Corinth and the whole area surrounded by countless islands, particularly in the Aegean sea to the east of the mainland. The entire area of Greece is smaller than some American states.

Because the regions where people could get a living were cut off from each other, they tended to develop in their own way and had little to do with their neighbours. This isn't surprising if a town's nearest neighbour was on the other side of a mountain. The paths

between would have been difficult to use in the summer and virtually impossible in the winter. Only occasionally did the towns join together – for instance when the whole land was threatened by foreign invaders (and not always then!). Another exception was for the regularly held games.

Apart from these examples, Greek cities and towns often fought each other for economic reasons, occasionally out of fear or even jealousy. Each town or city state was called a 'polis', a word which turns up in modern English expressions such as 'metropolitan', 'political' and 'police'.

A polis was a single town set amidst farm land. Some, like Athens, were large. Most others were fairly small and there were very many of them. One guess says that there may have been 150 on the Greek mainland and ten times that number in the colonies and trading posts scattered all round the Mediterranean and Black seas.

Some city states were founded in wild countryside, others on the sites of more ancient settlements. In the latter case, the old palaces were destroyed or burnt, sometimes deliberately, and what had been the original city became the inner citadel or fortress in the new and enlarged area. Here the population could flock in time of danger.

Danger wasn't the only reason the citizens got together – they had to have meetings for the running of the town or city. The bronze age kings had gone and at first their place was taken at the city level by any man strong enough to reign by force. After a while, however, some city states developed a system of self government, replacing the rule of the tyrant with that of the people. The very word 'democracy' comes from the Greek for 'people's rule'.

Although the citizens in such a method of government could and did meet to decide policy and law, the only ones entitled to an opinion and a share in the law making were the free adult males. This effectively cut out women, foreigners and slaves, so it was not really true democracy as the modern world understands it.

The average town had houses and temples huddled in narrow, winding streets and both sorts of building seem to have developed from a common pattern. They were made of wood or brick, more rarely of stone and were squarish with a pitched roof, probably of thatch. The door was often protected with a small porch roof standing on two side columns, maybe tree trunks in their first form. The roads in which these houses and temples stood were normally of beaten earth, sometimes dressed with a layer of gravel.

This was the sort of town in which Greeks of the early classical period lived. The largest of all the city states was Athens.

Early Greek town

127

CHAPTER 8

The early days of Athens

We've managed to obtain a guide to show us round Athens. The time is the end of the dark ages and the beginnings of classical Greece.

'Hello,' says the guide, 'my name is Kallias. My city is Athens. We are in a part of Greece called Attica. That's on the eastern side of the country, just above the line of the Gulf of Corinth.

'Athens, you may remember, was almost the only Greek city not conquered by the Dorians who flooded in from the north. What we did have was a flood of refugees from other parts of the country – all of them running away from the invaders. We were very overcrowded for a time.

'Then many of them migrated to Asia Minor and set up their own city states among the barbarians – you know, those who can't speak Greek and whose language sounds to us like "Bar-bar-bar"!

'You can see how large the city is. In fact it's the most extensive and thickly populated in the whole country. Sparta and Corinth are the next in size and importance. These walls run a very long way: over three miles with half a dozen gates.

'If we stand in the very centre of the city we can see, away to the north west, an open space or town square which we call the agora. It means "a plain", "a level, uncluttered area" or "assembly area", though it's very

difficult to keep the agora uncluttered. You'd be surprised at the number of people who want to put up buildings on the smallest patches of land round the edges. Of course, when we want to hold a meeting, all the market stalls have to be cleared away. But there are so many statues and monuments now that it's difficult to walk a straight line – at least along the borders of the agora.

'Now, if you look away to the south-east, what do you see?'

'A large flat-topped rock. A hundred feet high perhaps?'

'About that. What you are looking at is our Acropolis. If it weren't there, you'd be able to see right down to the south east corner of the walls. What am I saying? If it weren't there indeed! If it weren't there, it wouldn't be Athens. After all, the Acropolis is the original town.

'When cities began to develop, they outgrew their hilltops and spread out at the foot. "Acropolis" only means "highest city". I'm told that there were royal buildings there once. Now, of course, all you can see are temples. Just below the rock on the south side is our theatre. You can't see it from here but you can from the Acropolis of course.'

'But where is the Parthenon? Surely one of the finest buildings anywhere in the world. I don't see any sign of ...' We break off. The forehead of Kallias is creased into a frown. 'I'm sorry,' he says, 'I don't understand what you are saying.'

Of course he doesn't and it isn't really our place to tell him that in the future his city will be involved in a war with Persia and that the strikingly beautiful Parthenon will be erected centuries hence – partly as a monument to those who fell defending Athens from foreign invaders.

The agora with the Acropolis in the distance

Chapter 9 Greek civilisation

How the cities were ruled

If we were to ask a historian to give us details of the way the city states were governed, he would probably say something like this: 'To tell the truth, we don't know very much on this subject. About Athens, for example, or Sparta, we have some knowledge but for most of the other places, our information is either very scanty or it doesn't exist at all.

'We know that, during the bronze age, there were places in the Greek world that were ruled by royal families but when the Dorians invaded in about 1200 B.C. nearly all that sort of thing was swept away.

'Strangely enough, it was only in Sparta, the chief Dorian settlement that the idea of kings remained. The Spartans even went so far as to have two of them at a time. Mind you, the Spartan kings were really just army commanders, but they were members of a sort of council of elders: there were thirty elders all told. They had to be over sixty years old before they could take office and were then elected for life.

'In addition there were magistrates to look after the day-to-day affairs of the city. They were called "Ephors" and there were five of them.

The Spartan 'kings' sitting in the council of elders

Athenians voting

The Areopagus

'It was different in Athens. This was probably the first place on earth to use a system called "democracy" (see p. 127). It didn't happen overnight but took many years to develop.

'In the earliest times, Athens was ruled by nine rulers or "archons" drawn from ranks of upper class Athenians. They were elected by an assembly of all citizens who owned a certain amount of property.'

'It doesn't sound like democracy as we know it.'

'No,' says the historian, 'it wasn't. I think you already know that there were certain people who had no say at all in public affairs: women, poor people, foreigners and slaves. Archons ruled for one year only and then retired to a sort of House of Lords which met at a spot called "Areopagus" (The Hill of the War God). To begin with, it had wide powers but these were slowly cut away by a number of Athenian statesmen such as Solon, Cleisthenes and Pericles.

'Although most people could read and write, we don't think that early laws were written down. Most people knew the main ones by heart – just as modern people can recall a proverb to fit any kind of happening. Mind you, men tended to disagree as to which law ought to be applied. Some of the laws probably contradicted each other – but then, so do our proverbs. Don't say you've never noticed that "He who hesitates is lost" and "Look before you leap" mean absolutely opposite things. So with Athenian laws, which must have needed tidying up.

'Draco, an archon in 621 B.C., was the first to codify the laws and write them down. Some of them had such severe punishments laid down, that we still use the word "Draconian" to refer to modern laws with harsh penalties.

'By the 5th century B.C., the Athenian Assembly met almost once a week and every male Athenian over 18 was entitled to be present and to speak for or against any proposal and then to vote on it.

'Anyone could make his way to the Pnyx, the hill to the west of the Acropolis, where the Assembly met and argued about taxes, temples, treaties, road building, war and peace, or anything else that arose.

'A lot of the actual work (in carrying out the wishes of the Assembly) was done by the "Boule", a council of 500 men, chosen at random to serve for one year only. Anyone could be a member of the Boule but never more than twice in a single lifetime.

'For nearly two centuries, Athens led the world with its democratic way of life, until the city was captured by the Macedonians in 322 B.C.'

Solon, Cleisthenes and Pericles

Solon

Pericles

'These were the three men who did most to bring democracy to ancient Athens,' says our historian, 'so it might be a good idea to find out something about them.

'Let's take Solon first. He was a magistrate or archon, elected in 594 B.C., with special powers to do something about the laws – poor people had complained about the harshness of the code of Draco and rich people complained that there was too much unrest and disturbance.

'Solon's first decision was to ease the birth qualification for membership of the Areopagus: from then on you didn't need to be born an aristocrat to be a member. Solon then did away with the savage custom of selling someone into slavery because of an unpaid debt. It was his idea to set up a court of appeal open to anyone who was dissatisfied with an ordinary court verdict.

'He decided to leave Athens at that point to see how the experiment would work in his absence. In fact things went rather well, although the rich complained that they had given away too much power and the poor maintained that they had got too little.

'Oddly enough, it wasn't under the rule of an elected official but during the "reign" of a tyrant, the self-appointed Peisistratus, that the common people became really free and the control of the land-owners was finally broken.

'Peisistratus seized power twice illegally – each time by a trick. The first time he pretended to be wounded

and acted as though he was being chased by a murderous enemy. He pleaded for an armed escort to protect himself and then used the men he was given to take over the government by force.

'He was quickly driven out but returned once more. This time he pretended that an ordinary (if somewhat large) woman, whom he had arrayed in golden armour, was really the goddess Athena. He arranged for her to drive into Athens in a chariot and to tell the people to trust Peisistratus. This they foolishly did and the tyrant returned to power for the next twenty years.

'When he eventually died, his two sons succeeded him. One died naturally and the other one was murdered. There might have been a successful revolt by the land-owners. Instead, there was a period of chaos lasting two years, after which order was restored by Cleisthenes who gave people back their freedom under the law.

'He rewrote the rules of government and broke the power of the aristocrats by redrawing the boundaries of the regions occupied by each land-owning clan. In this way, the areas of the old ruling classes were broken up into bits and pieces of land, scattered here and there throughout the entire land.

'Another invention of Cleisthenes was that of 'ostracism'. If a man had behaved so badly that the city would be better off without him, the citizens could write his name on a broken piece of pottery (the Greek for which is "ostracon") and put it into a large container. If a man received more than 6000 "votes" he was banished for ten years.

Pottery used in ostracism

'Another famous statesman was Pericles, the great nephew of Cleisthenes. By his time (after the long and damaging Persian wars) democracy was as complete as it ever would be in Athens. Pericles presided over what has come to be looked on as a golden age.

'Under him, Athens blossomed as the capital, in all but name, of Greek art, liberty, architecture, sculpture, drama, poetry, history, philosophy, science, politics and many other human activities.

'Athens had become almost an empire, controlling the whole of the Aegean and much of the Greek mainland. Her allies paid her money to deal with their possible enemies. The Athenian navy protected them and Pericles used whatever money was left over from ship building to beautify his city. It is from this period that the superb entrance gates to the Acropolis were set in position and the world famous Parthenon erected on the rock's flat top.

'As far as public life was concerned, Pericles said that the law should be fair for all and that men should be honoured for what they had done, not for who they were. Violence was to be avoided and men must learn to give and take.

'By now the ancient ruling council, the Areopagus, still packed with aged archons, no longer had any powers beyond that of trying murder cases. The running of the city and its surroundings was the responsibility of the Assembly whose meetings anyone could attend.

'The command of the army and navy was entrusted to ten generals elected each year: these were posts of far too great importance to be left to a chance ballot. In fact Pericles himself continued to serve as an army general almost until the day he died in 429 B.C.'

Peisistratus and the pretended Athena

133

Everyday life

Harvesting grapes and olives

Many Athenians got their living from the soil. The richest had their farms nearest the city so that they could actually live in town houses, leaving their slaves and employees to do the hard work on the land. Their day consisted of rising from a couch, washing, break-fasting on a lump of bread dipped in olive oil or wine and water, and starting out on a tour of inspection.

Depending on the time of year, farm labourers would be breaking the soil with iron-shod ploughs, harrowing, broadcasting barley seed, hoeing, weeding or reaping. Attica, the area around Athens, was not all that suitable for the raising of cattle or the growing of wheat, so most farms grew barley, beans, lentils, grape vines and olive trees.

A man who had no need to supervise a farm would base his life entirely on his city house. This probably had rooms leading off an open courtyard. The house itself might have a stone foundation on which stood the timber framework and sun-dried clay brick walls. A porch roof supported on columns led into the main part of the house. This doorway was the only opening on to the narrow street. What windows there were mostly faced on to the central courtyard. bedrooms were behind the courtyard or even on an upper storey.

The roof was much less steep than those in modern Britain, for rainfall was seasonal and fairly low. What rain there was could be collected in a large stone cistern. The roof was made waterproof with thatch or clay tiles.

There were no separate pavements specially for walkers around the buildings, but the roads themselves were sometimes paved or gravelled. Gangs of slaves swept the streets, being careful not to tip any rubbish into the drainage ditches.

Once inside the house, the master would bolt the main door. His personal possessions were mostly kept in cupboards and his stores in well-built rooms, both of which could be locked. There was not very much furniture – a few small, three-legged tables together with some chairs and stools for the women and children to use at meal times. The master himself lay on a long low couch to dine. However, most families had a fine collection of painted pottery (see p. 138).

If the master had to go out, he would take down his cloak from where it had been hanging on a nail in the annexe to the main reception room. Other items similarly hanging on nails might include his lyre (or small harp), his strigil (or bathtime body scraper), together with his military equipment – sword, spear, shield and leg guards. All Athenians had to do military

Coins of the period

service and the richer a man was, the more equipment he had to supply. A poor man might only be able to afford a spear, whereas a rich one had to supply a riding horse (a war chariot in earlier times).

There were occasional housing shortages, particularly in war time when house building had to stop. A citizen could buy or rent a house in more peaceful times but he might, like Diogenes, sleep in a huge, broken and discarded wine jar.

The master, then, goes down to the agora, or public square, often used as a meeting place, but mostly given over to market stalls. Maybe he is doing the shopping. By now Athens is minting its own coins, which makes such expeditions easier. A slave walks behind carrying a basket for the purchases.

Many of the errands can be done at the wooden stalls standing in rows across the agora – items such as meat, fish, bread, poultry, fruit, vegetables, herbs, olive oil and flowers.

Other goods and services can be found in the rows of permanent shops at the sides and rear of the square. If he wants ironware, he will go to the blacksmith's, whose fireside is a favourite meeting place for friends on a cold morning. In the summer, such 'get-togethers' will probably be at the barber's or shoemaker's. Other businesses carried out in the colonnade of shops will include the carpenter's workplace, the doctor's surgery and the teacher's school.

The master might attend a meeting of the Assembly, act as a juryman in a court case, or merely stroll round, greeting old friends, hiring a servant, or watching one of the professional entertainers – a juggler, conjuror or acrobat.

He might go home for a light lunch or buy himself a snack at a nearby stall. When he has had enough of the agora he will go home or to the house of a friend for the day's main meal and some serious talking and drinking.

Town house

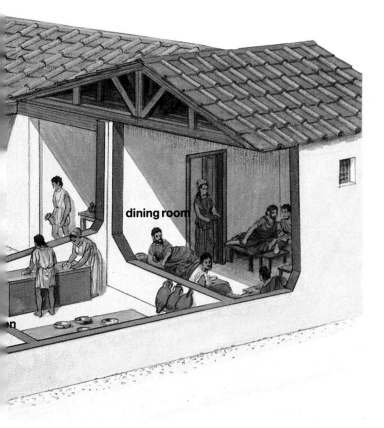

dining room

Other members of the family

While the master was out at the agora, what were the rest of the family and relations doing? It has to be said straight away that ancient Athens was a man's world: decisions of all kinds, from simple hearth and home ones to those dealing with peace and war were an all-male affair.

A young Athenian woman was married to a suitor chosen by her father. Love hardly entered the matter at all – father picked a likely candidate on the ground of his birth, breeding and worldly goods. Even an old or ugly husband would be acceptable if the other conditions were met.

The wife was expected to raise the children, to feed and clothe the family and to know her place. As a child, she had to pick up what education she could. Girls were rarely educated formally: only her brothers were sent to school, while she stayed at home learning how to prepare and cook food, and how to tailor clothes from the cloth she had woven on her loom.

This is not to say that women did nothing but bathe, chat to friends, paint their faces with cosmetics and have their hair done. Some Greek women were strong personalities in their own right. Women did not vote or speak in the Assembly but there is no doubt that many of them got their menfolk to put forward a particular point of view. There is evidence that women attended the theatre (although never as actresses) and they had their own athletics meetings and festivals.

A Greek woman's sons were only entirely hers until they were about six or seven, when they were sent off to one of the numerous day schools in Athens. Let's ask one young man about his day at school.

'My name is Timon,' he says, 'I am eleven years old and I have been at school now for nearly five years.'

'What time do you get up?'

'I rise at dawn. Our rooster wakes me up early. My father says we borrowed rooster breeding from the Persians, but how my ancestors got themselves up before we had chickens, I don't know.

'I wash in cold water and my slave pours water all over me when I've finished. I dry myself and put my tunic on. In winter, I wear a cloak as well – and sandals also. In summer I go barefoot indoors and out.

A woman weaving

'I eat a bread roll and wash it down with wine for breakfast. I say "wine" but it's really only water coloured pink with a little dash of wine. Even the grown-ups don't drink wine neat: they dilute it with more than the same amount of water.

'I walk to school which is a small corner of a building in an arcade of shops just off the agora. I give my personal slave, or pedagogue, as I call him, my writing tablets to carry on the way. He will protect me to and from classes and wait while I learn. I give the teacher the coins he charges for his lessons and we begin.'

'What do you learn?'

'History and Greek literature – and of course, how to read and write. We copy lines of Homer on to these waxed tablet boards with a pointed stick. The other end is blunt and flat. We use it to smooth out the wax if we make a mistake. We learn arithmetic with a bead frame, pebbles on the ground, or even on our fingers. Some masters teach geometry and nearly all of them will tutor us in singing, speaking and playing the lyre or flute.

'Later on we strip off in the nearby gymnasium and practise running, jumping, wrestling, boxing, throwing both the javelin and the discus and many other sports.

'Then I wash, dress and go home. I can play toy soldiers with my brothers, while my sister (provided that she isn't helping my mother) has some rather nice dolls to dress and play with.

'If there are no guests, we children sit up to the table on stools, while father reclines on his couch. If there are guests, we eat separately before going to bed for the night.'

A Greek school

CHAPTER 9

Art and pottery

When we looked into an Athenian house (see p. 135) we mentioned that most families had a collection of rather fine decorated vases. The potters of Athens were so famous for making these that their output was sent all over the Greek world by traders and merchants.

Although the earthenware is only one example of Athenian art, which also includes painting, coinage and sculpture, it is most important for us because it is the the one thing that has lasted down the centuries. A good deal of our knowledge of Greek everyday life comes from the pots painted with human figures, usually black on an orange background or the other way round.

Woman spinning

Cobbler

Women fetching water

Fisherman

Huntsman

Carpenter

Ships and trade

As the population of Greece grew, the country was unable to produce enough food for all the extra mouths. Trees were cut down for charcoal (used for metalworking and cooking) and timber (used for house and ship building): much of the soil was washed away by winter rains.

In fact, the only crops that would grow at all well were grape vines for wine and olive trees for olive oil – the cooking, lighting and washing oil of the ancient world. It was a matter of common sense to send these plentiful products abroad and to import the grain which Greece needed.

Exports included not only olive oil and wine but also silver from the mines at Laurium near Athens. One other export has already been mentioned – the huge quantities of painted pottery which found its way all over the Greek world. Athens took over the role of chief pottery maker from the city of Corinth in the middle of the 6th century B.C. and kept it for more than two hundred years.

By now Greece had colonies all round the Mediterranean. We've already seen how adventurers settled on the west and south-west coasts of what is now Turkey, together with the islands of the Aegean. Colonists also took over the islands off the opposite, or western coast of the Greek mainland, settled in southern Italy, North Africa, Spain and cities such as Massilia (Marseilles) in the South of France. Stranger still, perhaps, to modern thinking, they started building trading posts and versions of the Greek 'polis' around the shores of the Black Sea in what is now Russia.

The Black Sea colonists were following in the footsteps of the mythical Jason and the Argonauts who sought the golden fleece at a place called Colchis. The voyage was repeated in the 1980s by Tim Severin and his volunteer crew sailing a specially built reproduction of an ancient Greek merchant ship. The modern voyagers didn't meet multi-headed serpents nor fight warriors who grew from dragon's teeth but they did prove the journey, though difficult, could be done (see

Greek merchant ship at sea

p. 162). In fact, Athens got a good deal of the grain its citizens needed from south Russia.

Greek merchant ships were less than one hundred feet long, with a rectangular sail on a single mast. The sail was mostly used in favourable winds, the men rowing only when the wind was against them or when manoeuvring.

Sea travel was uncomfortable and dangerous. Ships had open holds and benches for the rowers. There was little in the way of decking, the crew sheltering under a spread canvas if it rained hard.

At night, or in really bad weather, the vessel was beached and hauled up on the sand. This was because Greek captains tried always to keep in sight of land when sailing, which isn't possible in the dark. Of course there were no compasses or other navigational aids. They managed perhaps fifty or sixty miles a day, on average.

Athens imported metals and metal goods, hides, furs and slaves, as well as grain. The last mentioned accounted for two thirds of all the cereals Athenians needed – some from Egypt, some from Russia. Not long ago, archaeologists discovered the ruins of a Greek grain port at Olbia in south Russia.

Greek shipwrecks of the period are occasionally found. One such vessel had carried wine in large, clay jars called amphorae. A few were unbroken and still stoppered with the wine inside. Needless to say it hadn't 'kept' and was quite undrinkable.

Military ships were a little longer than cargo vessels and had part of the prow sticking forward some ten or twelve feet. The commander tried to use this 'beak' to ram an enemy ship. Failing this, he aimed to row alongside it, ordering his men to 'ship' their oars at the last possible moment. With his own oars out of the water, and by skilfully using the steering sweeps, he hoped to snap off the enemy's oars like carrots.

All Athenians had to do military service which might be in the army or the navy. However the rowers were paid professionals: they had to be when vessels with two or three banks of oars were introduced (biremes and triremes). A citizen could find himself serving as a sailor one day and elected admiral the next. Of-course, he could be just as quickly reduced to the ranks again, especially if he were unsuccessful.

Divers using water probes to investigate Greek shipwreck

The Gods

Hera and Zeus

Athene

Apollo

The very earliest Greeks probably worshipped an earth mother goddess but later invaders brought a male deity with them. In the classical period, religion seems to have descended from a mixture of the two beliefs.

Let's ask this Athenian what he believes in and worships. 'Is there a service in your temple today?' we ask him.

'Service?' he says, 'I don't know what you mean.' We explain and his face clears. 'Oh no,' he says, 'The temple is the home of the god and shows how important the town is but we don't worship in there.'

'Where do you worship then?'

'At any shrine or altar of the particular god we want to talk to. I'm not sure that 'worship' is the right word: we may want to thank the god, to praise him, or plead for something – maybe even bribe him.'

'You have lots of gods then?'

'Oh yes. Some say there are almost as many of them as there are people in Greece. Of course, there are important ones who are known all over the land but every town, village, house, field, fountain, stream, forest, or what you will, has its own spirit.'

'Tell us about the well-known ones.'

'Well, to start with, there's Zeus, the father of the gods. He lives on Mount Olympus with his wife Hera and about ten other Olympians, as we call them. Zeus is the king of the gods and controls the weather, sending sunshine or thunder and lightning at his will. Hera ill treats the girls her husband falls in love with but she also looks after married women and is interested in the bringing up of children.'

'Who are the other deities?'

'There's Apollo, the sun god, who is supposed to be the patron of archery, music, truth, fortune telling, healing, law and order and moderation in all things. His twin sister is Artemis, the goddess of hunting, guardian of cities and young animals, protector of women.'

'How can she guard animals if she's the goddess of hunting?'

'You have to forget one of those if you're interested in the other one – just close your mind. Now, where was I? Oh, I know – Aphrodite, goddess of love and beauty, Demeter goddess of farm crops. Would you like to hear a story about her?'

We nod and he continues. 'Hades, lord of the underworld which was named after him, carried off

Hades carries off Persephone

Demeter's daughter, Persephone, to be his bride. Demeter then refused to make the corn grow or the fruit to ripen until she got her daughter back. The people of the land of Greece began to starve, so Zeus talked to Hades and got him to agree to let Persephone come back to the world for eight months of every year. The remaining third of the year she was to spend in the underworld. This, we believe, is how the seasons started.'

Privately, we think this might be a folk memory of ancient famines caused by climate changes or soil erosion but we let him go on.

'Hermes is the son of Zeus and the messenger of the gods. He also protects flocks and herds and is the god of trade and the market place. Among those who look upon him as their champion are mischief-makers, wayfarers, orators, thieves and writers!'

'Poseidon is the god of the sea, Ares the god of war. Hera, his mother, hated Ares for the deaths he caused but Hades loved him for the extra souls he sent to the underworld! Hephaestus, the lame, is the god of fire and of blacksmiths and armourers. He is a clever craftsman and is supposed to have made Pandora, the first mortal woman. Dionysius, god of wine, is a symbol of revelry who gave man a gift which could be used or misused.

'There are many other supreme beings who are widely known – for instance, Pallas Athene, the patroness of our own city of Athens. Then there's Prometheus, the original fire god, who was dismissed and punished for giving Mankind the secret of fire. Iris is the goddess of the rainbow and Pan, the god of flocks and woodlands. The lesser spirits include Naiads and Dryads who were nymphs of water and trees. I suppose you've heard of centaurs? You know – half man and half horse?'

We nod but we think centaurs may be another folk memory – perhaps of the first Greeks ever to see a man riding a horse. Our musings are cut short as our friend speaks again.

'Also we sometimes revere the old heroes – Achilles, Heracles and—'

'Hold on. That's a lot to take in.'

'There's more.'

'I'm sure there is but I reckon that's enough to think about for the time being. Thank you for your information.'

Chapter 10   The Persian wars

The Persian Empire

A map showing the Persian Empire at its greatest extent

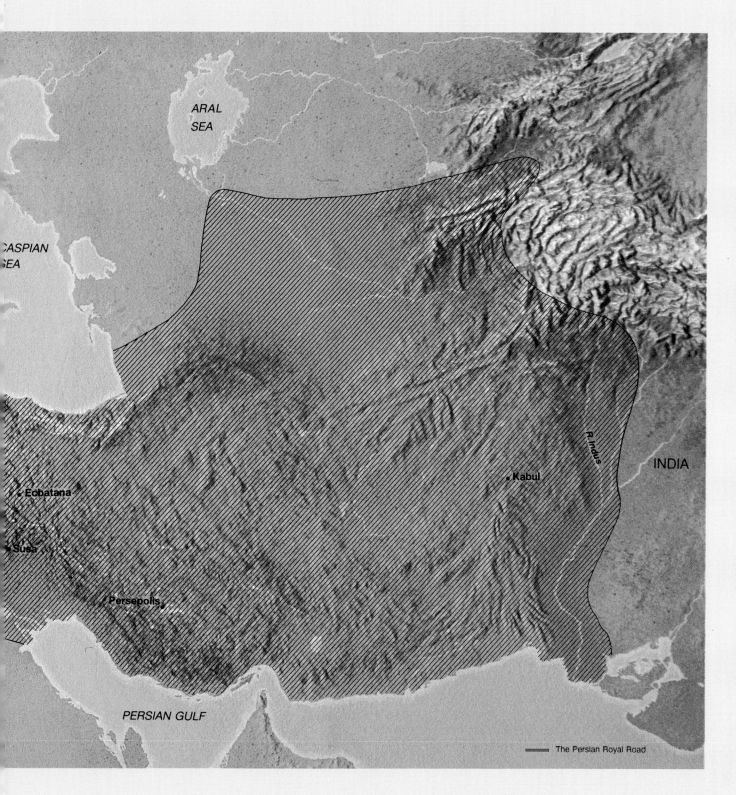

ARAL
SEA

CASPIAN
SEA

INDIA

R. Indus

Kabul

Ecbatana

Susa

Persepolis

PERSIAN GULF

The Persian Royal Road

Persian rulers

Persian soldier

Cyrus the Great

It seems incredible that an unimportant tribe in the near east should have been able to conquer its neighbours near and far and to become the largest and most powerful empire the world had yet seen. Even more remarkable is the shortness of the period during which Persia was the supreme country.

Its greatness started with the conquests of its mightiest monarch, King Cyrus, in the middle of the sixth century before Christ. This magnificent empire was conquered and finally shattered, lasting only a little over two centuries.

The period is so short that a list of a mere dozen or so rulers is enough to cover it. The first king (as we've seen) was Cyrus the Great, who set the empire on its way by beating the Medes who had been the supreme power in the area. The last Persian monarch was Darius III, who was killed in 330 B.C.

The reason why the Persians were able to win battles so easily was to be found in the way they fought them. Every Persian had to be ready to fight – rich men had to provide their own horses and horse trappings. These became the cavalry, whilst ordinary peasants fought with short daggers and lances. Everyone had to learn archery, for bowmen were often the key soldiers of the Persian army.

Although many of the country's rulers were extremely good generals, it was the tactic which made use of archery that won battles. The cavalry might try to surround or drive off enemy mounted troops but first, the infantry wedged their wooden, hide-covered shields in the ground in front of them to act as a barrier. Then they loosed swarms of arrows at their foes.

In most cases, they never had to get into a situation where they had to engage in hand-to-hand fighting, because their enemies (mostly armed with long spears) never got near enough to use them.

Cyrus, who founded the Persian empire, did it by also conquering Babylon, Afghanistan and the Greek colonies in what is now Turkey. His son, Cambyses, defeated the Egyptian pharaoh, Psamtik III but failed to take Ethiopia. His army was destroyed by a sandstorm in Libya and he, himself, died in Syria on his way to crush a revolt.

After his death, a usurper tried to seize the throne but Darius I, a cousin of Cambyses, beat the rebels and restored the family to the throne. He divided the country into twenty districts called satrapies. These satrapies were occupied by the peoples originally subdued by the Persians. They paid taxes whilst the Persians did not.

Darius reorganised laws, postal services, weights and measures and set up a proper system of money. Although some of his foreign troops accepted gifts of things such as food, land, houses, furniture and so on as wages, others (in particular, his Greek subjects) insisted on payment in gold or silver coins.

Both Darius and his son, Xerxes, tried to conquer Greece, neither with final and lasting success.

Many of the remaining monarchs were named in honour of these two men until the last of them, Darius III, was defeated by Alexander the Great.

This impression from an engraved chalcedony gemstone shows a Persian horseman attacking a Greek soldier

The Battle of Marathon

The Greek colonies in Persian Asia Minor felt themselves threatened by Darius I. They were told that they must not only pay tribute to the Persian empire but also do compulsory service in the Persian army. In the year 499 B.C. they revolted against their rulers.

Athenians and some other Greeks from the mainland sent help and together they advanced on nearby Persian towns and sacked them. Unfortunately, the mainland Greeks then decided to leave their kinsmen to carry on the struggle on their own and they sailed back home.

Darius's army made short work of the rebels, destroying their fleet and capturing and burning Miletus, one of the chief Ionian towns. Many of the beaten Greek colonists were then exiled to the mouth of the River Tigris – over a thousand miles away.

When the news reached Darius in his capital city of Susa, he gave orders for the conquest of Greece. He sent his son-in-law, Mardonius, to start the invasion. Mardonius overran Thrace and Macedonia in the north of Greece, but then had his ships wrecked and had to give up any idea of going further south into Greece.

This was in 492 B.C., and shortly afterwards Darius sent ambassadors to the remaining Greek city states, demanding that they recognise him as their overlord. The messengers were told to ask for presents of Greek earth and water as a sign that the Greeks agreed to Persian rule. The envoys were siezed by the angry Greeks and thrown into deep pits and wells, with the message: 'If you want Greek earth and water, help yourselves!'

150

Persian envoy being thrown into a deep pit.

Darius was hardly pleased at this turn of events and in 490 B.C. sent a huge army in 600 ships under the command of his generals, Datis and Artaphernes. The plan was to land at the bay of Marathon and march overland to Athens.

The Athenians awoke to their danger almost too late. Miltiades, the Greek general, who came from Thrace in the north, had some experience of Persian battle tactics. He thought the best thing was to hit the Persians rather than wait for them to attack first.

While working out his plans, he sent Pheidippides, a well-known athlete, to run to Sparta seeking help. Pheidippides ran almost continuously for two days and nights only to be told by the Spartans that they were having a religious festival and that they couldn't start out until the next full moon. By the time Pheidippides had run back to Marathon he had covered over a hundred miles. He was also to fight in the battle.

Miltiades made an attempt to cut down the Persian advantage in numbers by stretching his lines of men across a narrow valley. He put his weakest formation in the centre and his strongest ones on the two wings.

The Persians were delighted to see the weakness of the lines in front of them and made ready to attack the Greek centre. However, the Greeks began to run forward when they were still just out of range of the enemy arrows. Their centre was swamped but the two wings closed on the Persians like the jaws of a vice. Vicious hand-to-hand fighting broke out and at the end of the battle, the Persian survivors lost their formations and ran for their ships, leaving 6,400 of their comrades dead on the plain of Marathon.

The Athenians lost only 192 men. They were buried in a common grave and the earth heaped up over them. The burial mound is still in existence and can be seen by the visitor to modern Greece.

The great empire of Persia was beaten but it wasn't a final victory for the Greeks, only a breathing space.

As for poor Pheidippides, he managed his long distance run and even survived the battle. Unfortunately, he was then sent to take the good news of the victory back to the citizens of Athens. He ran all the way, gasped out his tidings and then fell dead.

CHAPTER IO

Thermophylae

'My name is Ninaku. I'm an archer from central Persia. Ten years after our disaster at Marathon, Darius's son, Xerxes, our new king, has decided once and for all to beat the proud Greeks to their knees.

'Those Greeks seem to us simple soldiers to be far too cunning for their own good. I fought at Marathon and I should know. After that battle, we went on board our ships and sailed for Athens, hoping to catch them by surprise but the devils had marched back and were waiting for us. We had to leave empty-handed that time but we won't be put off on this campaign.

'Let me tell you how Xerxes got our huge army over from Asia to Europe. There's a stretch of water just over a mile wide between the continents. It's called the Hellespont. Instead of sailing across, the king gave orders to make two boat bridges. Each one had more

than 300 vessels held in place by stem and stern ropes tied to heavy boulders which were then dropped down to the sea bed. The ships were joined side by side with thick ropes across which stout planks were laid.

'These were spread with straw, topped with a thick layer of earth. This was supposed to help the horses, as were the canvas sails rigged up on each side all the way across to screen the sight of the sea from the animals.

'You can imagine the chaos if one or two had reared, shied or bolted! I don't know about the horses but there were a few of us who were happy not to see the waves. I can remember feeling uneasy in one place where there were gaps between the planks. It was bad enough to catch sight of the water below but I couldn't help thinking we were half a mile from the nearest land – and I can't swim.

Crossing the Hellespont.

'At last all the army was over – Ethiopians draped in leopard skins, us Persians in our woven cloth uniforms, Indians in cotton materials, other warriors in goat skins – you never saw so many styles of dress, nor so many shades of skin colouring – all the way from dark brown to light pink.

'I've heard a rumour that there were two and a half million in our army – one fellow thought it might be more than *five* million! All wrong, of course. Men came ashore on the Greek side at the rate of about one every three seconds: admittedly, they were doing that non-stop for a week but even so, it only comes to about two hundred thousand men. Work it out for yourself.

'We moved southward down the coast till we came to a narrow pass between the mountains and the sea. Our spies told us that the Greeks call it 'Thermopylae', which means "the gate by the hot springs".

'There we found three hundred Spartan warriors under their king, Leonidas. We tried to force our way through but the pass was so narrow, we couldn't use our superior strength.

'Then we had a stroke of luck. After several unsuccessful attempts to smash the Spartans we sent a spy to look over their camp. He reported back that they were doing exercises and combing their hair. Xerxes laughed until one of our captains told him that the Spartans only did that when they were prepared to fight to the death. Xerxes grew thoughtful but then our spy produced a Greek traitor he had met who was willing to show us another way through the mountains.

'We moved in single file along the steep rocky paths until several thousand of us had passed. Then we attacked the Greeks from front and rear at the same time. They fought like tigers until their weapons were broken and useless. Then they used their bare hands.

'At last they had all fallen and the way was clear for us to descend on Athens. We were sure it would be easy this time, as the rest of the Greek army had withdrawn to defensive positions well to the south of Athens. Nothing would stop us now.'

Salamis

Women and children being evacuated

Realising at last that nothing could now keep the Persians from their city, the Athenians put a bold plan into execution. The first part was to evacuate the women and children to nearby islands and enlist nearly all the able-bodied younger men into the navy, which was still in existence and so far unbeaten.

Only a handful of defenders guarded the deserted streets of Athens. The Persians swarmed in through the gates and attacked the Acropolis where remnants of the Greek garrison were holding out. So well did they fight that it was a fortnight before they were overwhelmed.

The Persians then proceeded to smash, burn and destroy every monument, building, temple and statue they could find. Destruction was nearly complete. When the Greeks finally retook their city, they allowed some of the damage to remain unrepaired for decades as a warning to the citizens.

Themistocles, who had risen to power during these troubles, resisted demands that the Greek fleet be sent to support the remainder of the united cities' army, now guarding the Gulf of Corinth. He wanted to engage the Persian ships at a place called Salamis, not far from Athens.

It was a narrow strait between the island and the mainland and Themistocles reasoned that, as at Thermopylae and Marathon, narrowness might prevent the Persians deploying their full strength.

His problem was to trick the Persians into attacking him at the place he had chosen himself. He solved it by sending a messenger to Xerxes. The messenger pretended to be a traitor. He told the Persian king that he was in sympathy with the invaders and that the Greek sailors were so terrified of the Persians that they would sail away at the first sign of trouble.

Xerxes gave orders straight away to set sail for Salamis and to attack the Greeks immediately they arrived. The second part of the cunning plan of Themistocles was to tell his 'traitor' to let Xerxes know that if a Greek fleet were to be attacked without further ado, a good half of the sailors would change sides.

The Persians sailed confidently into the narrows at Salamis to meet their enemy. Greek ships appeared in front of them and then suddenly, another contingent showed up behind the invaders. Boxed in, they were at the mercy of the Greeks. The Athenian ships had rams and were smaller and more manoeuvrable than the clumsy Persian galleys.

Xerxes, watching the battle from a throne on the shore, could hardly believe his eyes. His fleet lost at least half its ships, the Greeks scarcely forty.

Xerxes, in despair, left for Asia, taking most of his fighting men with him. He left some under the command of Mardonius to renew the attack the following year. Facing the Persians was the combined Greek army of almost a hundred thousand men, led by Pausanias, a Spartan general. They were still outnumbered by their enemy but not by nearly so many as they had been the previous year.

The two forces met at Plataea. Mardonius decided to wait until the Greeks attacked and then destroy them with his mounted troops. It was a good plan but it came to nothing because of a Persian error. When the Greeks began to rearrange their battle order, Mardonius mistook the troop movements for a Greek retreat. He forgot all about waiting and gave the order himself to start the battle.

It was the wrong move. Pausanias's men took the shock and then counter attacked. Mardonius was killed, together with most of his foot soldiers. The rest fled.

The Greeks were not to know it but this battle in 479 B.C. was the last main engagement of the wars. From that time on, Persia was never again a serious threat.

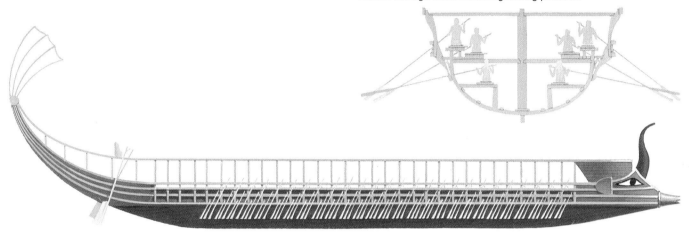

Section through trireme showing rowing positions

Athenian ship showing the ram at the prow

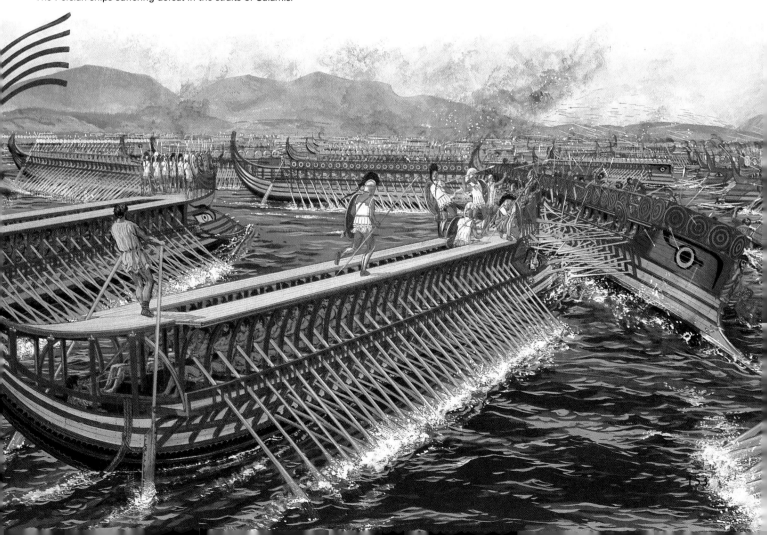

The Persian ships suffering defeat in the straits of Salamis.

Chapter 11 Pericles and the Golden Age

The wise men of Greece

Following the defeat of the Persians, there were almost fifty years of peace. Athens became the leading city state and enjoyed a period of prosperity together with a flowering of the arts and sciences such as the world had never seen before.

Under the leadership of Pericles, the city was beautified, its architects designed and erected splendid public buildings, and sculptors created many marble and bronze statues to adorn them. Its thinkers put forward all kinds of new ideas and its dramatists presented plays both serious and comical, so excellent that many of them are still performed today.

Not all the outstanding people listed below belong to this Golden Age but the fact that such a high proportion of them do, shows what a rich half century it was. The actual dates are 479 B.C., when the Persian menace came to an end, and 431 B.C., when the Peloponnesian war broke out. Perhaps you can work out which of these lived and worked during this period?
(Note: all dates given are B.C.)

Pheidias carving a statue

Kallikrates (5th century) A master builder and architect whose designs for the new Parthenon and the temple of Athena Nike on the Acropolis were accepted and used as part of Pericles's plan to make Athens the most glorious city in the world.

Ictinus (5th century) Many considered him the finest architect of his day and he was entrusted by Pericles with the construction of the Parthenon. He also helped design the Parthenon.

Myron (5th century) A sculptor whose bronze statues of animals and athletes were always in demand. His best known work, copies of which have survived, is the 'Discobolus' (discus thrower).

Pheidias (c490–432) This sculptor was a native Athenian. He worked on the statue of Athena Parthenos. When the architects had put up their buildings, he was entrusted with all the artistic decoration – including the friezes on the buildings of the Acropolis.

Herodotus (c484–424) Known as the 'Father of History', his work on the recent past of his own countrymen is one of the chief sources of information for what happened in the Persian wars.

Sophocles

Sophocles (495–405) Born near Athens, he became a great dramatist. He is supposed to have written over 130 plays, of which only seven have come down to us. Among the most famous of them are: *Antigone*, *Electra* and *Oedipus Rex*.

Anaxagoras (c500–428) A philosopher (Greek word meaning 'lover of knowledge') his idea was that the universe was made up of little beads of different kinds of matter. These were all mixed up to start with but something began to move them about and all the similar beads drifted together to make the things we see. He was condemned as an atheist ('anti-god') when he said that the sun and the moon were not divine persons but fiery, molten lumps.

Thales (640–550) A philosopher who was the first to suggest a scientific explanation of the universe rather than one of myth or religion.

Socrates drinking hemlock

Socrates (c470–399) A philosopher who conducted debates with his young followers on morals and religion. He was found guilty of corrupting youth and sentenced to death. He chose to kill himself by drinking hemlock.

Plato (427–347) Travelled widely and at one time was sold as a slave. He became a disciple of Socrates, whose work he carried on. His interests included the things that affect our conduct and character. He believed that the good citizen could only flourish in a just and orderly society.

Pythagoras (582– ?) He had some strange ideas about mathematics, dieting, religion and music. His famous theorem dealt with the relationships of the sides of a right-angled triangle.

Aristophanes (c445–385) He wrote 54 comedies for the stage, of which only eleven survive. The best known are *The Birds*, *The Wasps* and *The Frogs*.

Euripides (480–406) 18 of his 90 plays still exist and are still performed, including *Medea*, *The Trojan Women*, *Orestes* and *Bacchae*.

Aeschylus (525–456) Author of more than 70 tragedies. We know of only seven, including *The Persians* and *Prometheus Bound*.

Aristotle (384–322) Probably the first man to advocate the scientific method: 'Look carefully first, then make your theory'. Tutor to Alexander.

The doctor and patients

Hippocrates (c460–377) 'Father of Medicine', he was both physician and surgeon. We know of 70 of his essays on medical subjects.

Democritus (c460–357) The first to say that everything was made of atoms.

Thucydides (c464–c404) Wrote a fair and accurate history of the Peloponnesian war.

Empedocles (c493–c433) A philosopher who held that everything is made of earth, air, fire and water.

Demosthenes (383–322) Orator and statesman. An orphan, he studied law and to cure his stammer, he walked the seashore with his mouth full of pebbles and tried to outshout the noise of the waves crashing on to sand and rocks.

Slavery

Slaves working in the mines

Slaves working on a farm

My name is Enkales (Enk-a-lees) and I am a slave. I'm a slave because my father was a slave and his father before him. It's said that my grandfather came from somewhere to the south of Egypt once long ago. He was on a voyage across the Mediterranean when his ship was attacked by pirates. They stole the cargo and sold all the people into slavery.'

'Is that how people become slaves in Greece?'

'Not the only way, no. You could be kidnapped, captured as a prisoner of war or sold into bondage for debt. I don't think the last one is still used and I was told that the great Solon had done away with the custom of making a slave of any labourer who didn't work hard enough.

'It was Solon who freed all kinds of slaves; for instance, any Athenian who had to flee abroad to avoid slavery, any Athenian who had been sold in a foreign slave market or any Athenian who'd been made a slave here in Attica.

'My job is to look after the house, help with the

shopping, chopping wood and getting it in, buying charcoal for the cooking fire and fetching all the household water from the public fountain. I also do all the odd jobs that crop up around the house as well as walking the young master to and from school when his regular slave can't do it.

'It's hard work most of the time but I suppose I'm better off than some slaves. I'm talking about those who work in the mines. I overheard a house guest the other day. He had rented part of the silver mines at Laurium. He and scores of other mine men bought up to a dozen or so slaves each and set them to work. They had absolutely wretched conditions to toil in.

'Most of the time they worked until they dropped in hot, wet darkness, breaking their backs to fill leather bags with lumps of rock which they had smashed with pickaxes and crowbars. Their owners' attitude seemed to be "Slaves are cheap, so keep them at it until they fall exhausted." In fact, slaves aren't all that cheap—'

We interrupt to try and find out how dear they were

Slave auction

in terms we can understand. It seems that it would have taken the complete earnings of a modern average workman for six or seven weeks to buy a male slave.

'Anyway,' says Enkales, 'there are even now as many as twenty or thirty thousand poor devils slaving away in those silver mines.'

'Couldn't they complain?'

'You obviously don't know much about the set up in Athens. No slave is allowed to vote or speak in the Assembly and as for having a revolt – well! We'd never get enough of them to do the same thing at the same time. Why, they come from so many different parts of the world, you can't even find a language they all understand. Some of them don't speak a word of Greek – especially the mineworkers.'

'Do slaves work on the land?'

'Yes, but not as many as Sparta, or some of the other cities, use to farm with. Even so, it's been worked out that almost half of all the people who live in Athens are slaves. Many of us are house slaves and others work in quarries, docks or workshops, making things.

'I suppose the owners of these businesses have to be careful not to employ too many slaves or no free man would ever find work. As it is, most households have about three slaves on average.

'A slave can, if he's lucky, buy himself out. All he needs is to lay his hands on a lot of money. I've already said that house slaves are better off than those who work in quarries or mines but all of us suffer in a way I've not told you about yet.'

'What's that?'

'Well, if ever any one of us is called upon to give evidence in a court case——are you sure you don't know about this?'

We shake our heads.

'The rule is, that however a slave is connected with a trial, even if he's only an innocent bystander, he must be tortured first before his evidence is taken, because they believe he will tell lies otherwise!

'You can see that it's not such a golden age for us!'

157

CHAPTER II

Clothes

Clothing fashions changed very little throughout this period – certainly not as much as they have in modern times. Greek clothing needed no skilled tailors to make it fit and yet it remains among the most elegant of styles that human beings have ever invented. In fact, sculptors and painters of the last few centuries of our own age have sought to give their, often royal, subjects grace and dignity by showing them in Roman toga and tunic, or in the Greek equivalent of himation and chiton.

A chiton (pronounced kye-ton) was a loose tunic worn next to the skin by men, women and children. It was not much more than a tube of woven material of either linen or wool, with armholes or short sleeves. It was pinned or sewn together over the tops of the shoulders. For men and boys it did not reach the knee and was either its natural light colour or bleached white. For women and girls it was ankle, or even floor length and might be dyed or patterned in colours.

In both cases it was hitched up with a simple girdle of leather or cord around the waist. No underclothing was worn – if the person concerned was cold in the winter, he or she might wear more than one chiton.

Over the chiton went the himation, a woollen garment that was merely draped on the body, round the waist, over a shoulder, under the opposite arm and then back over the same shoulder. It was recognised as a sign of elegance and good breeding to have your himation arranged properly: too short and your neighbours sniggered; too long and it dragged in the dirt.

In the latter case, it meant a visit from the travelling laundry-man, or fuller, who collected the soiled clothes, and treated them with various substances such as nitre, potash, or an aluminium salt, known as fuller's earth. With the latter, the fuller made a paste which he dabbed or spread on the dirty linen, particularly if there was a greasy stain to be removed. When the stuff was dry, it was broken and crumbled, the last traces being removed with a wire toothed comb or brush. Then the whole garment was rinsed in clear water. If a bleach was desired, the cloth might be hung up in sulphur fumes.

These processes, unfortunately, left the materials rather less waterproof than when they were first made, so that wearers were more anxious to find shelter when

Greek dress for women

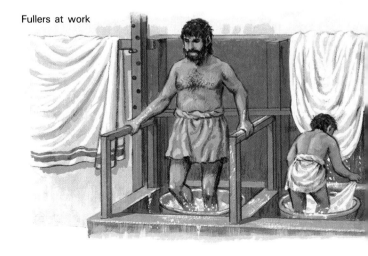

Fullers at work

it rained. Strangely enough, long sleeves, which would have given some protection, were never fashionable, being left to workmen to wear. The chitons workmen wore were usually dark-coloured so that they didn't show the dirt.

Clothing was made by hand, either in a workshop or by the farmer and his wife. If they didn't own sheep, poor peasants probably wore clothes of soft leather.

As sheep had to be sheared, the wool washed, combed, spun and woven, the resulting garments were extremely hard wearing but rather expensive.

Because of their cost, the Athenian's himation and chiton were a tempting target for thieves. If a citizen bathed or took exercise, he did so naked and should have had a slave to guard his things. In the absence of a guard, the clothes were liable to be stolen. In fact, some thieves were bold enough to snatch the himation from a man's back in the street, particularly at night.

In the house of a friend or at home, the Athenian went barefoot but a sort of sandal was worn in the street. Country folk wore stouter boots and poorer peasants wooden-soled 'flippers' held on with thin leather thongs. If a cobbler was making a pair of shoes, he would ensure a good fit by asking the customer to stand on the leather. He would then cut round the shape of the customer's foot.

Beards and hair had been long at the time of the Trojan war but they were shorter during the Golden Age. Men didn't often go clean shaven until the age of Alexander. Women tried a variety of hairstyles and were fond of wearing jewellery, especially engraved precious and semi-precious stones.

By the way, if you saw an Athenian with very short hair, he might be in mourning or he might be a mean man trying to save money on trips to the barber.

Greek dress for men

Greek hairstyles and beards

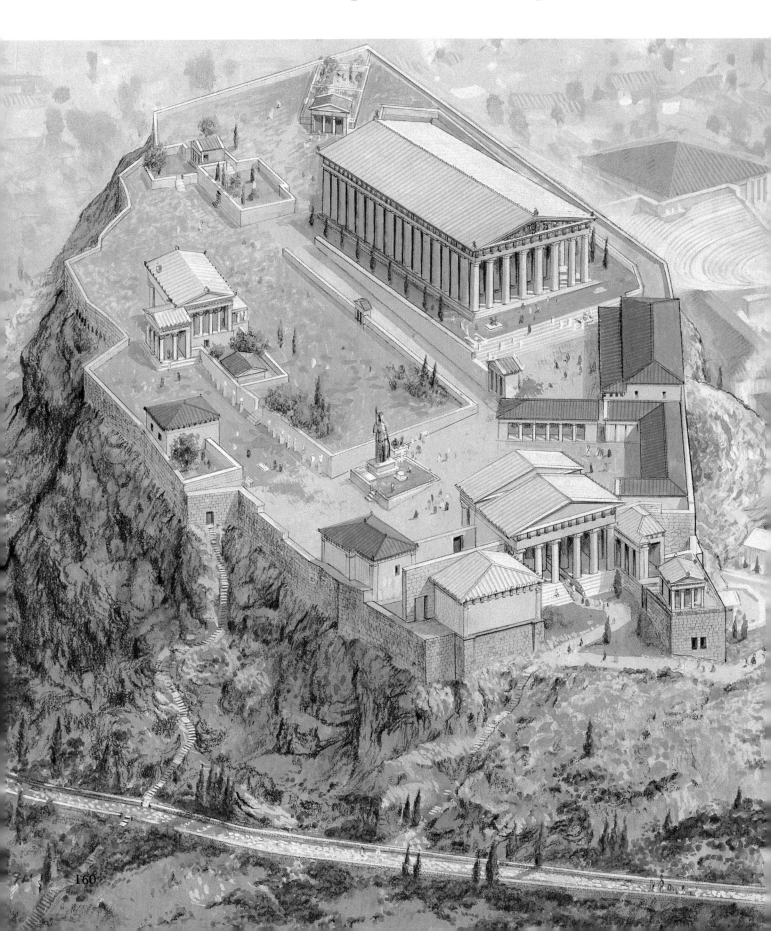

We've heard how the Persians had left Athens in ruins. The defenders of the inner fortress, or Acropolis ('highest city'), had held out for several days before finally giving in. It seemed that the temples and other buildings on the rock had taken the brunt of the Persians' anger.

For a while, the fire-blackened remains were left as a monument for the citizens to see and it wasn't for decades that a decision was taken to rebuild. In the meantime, one of the destroyed temples was replaced with a temporary wooden building while Pericles looked about for men to do the reconstruction.

The men he chose were Ictinus and Kallikrates to design the new temple and supervise the workmen, plus Pheidias to provide the 500 or so sculptures that were to adorn the finished structure. The work began in 447 B.C. and took fifteen years.

The top of the rock was smoothed and levelled to take the base, then the fluted pillars were put up – seventeen along each side and eight across the front and back. The original measurements of the building were: nearly 230 feet long, about 100 feet wide and 65 feet high. The tops of the 58 main columns were joined by flat stone slabs and a shallow triangle of stone was set up at each end, later to be filled with sculptures. The rest of the roof was made of wood with tiles on top.

The citizen visiting the temple would perhaps make a sacrifice on the altar just outside the main doors before going in to pray to the goddess, Athena Parthenos. No ceremonies were conducted inside the temples.

Inside the rows of columns was a passageway all round the main building. In a back room was a store for the treasures, but in the main room, facing the front door, stood a huge statue of the goddess, at least 40 feet high.

Pheidias had made a wooden framework and covered it with carved ivory for the lady's hands, arms, neck, head and face, plus moulded gold for her head-dress and draperies.

Unfortunately, the statue no longer exists: it was taken away to Constantinople a thousand years later, where it was destroyed by fire some time between the 6th and 10th centuries of our own times.

The ancient Athenian worshipper would have seen the giant statue only dimly. There was no lighting save that which entered through the main doors, or was reflected up from a pool of still water at Athena's feet.

From the outside, the temple still appears in modern times to be a marvel of proportion but the builders had worked cunningly for effects. The straight lines you can see are nearly all a little curved and the gracefully tapering vertical columns bulge at one point and actually lean inward slightly.

With the right weather conditions, the visitor today will experience a stiffish breeze as he goes through the Propylaea (front gates), a magnificent entrance way to the top of the Acropolis. Looking back the way he had come, he would be gazing in the direction of Sparta and somewhat to the left of that, down to the Piraeus, the road to which was once protected on each side by walls four miles long, so that ancient Athens couldn't be cut off from its port and be starved out in a siege.

Passing on to the rock proper, he would see on his right a small temple dedicated to Athena Nike (goddess of victory). To his left was the Erechtheion, with one of its porches supported by Caryatids (carved stone human figures) rather than columns.

Nowadays, most of the sculpture has long since gone. What still exists is in museums and is a plain yellowish white. It's difficult to imagine Greek statues as they nearly all once were – painted pink for skin, yellow for hair and with red and green clothing on a bright blue background.

The Parthenon still looks wonderful but there is nothing inside it. In fact, it's surprising that there is as much left as there is. It remained a Greek temple for a thousand years, was turned into a Christian church for the next thousand and into a mosque during the Turkish occupation. The Turks later used it as a gunpowder store. Then a 'lucky' shot from a Venetian cannon landed right on the explosives and blew the inside to pieces.

The sculptures from the walls of the Parthenon treasury were brought to Britain by Lord Elgin and may be seen in the British Museum. They show a procession of 192 youthful horsemen – probably representing the 192 soldiers killed at Marathon.

Greek parents often told their children stories of Greece's heroic past. The tales were literally about heroes and heroines, although many of these fantasies also dealt with gods and their adventures. The themes of these stories were used extensively by poets and playwrights. Here are brief outlines of two 'hero' stories:

Herakles (called Hercules by the Romans)

His ancestors were descended from Zeus and he was supposed to be the bravest and strongest man who ever lived. He was so hated by the goddess Hera that she sent snakes to attack him in his cradle but the baby Herakles strangled them. Because of a crime committed by his father, he was ordered to make amends by carrying out a series of almost impossible tasks, or 'labours', as they were called. There were twelve of them:

1. He had to kill the 'unbeatable' lion of Nemea. He closed with the beast and strangled it with his bare hands.
2. He slew the Hydra, a monster with nine heads.
3. He was sent to capture the golden-horned stag of Arcadia, which he did after tracking the animal for over a year.
4. Another animal's capture was demanded – that of the giant boar of Erymanthus. He chased the animal so hard it became exhausted and thus easy prey.

5. He was given the chore of cleaning out the Augean stables in Elis, an enormous building with a thousand stalls. He managed this by altering the course of two rivers so that they would run through the animals' quarters and wash them clean.
6. He shot with his bow and arrows the birds that were eating the grain in the countryside of Stymphalus.
7. He captured the bull of Minos.
8. He trapped the man-eating mares of Diomedes in Thrace.
9. He persuaded Hippolyte, queen of the Amazons to give him her girdle.
10. He laid hold of the cattle of the monster, Geryon.
11. He had to obtain the golden apples of the Hesperides. Only one person knew how and where to get them. This was Atlas, whose job was to support the sky on his shoulders. Herakles held the sky for him while he went off to get the fruit.
12. His last labour was to descend into Hell to capture Cerberus, the three-headed dog of Hades.

There were many other stories told of him.

Jason and the Argonauts

There was a mention of Jason on p. 140. Here is a tale told about him and his crew.

Phrixus and his sister, Helle, were escaping from danger on a ram with a golden fleece. The ram could fly. Helle fell off into the sea and drowned. The waters have been called the Hellespont ever since. Phrixus landed safely, made his way to Colchis on the Black Sea and sacrificed the ram. He hung its fleece in a sacred grove where it was guarded by a dragon that never slept.

Years later, Jason was persuaded to go and seek this golden fleece. He had a special ship, the Argo, built to a new design. It was the first Greek war galley. Jason called for fifty volunteers, among whom were Orpheus, Polydeuces and Herakles.

After many adventures, they gained the Black Sea and sailed to Colchis on its south eastern shore. The local king would not give up the fleece until Jason had tamed the royal animals. These were fire-breathing

bulls with bronze hoofs. Jason must harness them and plough the field of Ares. Then he had to sow the field with dragon's teeth.

He did this but was surprised to find a fully armed warrior springing from each sown tooth. However, Jason and his crew slew the warriors and with the help of Medea, the king's daughter, took the fleece and escaped to his ship.

One version has the Argonauts travelling home via the River Nile and overland through Libya to the Mediterranean. Another ending of the story makes them sail up the Danube and down another river to Italy.

One interesting footnote was the discovery that some ancient gold prospectors, instead of 'panning' for the precious grains had actually pegged out fleeces in likely rivers and, if lucky, would take them out glistening with gold. Could the story of Jason be a reflection of this fact, just dimly remembered?

Music

Although some tunes with musical notes have been found at Delphi, we don't really know what Greek music sounded like. There were no record players or tape recorders in those days, so all we can do is to make some guesses based on pictures and writings.

We know that in almost every society without a written language, stories, histories, moral tales and so on were passed on from person to person down the generations. If there was a mistake, a mishearing or misunderstanding, perhaps even a simple failure of the memory, the details could become distorted to a greater or lesser extent.

The best way to learn something by heart is to set it to music in the form of verse. Greeks excelled at epic poetry which was often a straightforward account of some historical happening. Their other verse form was lyrical poetry which dealt more with human feelings.

When poetry was recited to music the accompanying instruments were either a pipe-like flute or oboe, sometimes played singly, sometimes in pairs. The other common instrument was the lyre.

The simpler pipes had holes for the fingers to change the pitch and a musician learned to cover half of a hole to get an 'in-between' note. The average pipe was made of hardwood or bone and had a double reed. It probably sounded a bit like a somewhat nasal 'drone' on a bagpipe.

When a player put two pipes to his lips at once, he obviously got them to harmonise, but which one carried the tune and which the descant or how it was done, we just don't know.

The small portable harp, or lyre, came in two kinds. There was the formal or ceremonial lyre, the 'kithara'. The guitar and zither probably owe both their name and their very existence to this instrument. It had seven strings with a wooden sounding board and a plectrum, for plucking the strings, which was tied to the wood to stop it being lost.

The everyday lyre also had seven strings but it was made of cane, wood and horn with a sounding board made of animal skin stretched over an empty tortoise shell.

Flutes and lyre

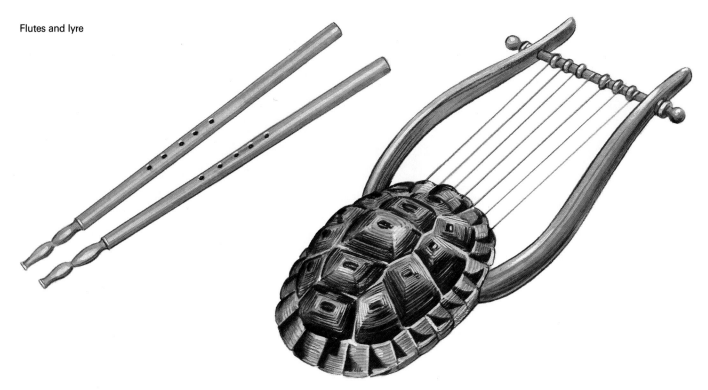

There were probably small drums and the army certainly had a metal horn which could produce two or three notes when the player vibrated his lips and blew harder or softer.

Goatherds and shepherds amused themselves playing on the pan pipes, or syrinx. This was a set of hollow stemmed whistles of gradually increasing length bound together side by side. This is still in use on parts of the Black Sea coast.

The last instrument the Greeks developed was a kind of organ. It was worked by water pressure which drove air into the chosen pipe. The player made the choice by moving a lever.

Going back to the beginning of things, we know that music was important even in Minoan times, for there are pictures of Minoan musicians. By the time of Homer, it's fairly certain that nearly everyone could both play and sing. Music was always a main subject in Greek schools and also a necessary part of everyday life.

Hymns, folk and work songs were sung at various festivals, whether of a religious or sporting nature. They could be sung at weddings or after a successful harvest of grapes or olives. Athletes and warriors often trained to a rhythmic melody. Even drama, which the Greeks practically invented, grew out of music and dance.

Pythagoras, the mathematician, made an important musical discovery. If you stretched a string and arranged it to sound 'C' when plucked, you could divide it into 120 parts and produce a range of notes over a couple of octaves by 'stopping' the string at 30 parts, 40, 45, 60, 80 and 90. He was the first person to discover the octave itself.

It is interesting that the words 'chorus' and 'choir' come from Greek words, as do 'harmony', 'orchestra' and 'music' itself.

Double flute player and lyre player

A day at the theatre

Cimon is a mask maker. He is going to do two things: he'll show us one way of making masks for the stage actors and tomorrow he is to take us to the theatre.

We are in his workroom and he is about to start work on the face of the actor sitting on the stool. He begins by rubbing olive oil on to the actor's face. He is a young man and will take the part of a queen. Women do not act in ancient Greece. They are allowed to watch the play but not to take part.

Cimon ties narrow strips of linen around the young man's head until his face is almost covered. Only the nostrils and the mouth have been left free. He then puts on further strips, criss-cross fashion, which have been dipped in a flour and water paste. While he is doing this, he talks to us.

'You'll have to get up early tomorrow,' he says, fixing another strip in place. 'The theatre doesn't have much in the way of lights, so the performance starts at dawn and goes on all day.'

'What a long play!'

'No, it's three plays – four really – three tragedies and a farce at the end. Don't forget to bring some food and a cushion.'

'How did drama start in Greece?'

'Some people will tell you the origin was in Crete but here, in Athens, it began with hymns to Dionysus, the god of wine, for a good grape harvest. Everyone came together to sing and praise the god. Some danced as well.

'Eventually the celebration was held in the agora. A fellow called Thespis started to sing or speak on his own. He stood on a farm cart and did solos.'

'Actors are often known as Thespians,' mumbles the young actor.

'Keep your jaw still. I'll do the talking. Where was I? Oh, I know – I was saying about talking on your own. It wasn't long before the hymn had turned into two or three solo parts for the actor, with a chorus making comments and descriptions of things the audience couldn't see.

'There were fifty in the chorus and they danced and sang in a circle about eighty feet across, at a place just below the Acropolis. People sat on the hillside looking

Making a mask

down on the "orchestra", as we call the circle of the chorus. In the middle is an altar to Dionysus.

'The next developments were a raised stage for the actors and plays not necessarily about Dionysus, or indeed any god. The audience were given wooden benches to sit on and eventually horse-shoe shaped rows of stone seats were made. A "skene", or small building was put on the higher stage, from where the actors could come on and go off.

'Mostly, we see tragedies – by Aeschylus, Sophocles or Euripides. When there's a festival like the one tomorrow, we put one of our archons in charge. All the authors send him a copy of their new plays and he picks the ones that are to be seen. He also gets in touch with a rich citizen, or choregus, who'll pay for the production. The city provides the actors' wages and even gives ticket money for the very poor. Everybody has to attend.

'Costumes are elaborate, in bright colours and often padded. You may be sitting in the back row and you must be able to see which character is which. You can hear all right, no matter where your seat is.'

'Oh,' we say, 'is that why they have masks?'

'Of course. You may be too far away to see the face, so we make them larger than life – even grotesque. There are only two or three actors, which means each will play more than one part. I've made masks with two faces, so the actor can quickly change expressions or characters by moving the mask round.'

As he speaks, he is cutting through the linen strips at the back of the actor's head. 'Now,' he says, 'I can build up the lips, nose, cheeks, or any other feature with rolls of linen and smooth over all with white plaster. I coat it with a thin glue, let it dry and then paint it. Of course, some masks are made of wood, cork, or even thin metal.' He sets the mask down on a bench and we thank him.

A modern performance of a Greek play in its original setting at Epidauros

The next day we queue up with him before dawn to get into the theatre. He has bought a couple of little, round metal tokens with a seat row and number on them. We take our place, arrange the cushions and slip the food basket behind our legs.

Cimon has a question. 'Your language uses our words for theatre, scene, drama, tragedy, comedy, orchestra, chorus, and many others, doesn't it?'

'Yes,' we nod, 'Why do you ask?'

'Do you know the Greek word for actor? No? Well, it's "hypokrites".'

'Oh yes, of course – one who pretends to be something he isn't!'

Plan of theatre

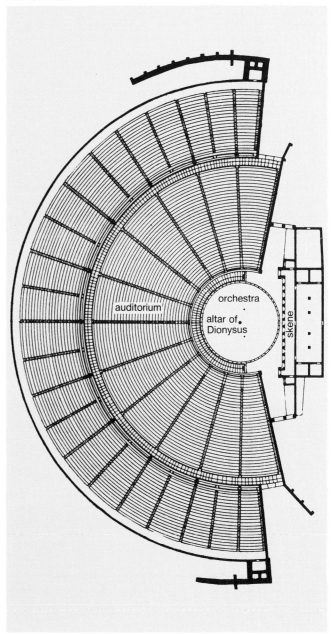

167

The Oracles

View of Delphi today

The Hypogeum

Greeks were a religious and also a superstitious people, which is strange considering that they also believed strongly in the powers of reason. Because they held many illogical beliefs, they saw nothing odd in consulting fortune tellers to find out about the future.

The fortune teller was usually a priest. He might try to find out what was to happen to you by working out meanings from the insides of animals slaughtered for sacrifice, or from the flight of birds. There were ancient places where many of these priests had come together.

In Greece alone there were over two hundred and fifty temples or shrines where you could find out about the future and there were many others throughout the ancient world. For example, on the island of Malta there is a temple called the Hypogeum, possibly more than 4000 years old.

Visitors to the Hypogeum are shown an opening in the rock of the underground chamber which would amplify sound but only of men's voices. A priest would speak his answer into this natural 'microphone' and the enquirer, unable to see the priest could not fail to be

impressed as the reply to his question rolled and thundered around the rocks.

At Dodona, near the modern boundary between Greece and Albania, there was an oracle or seer in the form of an ancient oak tree. Visitors would ask the priests to advise them on a business deal, or about a family or farming matters. The priests would listen to the noise of the wind in the tree's branches and interpret the sounds as a response from the oracle.

The statue of Hermes at Pherai in Thessaly gave advice in an even odder way. The truth seeker put a coin on the god's altar, lit the holy lamps, burned incense and then thrust a finger in each of his own ears whilst hurrying away. At a certain distance he removed his fingers and the first thing he heard anyone say about anything was the answer to his enquiry.

However, the most famous oracle was the one at Delphi, just north of the Gulf of Corinth and set part way up the foothills of Mount Parnassus. There were temples, treasure houses and an athletics stadium farther up the 8000 foot high mountain. In later years the site was neglected and overgrown. A peasant village was built over it. Not until 1893 were the mean little huts removed and the site uncovered. From archaeology and from writings, we have found out a good deal about it.

The place, a fairly lonely and romantic one, was ancient in Mycenaean times. Legend has it that a dragon, the Python, was slain by Apollo who founded a centre there. The chief priestess, the one who made the prophecies, was called the Pythia, or Pythoness.

Private individuals, groups, city councils and even kings consulted her. They wrote down what they wanted to know and their requests were taken into the temple of Apollo, where her underground chamber was to be found. The Pythoness sat on a golden stool and breathed in the vapours that came up from a vent in the floor. To make sure she was drugged, she chewed laurel leaves. Her ravings and mutterings were taken down by the attendants who then said what they thought the meaning was.

The Pythoness

This was then taken out and delivered to the enquirer, often in such a way that more than one meaning could be taken from it. You may remember how king Croesus had asked the oracle if he should go to war against Persia. The Pythoness told him that he would bring a great empire to an end if he did. Croesus took it to mean the destruction of Persia but unfortunately, it was his own empire that fell!

Athenian citizens had enquired about the best defence against Xerxes in the Persian wars. The oracle had advised 'wooden walls'. Fortunately it was decided to build more ships rather than a timber fence all round the city.

The last message that we know of from the oracle was delivered to a messenger from the Roman emperor Julian in 361 A.D. It said, 'Tell your king that the good times are over; that there is no roof nor magic laurel tree for Apollo and that the holy spring has ceased to flow.'

By that time, many previous Roman emperors had robbed the site of much of the treasure given by grateful pilgrims, and earthquakes had laid the buildings low.

Chapter 12   Athletics and games

Legend of Pelops

When asked how the Olympic and other games had started, the Greeks, as usual, had a story which explained their origin.

King Oenomaus of Pisa in Elis had a daughter called Hippodamia. To make sure she would marry a man of the right heroic kind, the king decreed that anyone might have her as a bride if he could carry her off in his chariot. The condition was that Oenomaus would chase after the suitor and if he caught up with him would spear him in the back. At the time of the story, there had been more than a dozen unsuccessful hopefuls.

It was very unlikely that anyone at all would win, as the king's horses were magic ones, a present from a god. However, a young man named Pelops, who wished to marry Hippodamia, also had a team of magic horses. At last there would be an even contest.

Perhaps there might have been if Pelops had trusted to luck. He didn't leave things to chance, however. He bribed the king's charioteer to replace the lynch pins on the royal chariot with similar looking ones made of wax.

The chase was to have been from Elis to Corinth, fifty miles away but only a fraction of that distance had been covered when the wax pins sheared through and the wheels came off. The old king died in the accident and Pelops married his bride.

They lived happily for many years. When Hippodamia died, Pelops ordered games and races to be held in her honour as part of the funeral rites.

This, the Greeks were sure, was the beginning of the Olympic games.

Olympia

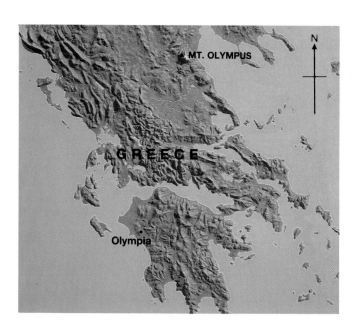

Olympia now

Warrior and horse

Those who know only a little about Greek history often confuse Olympia with Mount Olympus. The last named was the fabled home of the chief gods of the Greek world, whilst Olympia was the site of the games which were held every four years, a period known as an 'Olympiad'. The two places are almost a three hundred mile journey apart. Mount Olympus is in the north east of the country and Olympia is in the south west.

Olympia was in ancient times a sanctuary, or holy place, not a city. It lay in a valley at the foot of Mount Kronos. It was the site of the nationwide 'games' for over a thousand years until the area was abandoned and forgotten.

The river flooded, landslides occurred and both the buildings and sporting arenas became covered many yards deep in sand, silt and mud. So thoroughly were they buried, that there was some argument in the last century as to the actual situation of Olympia.

The first main excavation was done by a German team in 1876. The diggers were partly helped and partly hindered by the habit of local people of raiding the area for building stone. Where the villagers had used spades, the Germans could see what was worth following up. Unfortunately, much of the masonry that could have provided information had gone.

In spite of this, the list of ancient Greek things that were recovered makes interesting reading. To begin with, there were more than 13,000 small or medium-sized bronze objects, many of them given to the local temple as a thanks offering for a victory. There were also over a hundred statues or sculptures, over a thousand terra-cotta objects, together with countless inscriptions and monuments plus an almost unbelievable six thousand coins.

The diggers found the site of the altar to Zeus where athletes promised to keep the rules. They also found the foundations of a huge building, called the Leonidaion, where important guests stayed. There were so many ordinary visitors when the festival was on that they probably had to put up tents or sleep in the open air. Even the officials had tents to live in which could easily be picked out, since they were always made of snow white material. Priests had a permanent building and there was a row of small store houses where gifts offered to the gods were kept.

The stadium, 606 feet long, was where the foot races were run and next to it was the palaestra, or wrestling arena. Somewhere nearby, there must be a horse and chariot racing course. The Germans never found it, in spite of the measurements given by ancient writers – two thousand feet long and several hundred feet wide.

Bronze ram's head

How the Zeus statue might have looked.

The temple of Zeus was represented by foundations and the stumps of fluted columns. At one time there had been a forty-feet high statue of the god made by Pheidias, the artist responsible for the Athena statue in the Parthenon. The Zeus statue was one of the seven wonders of the ancient world.

The excavators even found the workshops where the sculptor had produced his masterpiece. Pieces of the mould for the god's gold draperies were found but more remarkable still was a fragment of broken pottery with 'I belong to Pheidias' scratched on it.

Zeus was not the only god with a shrine and many of the visitors spent as much of their time on religious matters as they did watching the games. As well as priests, worshippers, athletes, trainers, judges and officials, there were horse traders, food hawkers, pedlars of wine with their bulging goatskins plus sellers of trinkets, souvenirs, amulets and small objects to be presented to the various temples.

At one time there had been an oracle at Olympia, similar to the one at Delphi. Legend has it that the games had been abandoned several centuries before Christ and in a period of chaos, civil war and plague, someone asked the oracle what could be done to restore peace. The answer was given that temples and shrines should be repaired and the games begun again.

When they did, a record was kept of the events and their winners. In 776 B.C., when the thousand year cycle of athletic events was started, a man named Coroebus had the honour of crossing the finishing line ahead of his competitors and rivals – the very first Olympic champion.

The Olympic games

Crowning the victors

We've seen that the Olympic games were first recorded in 776 B.C. They took place every four years until 393 A.D. when they were banned. They were therefore held no fewer than 292 times.

At first, this purely religious festival had very little to do with athletics – for several Olympiads, one 200 yard sprint was the only race held. Even when other contests were added, they were packed into one day. Only later were there four days of events with a fifth day for prize giving. The prizes, by the way, were officially nothing more than head bands of wild olive leaves.

However, when the victors returned home, they often found that their own city would give them a pension, free them from paying taxes or feed them for life. Only in Sparta was the reward a place in the front line of soldiers in the next war!

Spectators and competitors were locals at first but eventually they came from all over the Greek world – not just the mainland but also from the colonies along the shores of the Mediterranean. A truce was proclaimed for the period of the games: civil wars stopped long enough for athletes and audience to get to the games and back to their own cities again.

The spectators, perhaps 20,000 in number, tended to group themselves into factions around the running track, rather like the separation of home and away team fans at a modern football match. The crowd was entirely male: women were forbidden to watch or take part. In some places, including Olympia, women held their own games after the men had left.

The opening event was usually a chariot or horse race. Small chariots drawn by four horses raced round the hippodrome (horse track) in clouds of dust. Fitting out a chariot and team was expensive and only rich men could afford to enter. Sometimes as many as forty chariots were ranged along the starting line.

The race consisted of several circuits of the track. A twelve lap race was just over nine miles but few vehicles finished the course. Chariot drivers were the only athletes wearing clothes – perhaps to protect them in case of an accident.

The rest performed naked. Trumpet calls signalled the appearance of contestants, judges and officials through a narrow corridor into the stadium.

The athletes had been practising for almost a year under their own personal trainers. Even the judges were compelled to come early to be taught how to do their job. They had two weapons – a long cane or whip to punish minor law breakers and the power to fine those who cheated deliberately. The money went towards the cost of statues of the gods, on the bases of which were inscribed the names of the cheaters.

On the day itself, the contestants had risen at dawn, prayed to their own gods and promised at the altar of Zeus to keep the rules. Now here they were in the arena. They stripped and oiled their bodies. A herald called for them to take their marks and they fitted their bare toes into a grooved stone which served as a starting block. Another trumpet signalled the 'off' and the athletes ran for all they were worth.

The short race of 200 yards was added to as the years went by. A middle distance race of 400 yards was run and then one of nearly three miles. Curiously enough, there was never a marathon event.

Other events were tacked on – boxing, wrestling, discus and javelin throwing, weight putting and long jumping were some of them. The best performers usually entered the 'pentathalon' (five contests) and the really tough ones the 'pancratium' (all strengths) which was a cross between boxing and wrestling, with almost any kind of attack allowed, short of eye gouging, biting or finger breaking.

If he still had his fingers and could use them, a losing fighter could raise one as a sign of surrender. Sometimes the holds were so fiercely applied that the wrestlers could not free themsleves and had to be prised apart.

When the main events were over there were 'mini' Olympics for the heralds and trumpeters, followed by wrestling and races for boys. One vase painting shows a young hopeful performing the long jump. He is holding 'halteres', or dumb-bell shaped weights in his hands. He held them behind him and threw his hands foward as he jumped. The weights were supposed to increase the length of his jump.

This technique was widely used but not, oddly enough, for the high jump, which was not an ancient Olympic event. Neither, it seems, was swimming, even though the remains of a modern sized swimming pool have been found.

Other games and pastimes

Olympia was not, of course, the only place where an athletic festival was held. There were many of them. In Athens, there were seventy public holidays a year. Every four years there was a week-long festival in honour of Athena at which, in addition to the usual running and jumping, there was a torchlight relay and a boat race.

The three most famous games after the Olympics were the Pythian, or Delphic, the Isthmian and the Nemean. Prizes for winners were laurel leaf wreaths at the Pythian games, pine needle or wild celery crowns at the Isthmian and headdresses of wild parsley or celery at the Nemean.

The Pythian games were held, like those at Olympia, every four years, whereas the festivals at the Isthmus and Nemea took place every two years. Prizes at some of the lesser known festivals included money, jars of wine or oil, clothing and cloaks, or shields, swords and armour.

The same kinds of events were staged at most of the festivals but at Delphi there were also contests to find the best flute or lyre player, or the composer of the best tune. Soon, other organisers were including music in their programmes.

As well as these official contests there were many other sports in which the Greeks indulged which were never, as far as we know, part of a festival's games. We don't know much about them apart from sculptures or vase paintings but it seems they played a kind of football and there is one illustration of a game which looks suspiciously like the start of a game of hockey.

Game resembling hockey

Bowling a hoop

Wrestlers

There were also 'impromptu' games, sports and pastimes indulged in by children and young people generally. It's not surprising to find that many of them are well-known to modern people, as they turn up almost anywhere and in almost any period of history.

Arm wrestling, leap frog, tops, knucklebones (five-stones or jacks), skipping, tug of war, hoop bowling, 'he', 'it' 'touch' or 'tag', pickaback fighting, blind man's buff, marbles and various ball games are just some of them.

A great many of these were played by young children and some, at least, have served to introduce the youngster to the adult sport. A lot of boys must have played with toy bows and arrows, or tried hurling a straight stick as a prelude to javelin throwing. Perhaps they even twisted a strip of thin leather or cloth round the shaft, as grown-ups did, to make their stick revolve rapidly and keep it on course. It's even more certain that boys practised wrestling, just as they've done throughout the ages.

Among young men, there was a game that doesn't seem to have led to anything, except drunken amusement. It was called 'kottabos' and was played at the end of a party.

The performer took a little wine in his wide rimmed drinking cup, and flicked it at a target – perhaps a statuette, or aimed it into an empty bowl. Greeks half believed that if you were good at it, you would be lucky in love.

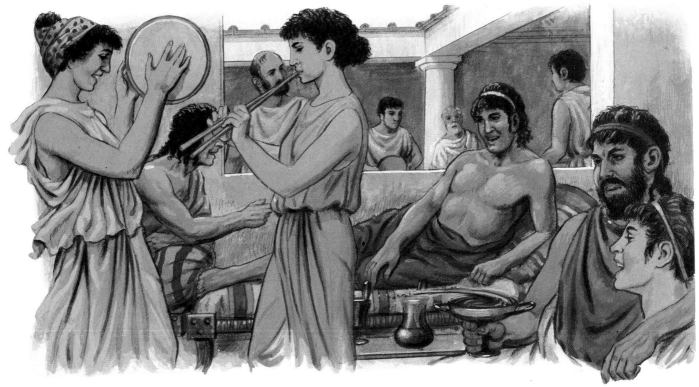

Chapter 13   The Peloponnesian wars

Sparta

A visitor to Sparta was once invited to a meal. He later told a friend that the food was so awful, he could scarcely eat it. When he described the haggis and black broth he was given, the friend said, 'You were lucky to get special treatment – normal Spartan food is much more unpleasant!'

The reason for the poor food was that Sparta was on a war footing and had been for two or three centuries.

In the early days most Greek cities were very similar to each other but after the Dorian invasion, Sparta became the chief city of the newcomers while Athens was the virtual leader of the original Achaeans.

After a while, the harsh conditions in Sparta were relaxed as the Spartans subdued the peoples round about them. For a time cultural activities flourished. Fine pottery was produced and exported; festivals of music and poetry were held.

Then one of the subject peoples rebelled and had to be put down by force. Spartans were afraid that they might not be so lucky next time – unless they were well prepared. After all, the helots, as these semi-slaves were called, outnumbered Spartan citizens by at least seven to one.

The Spartans thereupon made up their minds to turn their city into an army camp. They stopped trading with the rest of Greece and refused to use the new coin money, preferring to go on using iron bars as currency. In future they would only be soldiers and the helots would have to do the farm and other general work. Helots were beaten if the amount of food they produced fell short of what was demanded and could be put to death if they complained.

The only way to maintain this state of affairs was to give every Dorian Spartan a military training.

This began more or less at birth. If a boy baby was weaker than average anywhere in Greece, his father had the right to refuse to bring him up and the wretched child could then be abandoned to die of exposure or be killed by wild animals. In Sparta, the father had no choice – the decision was made by a board of officials and there was no appeal.

Even if the boy was accepted, he was taken from his mother at the age of seven and sent to a military school.

Spartan soldier

There he was subjected to an extreme form of discipline. He ate very poor food, slept on heaps of rushes, wore a thin tunic winter and summer and went barefoot even if there was snow on the ground.

Boys often went hungry and had to steal food. This was encouraged as good practice for the soldier's trick of 'living off the land'. However, if a food thief was caught he could only expect severe punishment and the jeers of his friends.

Spartan boy stealing food

Spartan boys must never show emotion or any sign of weakness. There were even whipping contests to see which youngster could stand the most punishment without crying out. There were cases of lads being beaten to death sooner than show that they were hurt.

The endless military drills and exercises were punctuated every week or so, when the boys were paraded and inspected to see if there was any spare fat on them. The training had no let ups and there were no holidays.

When the youths grew up and began to think of getting married, they would remember that no one was allowed to marry until he was twenty, nor could he live with his wife for another ten years after that.

It is interesting to compare this sort of career with that followed by a young man in Athens (and other Greek cities). The Athenian might or might not have an ordinary education to the age of 18. Thereafter he did only two years military training, compared with 23 years in Sparta.

Sparta itself had no walls because it was thought that the citizen would fight all the harder when he was attacked if he knew there was no other defence. For a similar military reason, no lights were to be shown in the city at night, so that people could get used to moving or even marching in pitch darkness.

Little evidence of a cultured Spartan civilisation can be found from this rigidly controlled age – no great art in the form of sculpture, architecture, poetry or drama. Athens showed the world the first workings of democracy by way of freedom of speech and thought plus the ability of each Athenian citizen to express his own personality in his own way.

Athens and Sparta were rivals for the leadership of the Greek world – first one was on top and then the other. Eventually, as we shall see, the rivalry became so intense that a civil war broke out.

Boy being checked for excess fat

179

Why the war started

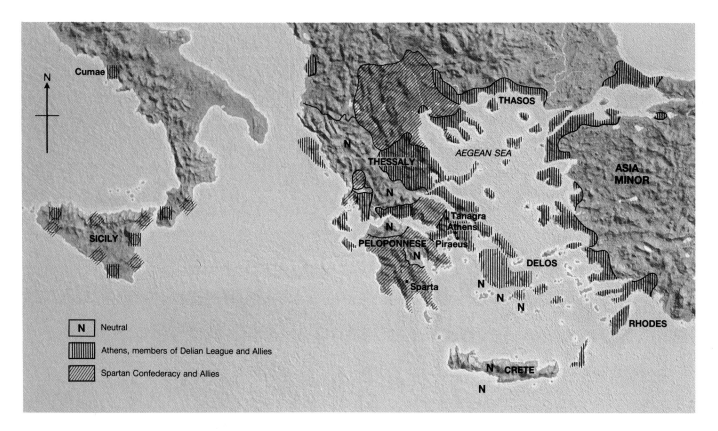

It was probably the defeat of Persia that led to the Peloponnesian wars. The Peloponnese was the southern part of Greece, controlled by Sparta. It was named from the legendary king Pelops (see p. 170).

Athens to the north had made certain that Greece was not occupied by the Persians and wanted to ensure that they never did so in future. So they began to recruit allies, each of which promised to help any of the others if they were attacked.

This joint alliance was called the Delian League because it was originally based on the island of Delos, lying half-way between Greece and Asia Minor.

The trouble was that not every colony or city state wanted to join the League. Those that were reluctant were forced in one way or another to become 'allies'. The unwilling members quickly sank to the position of underdogs, to be ordered about rather than consulted as friends or equals.

By the time Athens under Pericles had gathered together most of the mainland city states, the Aegean islands and the colonies in Asia Minor, the whole thing was much more like an empire than a partnership. Severe measures were taken against any city that tried to break away. Athenian leaders chose to look upon these as traitors who were about to join the enemy, even if they were merely fed up with being told what to do by Athens.

One such was Thasos, an island off the northeast coast of Greece. In 463 B.C. Athens sent war galleys to teach her a lesson. Thasos' fleet was defeated, her ships confiscated and her defences torn down. She did what others had done when faced with the same problem – she asked Sparta for help. Unluckily for Thasos, Sparta was too busy to do anything – all her attention was fixed on a revolt of her own slaves.

Incidents like these angered the Spartans. Nor were they the only ones to be annoyed. Many of Athens' subject cities complained that the tax or tribute money which was supposed to be spent on ships to protect them from attack was actually paying for city improvements in Athens itself. A leading Athenian might have replied that the complainers had neither been occupied or raided, so what was wrong?

It wasn't long before Athens seemed to be looking to extend its empire into the western, as well as the eastern, Mediterranean. This, too, made Sparta uneasy, for their own corn supplies came from Sicily where there were many Greek colonies, as there were in southern Italy and the Mediterranean coasts of Spain and France – Marseilles started as a Greek settlement.

Sparta found that she had to build up her own league of friendly cities. In 457 B.C came one of the first actual clashes between the two rivals. A little to the north of Athens, the armies of the two 'super-powers' of those days met at a place called Tanagra. It should have been an easy win for Sparta as their army was far

stronger than that of Athens, which was basically a naval power. However, the Spartans only just won in spite of the cavalry from Thessaly changing to their side in the middle of the battle.

This was an unusual event: fighting between the two cities had been rare; now it was to become more common. Sparta's citizens grew convinced that an all-out war was inevitable.

Athens was quite content to sit behind her defences – the city was surrounded by walls, her port, the Piraeus, also had walls and the two places were connected by a road with a high wall on each side. The Athenian fleet was large and strong. Food supplies were protected, so what could happen to Athens? Sparta's army was the strongest in Greece but surely, if it tried to attack Athens, it would soon exhaust itself in the countryside, wouldn't it?

Sparta declared war and Athens ordered all the countrymen to leave their villages, bring their valuables and shelter inside the walls.

Athens and its harbour, Piraeus, showing defensive walls

Soldiers and battles

Our knowledge of the weapons soldiers used and the armour they wore comes from two different sources. On the one hand we have brief written descriptions and representations of fighting men in statues and painted pottery. Our second source is an unexpected place. We have to journey to Olympia, the site of the ancient games.

The arenas were only occupied intensively for a week or two every four years. Those sent to get things ready found that the wells dug last time for drinking water had mostly caved in. It wasn't worth the effort and expense of providing wooden shuttering or a brick lining for something so rarely used, so the advance party cleared the ground by sweeping everything into the old wells and filling them in with the sand dug out of the new ones.

Modern excavators found over 150 wells and the 'rubbish' they contained included old war trophies which had hung on poles until the wood rotted. That was when the orderlies tipped them into the holes and buried them.

Warrior departing for battle
Shield boss

Corinthian helmet
Captured Persian helmet

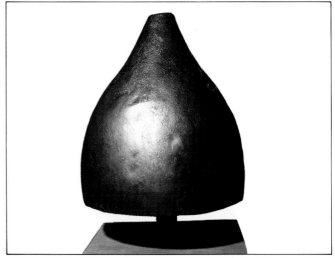

Phalanx

The war trophies were mainly helmets but there were other military bits and pieces – shields, breastplates, shinguards or greaves and protecting plates for foot and arm. One helmet is inscribed, 'A helmet of the Medes, taken by Athenians' and may be a relic of the battle of Marathon. Another one bears the name 'Miltiades', the actual commander at the same battle.

Back in the days of the Trojan war, the fighting was largely a matter of single combats between warrior heroes who rode to war in chariots. At the time of Pericles, campaigning was usually in the summer months and a whole war might depend on the outcome of a single battle.

The Mycenaeans seem to have measured the riches of a man in weapons and it was not unusual to find a burial accompanied by twenty or so bronze swords. Certainly, by the time of the war against Sparta, wealth determined what sort of soldier a man was. A land owner would be expected to provide a horse, in addition to the arms required of one not so well off.

Even though the bronze age had long given way to the iron age, many weapons and body protecting plates were still made of bronze. There are examples of bronze swords with iron edges. Iron was heavier than bronze and if made (perhaps accidentally) with the right proportion of carbon to iron, the resulting steel would take a better edge.

All sorts of weapons were employed – swords,

spears, bows and arrows, daggers and even lariats which some members of the Persian army used. In both Athens and Sparta, the vastly lengthened lance (perhaps 15–20 feet long) was the main weapon of the phalanx.

This was a square formation of foot soldiers, or hoplites. The first four or five ranks could point these lances forward, presenting a moving fence of spikes. Phalanxes might be strung out in various formations across a road, thus blocking it, or plugging a narrow valley.

There was little need for complicated plans of transport or supply: the men brought their own equipment, plus enough food to see them through a few days' campaigning.

Nor was there much scope for clever tactics: the normal plan was to 'steam-roller' your men forward, meeting the enemy head on and hoping that he would be the first to break formation and run.

Cavalry was rarely used in the main battle, but was reserved to cover the army's flanks or to take part in chasing a beaten enemy.

Apart from battles, an army might be ordered to go crop raiding or to besiege a fortified town. The last mentioned was hardly ever successful, in spite of the use of siege engines of assorted types. After all, the Trojan war had lasted ten years and the defenders only lost to a trick in the end.

CHAPTER 13

Athens is conquered

'My name is Patroclus. I lived through this war, so I reckon I'm the best one to tell you about it. It lasted 27 years from 431 to 404, in your method of dating.

'Sparta, as expected, besieged us in Athens during the summers and went back home when the weather got bad. Pericles knew that our army was no match for the highly trained Spartans, but while the navy protected our food supplies, he was content to let our enemy waste his strength in useless campaigns in the nearby countryside.

'Unluckily for us, a severe bout of plague not only killed many of our citizens, it also carried off Pericles in the second year of the war. Those who took his place were not so wise and decided that the best way to beat the Spartans was not just to sit behind walls but to attack their friends.

'In the third year of the war, the island of Lesbos decided to drop out. We were so annoyed that some of us pressed for a fleet to be sent to massacre all the islanders. Eventually it was agreed that we should seize the deserters' fleet, pull down their walls and sell them into slavery.

'After ten years, both sides were exhausted and a peace treaty was signed, promising no more war for at least fifty years. The next thing we knew was that some more allies dropped out with others changing sides. Whether that was the cause or not I don't know but skirmishing broke out and the war began again the following year.

'With our new friends we felt up to tackling the Spartan army but we were over confident and we lost. Our new allies melted away. Then, two years afterwards, the leaders decided, unwisely, as I thought at the time, that we'd send a fleet to attack pro-Spartan cities on the island of Sicily. A man named Alkibiades was to lead it.

'He was young, handsome, intelligent and charming and seemed to be the ideal choice. A pity we didn't know him a bit better though. Just before the ships were to sail, Alkibiades and some of his cronies got drunk and ran riot in the streets, smashing several sacred statues.

'Some of us wanted to condemn him to death for insulting the gods but the final judgment was to take away his command and then to exile him. The next we knew, he'd turned up in Sparta to warn them of our plans.

Alkibiades and his companions destroying the sacred statues

'For us, the attack on Syracuse in Sicily was a disaster from start to finish and we had finally to retire, many of our men being caught and destroyed. Then Sparta set up a base in our countryside not far to the north of Athens, with the result that most of our slaves deserted and ran there for safety.

'The next blow was that we had to close down the silver mines because we couldn't protect them. For coins, the Assembly had to raid temple treasuries. Even after that, we were using copper coins with a thin skim of silver or gold on them.

'Twenty years into the war, a group of four hundred men took over the government and abolished democracy. Mind you, they only lasted three months before we threw them out. Then, would you believe it? Sparta asked for peace and we turned them down!

'By now the war had declined into a string of naval engagements. Our merchant fleet was due in from the Black Sea loaded with corn – very important to people like me who had been living on free hand-outs of food nearly all our adult lives.

'We heard that Lysander, the Spartan commander, had left to try and catch the food ships. We weren't too worried and sent our navy to engage him. After it had left, some of us felt a bit uneasy when we discovered that there were only half a dozen ships left in the harbour.

'Well, of course, we lost the war through sheer carelessness. The crews of our fighting ships were ashore foraging for supplies when Lysander and his Spartans caught them. There wasn't what you could call a fight – it was simply murder. You can guess the effect of this dreadful news in Athens.

'We knew that without grain from the Black Sea, we'd have to give in. We sent men to ask what terms the Spartans were offering. It was months before the answer came and by that time thousands had died of starvation. No food came in: Lysander had anchored 150 ships just off the Piraeus.

'Sparta's conditions were known at last and pretty terrible they were. We had to agree to being ruled by our enemies, to hand over all but twelve of our ships and to tear down all our defensive walls. We had no choice and did what they told us.

'The war was lost for Athens but scarcely won for Sparta. Nearly thirty years of conflict had left the whole of Greece bleeding. Although both we and Sparta recovered a little in the next few years, neither was ever again to attain the power and fame it had once known.'

The defeated Athenians demolishing their defensive walls.

185

Chapter 14   Alexander the Great

Early days

Alexander was born in the year 356 B.C. at Pella, the capital of Macedonia, the son of Philip, king of Macedonia and of Olympias, his wife.

From his father, Alexander inherited bravery, an athletic body, plus a good deal of intelligence and common sense. From his mother he got his extraordinary good looks, a romantic frame of mind and an acceptance of superstitious beliefs. Olympias may have been a priestess of a nature god religion. One of her fellow priestesses once told Alexander that he would never be a loser.

At the time of his birth, Alexander's father, Philip, was busy turning his small, semi-barbaric kingdom to the north of Athens, into the ruling power in Greece. After the ruinous war between Athens and Sparta, Thebes had become the leading city.

Philip slowly pushed out his boundaries, picking off one city state after another. His possible victims quarrelled with one another, each thinking that Philip would never attack, that he would be satisfied with what he had and they made no preparations against attack until it was too late.

Philip, unlike his son, cannot have been a very pleasing sight – he had a crooked back, a limp and only one eye – all the results of war wounds. It must be said, however, that he wasn't a complete barbarian. To start with, Macedonians spoke Greek, even if with a strong accent, and the king himself so admired the culture of Athens, that he appointed Aristotle, the great philosopher, to be tutor to his son and heir. His influence gave the boy a love of Greek literature and Alexander is said to have carried a copy of Homer's *Iliad* on all his future campaigns.

A story is told of how the twelve year old Alexander acquired his famous horse, Bucephalus, which carried him 'to the ends of the earth'. A horse dealer arrived one day with animals for sale. Philip was still a soldier and a countryman at heart, so he attended the sale himself and took his son with him.

One of the beasts didn't seem to have been broken. It had wild, rolling eyes and shied several times. Philip at first would not consider buying it until Alexander begged the king to allow him to try and ride the horse. Alexander had noticed that the animal seemed frightened of its own shadow, so he turned it towards the sun, all the while murmering calming noises and patting its neck.

Soon he managed to get on its back and before long, he had it tamed. From the shape of its head, Alexander called it 'Bucephalus' – from two Greek words, 'bous', an ox, and 'kephale', a head. Philip bought it cheap from the dealer.

When it eventually died at the great age of thirty, Alexander had reached the Punjab in what is now Pakistan and he built a city called Bucephala in its honour.

In his youth, Alexander rarely drank wine and seldom overate. He was therefore, even at the age of sixteen, in superb condition to take over command of the army while his father was away. In double quick time the young man had put down a rebellion of hill tribesmen on Macedonia's northern frontier.

When Philip returned to fight a battle against the combined Greek states, he took over the supreme command again but Alexander was put in charge of the left wing of the army. Philip led the right wing. Against Alexander was the famous 'Sacred Band', the elite of the Theban army. The young Macedonian led the charge which smashed them to pieces.

On the other side, Philip pretended to retreat. The Athenian soldiers ran after his men who then turned and caught them in a trap. This battle took place at Chaeronea on the plains of Boeotia and marked the end of Greek resistance to the king of Macedonia.

When the fighting was over, Philip embraced his son and told him that he'd have to conquer foreign lands, for Philip's new Greek kingdom, large though it was, would not be big enough for Alexander.

Philip was murdered at a relative's funeral and Alexander succeeded him as king. He was just twenty years old.

A corselet and shield found in the grave of Philip

The army

Alexander did not have to reorganise the Macedonian army – that had already been done by his father. Philip as a young man had seen what a poor state the knowledge of military matters was in and when he became king he had determined to do something about his own army.

We saw on p. 183 what the normal practice was – each city state made use of the phalanx as a battle formation. This was a group of men arranged in a block and armed with long spears. The most successful were those whose soldiers were the more determined, strong and courageous.

The commonest type of warrior was the hoplite, an infantryman. Cavalry was almost unknown before the Persian wars, except in northern Greece. The hoplite usually carried a round shield, a spear and a sword. These, together with his body armour, weighed over seventy pounds. Thus, the phalanx wasn't exactly designed for speedy attacks.

There were points to be made both for and against the phalanx. In its favour was the fact that magnificent discipline and loyalty kept it fighting. Against it was its weakness when tackled from either flank, particularly the right, or shieldless side.

So Philip made his Macedonian phalanx a defensive block rather than an attacking one. He gave the men even longer spears, up to twenty feet, in fact, and added cavalry wings.

To fight a battle, he preferred to have six divisions of 5000 men each in the centre plus blocks of men with an attacking role, armed with spear and sword, heavy horsemen on either side and fast, lightly armoured cavalry beyond them again. There were also groups of bowmen.

Philip had learned from the Thebans that it was better to pick a weak target rather than use the Spartan method of advancing against whatever was in the way. The Thebans, however much use they made of mounted soldiers, usually chose the phalanx to destroy the target. This was not Philip's solution. He preferred to send in whichever of his groups stood the best chance of winning, having taken into consideration the nature of the ground and the strength and position of the enemy.

This then, was the army that Alexander took over when his father died. He added another refinement – the attack from the rear. It was managed like this.

The advance was not in a straight line parallel to the enemy forces but on a slant or 'echelon', with the right wing leading. That wing would make contact with the opposing forces first. The rest of the enemy would naturally continue to advance until they reached the Macedonian left wing. There the light cavalry would hold them by charging repeatedly.

At the same time, Alexander's heavy cavalry on the right made a tremendous effort and smashed through the lines in front of them. They then wheeled left and took the foe from behind.

These tactics were never faulted and the words of the priestess that Alexander would always be victorious proved true.

Macedonian phalanx

Alexander and his army fording a river

189

Battles and sieges

From the previous page, it would seem that Alexander relied on pitched battles for his conquest of the known world. This is not really true. Of course, he certainly did pit his Macedonian troops against those of rulers who stood in his way but he relied just as much on siegecraft.

Before his father's time, the Greeks had known little of the art of capturing a strongly fortified city. Philip realised that without reliable siege methods, Greece would never become a nation, for the separate city states might have to be beaten one after the other. How do you do that if you can't get a walled city to surrender?

Philip knew full well that the inhabitants of a city threatened with a siege only had to retire behind their thick stone or brick walls and wait for the enemy to go away. Only starvation could make them give in and few attackers had the time or patience for that kind of operation.

He therefore built up a corps of siege engineers and brought in ideas of wall attacks from farther east, where they had been known to the Assyrians and other ancient peoples. Philip was never very successful with his ideas, in spite of the fact that he was probably the first European ruler to introduce missile hurlers such as mobile catapults and ballistae.

Alexander used these machines and also battering rams, siege towers and pontoon bridges to cross supposedly 'uncrossable' rivers. Siege towers on ships and an artificial pathway, or mole, were features of Alexander's seven month siege of the city of Tyre. Ever scornful of danger, the young king led the final assault in person.

To conquer Persia, which was his life's ambition, Alexander had to defeat 'the Great King' – Darius. The Persian ruler had not thought it worthwhile to confront Alexander and took no part in the first battle fought by the two old enemies on Persian soil. The Macedonians won handsomely and sent huge quantities of booty back to Greece.

Before the next important battle, Alexander was shown the famous Gordian knot. A chariot's pole was tied to a post in an ancient temple. He was told that

A siege tower with catapult

A battering ram

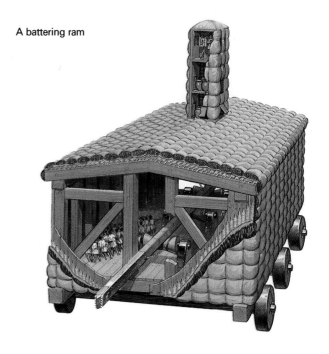

whoever could undo the knot in the leather would rule Asia. Alexander solved the problem by slicing through it with his sword.

The battle of Issus started with Alexander's troops strung out according to his pet plan, with the right wing advanced. One writer says there were over half a million Persians ranged against him but this must be a wild exaggeration.

Alexander led his men forward at a run, trying to avoid the enemy's arrows. They got to within striking distance of the Persian king's chariot. After many of his defenders had fallen, Darius fled the battlefield. Only a little while later, his men followed him and ran away.

Before the final battle with Darius, Alexander swept down the coast, into north east Africa and freed Egypt from Persian rule. Then he struck eastward, crossing the rivers Euphrates and Tigris with 40,000 infantry and a large number of mounted men.

They met the main Persian army at a place called Gaugamela, now in Iraq. The night before, the Macedonians had been astonished at the size of the enemy army, revealed by twinkling camp fires in the dark. The morning showed that it had not been an illusion – the enemy numbers were enormous, with soldiers from every part of the Persian empire, plus war elephants and even chariots with sharp scythe blades on the wheel hubs.

In spite of all this, Alexander threw his cavalry into a gap that had appeared in the opposing lines. They made straight for the unmistakable figure of Darius in his huge, decorated chariot. Hand-to-hand fighting raged towards the Persian ruler who, suddenly afraid, turned and galloped off.

Some time later when Alexander's men had swept away the tattered remnants of the once proud Persian army, the pursuing Macedonians caught up with Darius's chariot. The king's dead body was lying half out of it, apparently murdered by his own men.

Now, for the first time, Alexander could consider himself the ruler of the Persian empire.

Persian war elephant

The murdered Darius

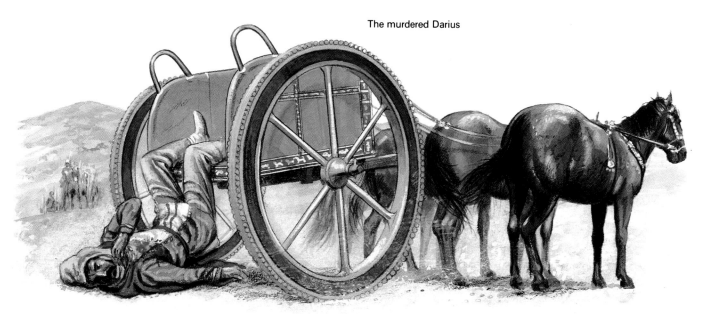

Persepolis

However, the business in hand for the Macedonians was the systematic looting of the treasuries of Persepolis. All kinds of valuables in gold and silver – cups and plates, jewellery, statuettes, crowns, tiaras and many other things were packed into containers.

These were then slung on the backs of mules and camels, lashed into place and then started on their long journey back to Greece. Among the objects sent, and ones that gave particular pleasure, were Greek statues that had been looted and captured during the Persian invasion of Greece – probably taken when the Persians had sacked Athens.

'So this is what it feels like to be an emperor!'

Even before Darius had met his death at the hands of his own officers, Alexander had entered the magnificent Persian capital that they called Persepolis. In Greek, the word means no more than 'City of the Persians'.

Alexander sat on the throne of the Persian kings and is reported to have said, 'So this is what it feels like to be an emperor.'

Already he was secretly making plans to unite Persia and Greece under one king and perhaps to extend the boundaries even farther to the east and south.

At the same time, Alexander's relationships with his old comrades were beginning to change. Once he had been a soldier among soldiers, enjoying the fighting, taking a leading part in the battles and spending the nights yarning and drinking with his friends. Now he was gradually realising that a king does not do such things.

The spell of the east was increasing its influence on him. Eastern luxury was soon to be considered normal – a strange idea for a man from a rough, hard and poor country.

The spoils of Persepolis being taken to Greece

Persian gold armlet

Persepolis on fire

It is said that the pack animal journeys were countless and this statement, for a change, was probably not much of an exaggeration. In addition to the things taken away, there are still in existence the remains of luxury objects which the Greeks smashed.

It was also said that Alexander and his men spent the night in drunken revels and that as a result, a fire was started accidentally which swept through the buildings of the Persian capital and utterly destroyed it.

The fire may have been accidental but it is just as likely to have been set deliberately. There are two reasons given for this. The first is that it was a signal to the Persians and their subject peoples that an age had come to an end.

The second, and probably stronger reason, is that this was an act of revenge – a reprisal for the Persian destruction of Athens and other parts of Greece.

Whatever the truth of the matter, no one will ever know now which it was – an accident or revenge. The fact is that Athens is still a thriving, busy city and Persepolis is nothing but a few forlorn ruins.

Alexander's last battle

Alexander led his army on forced marches, fought few pitched battles but did a good deal of skirmishing and put down many minor and major rebellions. Farther and farther the army went – right across the western part of Asia and down into the Indian sub-continent.

Constant campaigning, more and more bouts of violent drinking and lack of rest began to undermine Alexander's health. In spite of this he pressed on with what he thought were necessary reforms. In order to get obedience from his conquered subjects, he came to the conclusion that he must be considered more than merely a king but a living god instead.

He began to wear Persian clothing and behave the way he thought a god would conduct himself. During one of his frequent drinking bouts, one of his old comrades made a joke about Alexander's 'pretensions' to be divine. Alexander took offence and ordered him to bow down in an attitude of worship. The man, who had once saved Alexander's life, laughed and refused. The king scarcely paused: he caught up a spear and ran his friend through, killing him instantly.

Things like this now seemed to be of little importance compared with his ideas of world conquest. He realised that the only part of the old Persian empire he had yet to win was India.

So, in the early part of the year 327 B.C. he set out with an army now largely composed of local soldiers, although some of the Macedonians who had been with him from the beginning also went with him. He paused before crossing the high mountains guarding the approaches to India and subdued the country round about. During one of these campaigns, he captured a princess named Roxana and made her his wife.

Then he led his men along the Kabul valley and through the Khyber Pass, fighting fierce tribesmen all the while. They moved on through the Punjab and came to the River Indus.

Putting down local rebellions, making friendships and treaties and hoping perhaps to found more cities, many of them named after himself (there were already over seventy of these stretching all the way back to Egypt), he intended to press on eastward.

In fact, he needed to reach the river Hydaspes, a hundred miles away before the rains came and the river became uncrossable. Beyond the river he was sure, was the fabled 'Ocean', a mythical world river which many Greeks believed to encircle the entire earth.

When the army arrived on the banks of the Hydaspes, it was already beginning to rise. Alexander sent for vessels to be brought in pieces on wagons from the Indus. Then he confused the enemy king, Porus, by dividing his army into separate detachments and ordering them in different directions, so that the enemy didn't know what to guard against.

The boats were put together some miles from Porus's main camp. Alexander's army made their way

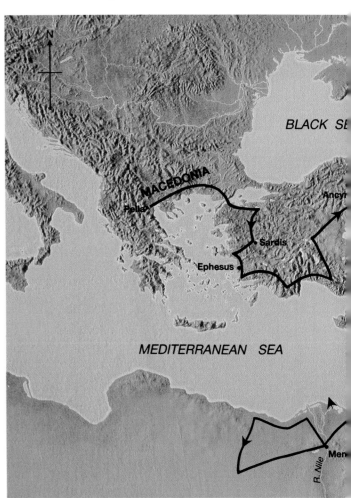

secretly at night, the noise of their passing being drowned by a violent thunderstorm.

Porus marched off to meet him with his chariots and elephants. Alexander put into operation a variation of his wheeling and striking from the rear tactic. On top of this, his infantry hurled javelins at the elephants and his archers fired arrows at them until the huge beasts, maddened by the attacks, charged dangerously against friend and foe alike.

Eventually, Porus, surrounded by his foes, surrendered to prevent a massacre. The battle, last of the four fought by Alexander, had lasted almost eight hours.

Alexander made it known that he intended to continue his progress eastwards. At last the army refused. The Greeks still with him had been away from home over eight years and had marched a distance very nearly equal to half way round the world. Alexander sulked for three days but even he had to give in at the finish.

The orders were given to turn round and head back towards Europe. The Great Expansion was over.

The elephants, maddened by pain, became uncontrollable.

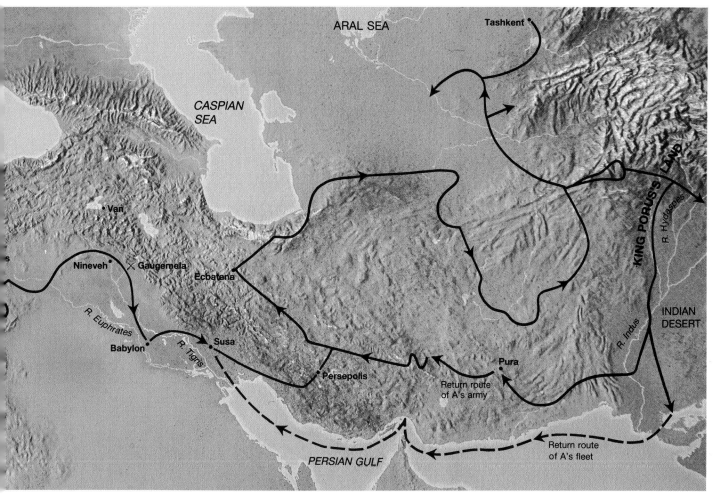

Death of a conqueror

Alexander did not lead his men back the way they had come. He had previously given orders to his shipwrights to launch eight hundred vessels on the Indus and he now proposed to go on board and sail down the great river to its mouth. Admittedly he was going south westward rather than to the east but the great conqueror still wanted to explore places unknown to himself.

As they descended the river, they became involved in many small wars and sieges. At one such siege, Alexander, in a fit of bravado, leapt with two other soldiers from the top of a scaling ladder into a hostile town. There he was hit by an arrow and would have died if one of his companions had not protected his fallen body with a shield until help arrived.

They reached the delta of the Indus and it was decided to explore a new route back home, the fleet sailing up the Persian Gulf and Alexander leading the 15,000 strong army along the shore line.

Difficult conditions forced the marchers to move inland and cross a desert where they almost ran out of food and water. Hostile tribes had to be put down before they could get even as far as Susa.

When Alexander found that some of the men he had appointed to govern during his absence had behaved badly, he had them put to death. On the positive side, more than 10,000 of his Macedonians had married native wives, and 30,000 of the local boys who had been taken and trained in Greece had now

Alexander is wounded

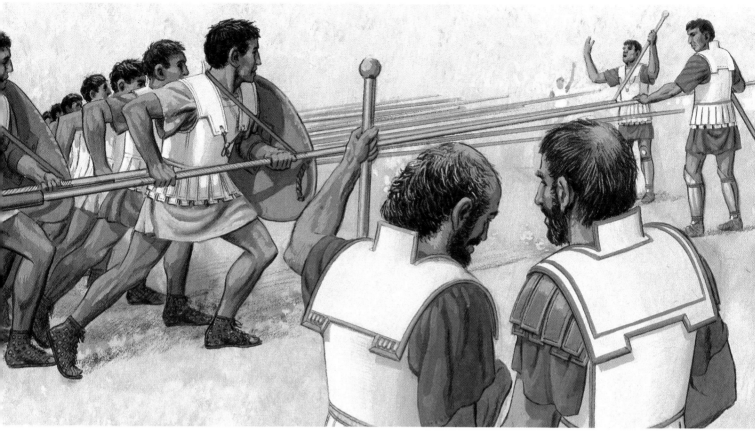

There were frequent exercises to keep the troops in practice.

returned as young men and been absorbed into the new army.

Alexander had a dream of a lasting peace between all men – Macedonians, Greeks, Persians and other barbarians – perhaps even extending to those who lived at the western end of the Mediterranean.

In the spring of 323 B.C. he returned to Babylon and began immediately to make plans for further exploration and conquest. His ideas for some sort of world government never really got off the ground.

He never stopped working away at his projects. Even though no expedition was under urgent consideration, Alexander went on organising troop exercises and reviews, sail-pasts and mock battles on the river, giving prizes to those who did the best.

The story goes that he had caught a slight chill and tried to shake it off by heavy drinking. However, the chill turned to a fever and even his magnificent constitution was unable to fight off the infection. Years of constant physical and mental effort had weakened him, as had the numerous wounds he had suffered in various military engagements.

He grew worse and when it became obvious that he wasn't going to recover, his physicians allowed his old Macedonian army companions to file past his camp bed to say their goodbyes. By this time, he was too far gone

Final respects paid to the dying Alexander

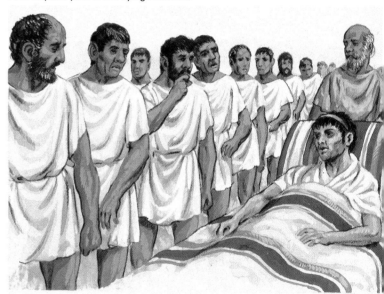

even to speak and could only greet each man with a faint movement of a hand or a glance from his eyes.

About a week before midsummer day in the year 323 B.C. he died. He was thirty-two years old and had reigned not quite thirteen years. During that time he had conquered a good half of the known world. His body was taken to Egypt and buried in his own city of Alexandria.

The empire is divided up

It was inevitable that Alexander's empire would break up, although it didn't happen straight away. Initially his officers had agreed to wait for his child to be born to Roxana, his wife. If it should be a boy, they would make him heir to his father's crown.

The ordinary Macedonian soldiers, on the other hand, preferred to hand over the empire to Alexander's half brother, who, unfortunately, was also a half wit. Eventually an agreement was reached under which both should rule jointly.

They might have saved their breath and their efforts. Not many years later, the son of Antipater, one of Alexander's generals, had both the heirs murdered, together with Olympias, Alexander's mother.

Murder of Olympias

Antipater himself took over the government of the European part of the empire. It was easy for him to do this, for Alexander himself had appointed him to run mainland Greece while the Macedonian army was away conquering the world.

Almost as painless was the siezure of power in Persia and Babylon by General Seleucus. He even extended his territory by adding Syria to his realm. He set up a new capital at Antioch on the River Orontes and his descendants ruled this part of the world for many years.

The third of Alexander's most powerful generals, Ptolemy, began to reign as king in Egypt, over part of the north African coast and also the Holy Land. His descendants included the famous queen, Cleopatra.

The boundaries of these three major areas, not to mention the many smaller ones, varied from time to time as the newly made 'kings' fought each other to enlarge or protect their kingdoms.

The next forty years saw the continuation of these struggles and during this time, the same kind of thing, although on a smaller scale, was going on in Greece itself. Alliances and leagues were formed, split apart, and reformed. Neither Athens nor Sparta ever again became leader of the Greek city states, although Athens in particular continued to be celebrated for her culture and philosophy.

We ought to take a look at just one of the many cities founded by the conqueror to see how Greek thought was flowering after being planted in foreign soil.

Alexandria in Egypt had become one of the leading Greek cities of the ancient world. Here was founded the Museum – almost the equivalent of a university. The city was also home to the best poets of the age, or at least those writing in Greek.

Among the thinkers of Alexandria who made important advances in science, mathematics, geography, astronomy and the arts of healing were Hero, Archimedes and Eratosthenes.

Hero probably lived somewhat later than the other two mentioned. We know from his writings that he had invented an early coin-in-the-slot machine for dispensing wine and also a primitive steam engine.

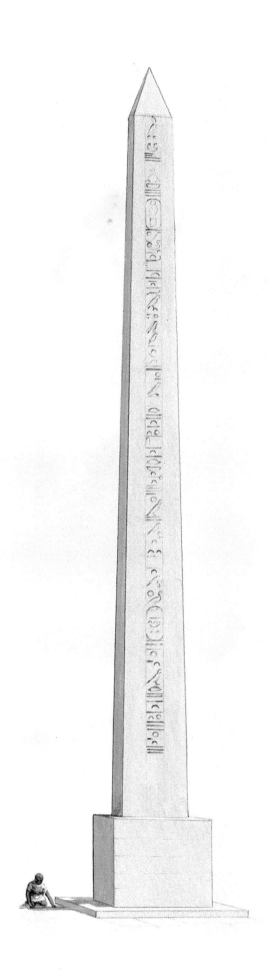

Eratosthenes measuring the shadow of an obelisk

Hero's steam engine

Archimedes, a native of Syracuse in Sicily, studied at Alexandria where he made great discoveries in science generally and physics in particular. He invented the Archimedean screw or helix for raising water and also (somewhat doubtfully) a method of setting fire to the sails of enemy ships by using huge magnifying glasses aimed at concentrating the sun's rays.

Eratosthenes was one of the first men to discover that the earth was round rather than flat. More important, he hit upon a method of measuring its size. He was told that on a certain day, the sun shone straight down a well at Syene, about four hundred miles due south of Alexandria, whilst an obelisk at the latter place cast a slight shadow.

From these scraps of information, he worked out that the world must measure 252,000 Greek stadia all the way round. This comes to almost 29,000 miles, a figure which compares very well with the modern calculation of about 25,000 miles.

So, in spite of the political collapse of Alexander's empire, Greek ideas, language and culture continued to hold sway over a large part of the known world.

Chapter 15   Greece conquered

The Romans come to Greece

A Roman soldier of 140 B.C.

Another city was becoming powerful in the Mediterranean at the same time that Athens and Sparta were reaching their peak. This was the city of Rome in central Italy. Until about 200 B.C. Rome was fully occupied in fighting a war against a rival city in North Africa called Carthage.

After Carthage and its general, Hannibal, had been dealt with, Rome was able to turn its attention to the eastern Mediterranean and in particular to one of Alexander's successors, Philip V, king of Macedonia. The Greek king had made certain of attracting Roman notice by entering into a treaty of friendship with Hannibal, the enemy of Rome.

On top of this, Philip had been trying to enlarge his kingdom by expanding into the territory of his neighbours. When he seemed to have designs on nations next door to Rome, or at least, only on the other side of the Adriatic, the Romans decided to interfere.

A three year war ensued, ending with the battle of Cynoscephalae. which almost turned into a farce. Both Rome's and Philip's army had each about 26,000 men – the Macedonians divided into two phalanxes of 8,000 men apiece, plus about 7,000 or so light troops and more than 2,000 mounted soldiers. The Romans had roughly the same number of heavy infantry, 16,500, together with 6,000 lightly armed foot soldiers and perhaps 4,000 cavalry. The Roman forces were commanded by Quinctius Flamininus, who could also call upon auxiliary troops and a certain number of war elephants.

Philip moved, first to one place and then another, seeking a suitably level battle ground, Flamininus followed him. Finally, the two armies, unknown to each other, made camp on opposite sides of the same low range of hills. The name 'Cynoscephalae', mentioned above, is Greek for 'dogheads' and refers to the shape of some of the rocky outcrops.

Next day there was a thick fog and parties of foot soldiers set out to look for each other. After wandering uncertainly for some time, a group of Roman light infantrymen met a similar force of Macedonians. The Romans were driven back, reinforced and driven back again. Luckily for Flamininus, his cavalry turned up in time to prevent a massacre.

When the mist had dispersed, Flamininus began to arrange his troops in battle formation, ordering his right wing to stand still, protected by a screen of elephants, while he personally led his left wing forward. Philip meant to stand his ground but was persuaded to advance, one phalanx leading the other. The command to lower lances was given and the Macedonians drove the Roman left wing some way down the hill.

The Roman right wing with its elephants then attacked the attackers – partly from one side. A Roman officer, seeing the success of this manoeuvre, wheeled some of his men around and took the Greeks in the rear.

The phalanx was not designed for this type of fighting and while the Greeks were trying to get into some sort of defensive order, Flamininus regrouped his left wing and attacked from the front.

The Macedonians could find no answer to this two- or three-pronged onslaught. When he saw defeat staring him in the face, Philip left the battlefield with a small mounted escort.

The Romans lost seven hundred men but the field of Cynoscephalae was strewn with 8,000 Greek dead. In addition, 5,000 of them were taken prisoner.

The Romans won because their army was organised in a more flexible way than the enemy – so that it was possible to alter a plan at the last moment in response to a changing situation.

This was merely the first encounter between the rising power of Rome and the declining power of what was left of Alexander's empire. It was not to be the last.

Greece becomes a Roman province

When the Romans withdrew from Greece in 194 B.C., Antiochus III, king of the Seleucid empire, tried to take their place. Unfortunately for him, his attack on Greece was far too slow and clumsy. It gave Rome time to counter-attack.

The form this counter-attack took was rather like the Roman plan for beating Carthage. Rome wouldn't attack Antiochus's invasion force directly, just as she hadn't tried to smash Hannibal's army in Italy. In both cases, it was decided to counter-invade – in other words, to draw off the enemy from his target by a campaign against his home territory.

The leader of the Roman forces was Lucius Scipio, whose brother Publius Scipio Africanus had been the successful general against Hannibal and Carthage. In fact, Publius volunteered to be his brother's second-in-command. He lent his considerable skill to the task of landing the Roman legions in Asia Minor. Unfortunately he fell ill just before the crucial battle was fought and Lucius was on his own.

To add to Lucius's difficulties, his own army of some 30,000 was outnumbered by the enemy's 60,000 or

more infantry, not to mention another 12,000 cavalry-men. However, Antiochus, instead of remaining in his fortified camp at a place called Magnesia, came out to do battle.

He seemed to be winning for a while but the Romans soon built up such a threatening force at an important point that the king took fright and bolted with the scattered units of his once proud army.

Roman peace terms were that Antiochus should take what was left of his army out of Asia Minor and leave it for the Romans to do with it as they wished. The treaty Antiochus had to sign was finalised as the Peace of Apamea in the year 188 B.C.

The scene shifts back to mainland Greece, as Philip V's son and successor, Perseus, sought to re-establish the complete independence of Macedonia. So, in 168 B.C. Rome sent a force under Paullus to deal with him.

He landed with his troops and took control of a mountain pass not far from the Macedonian camp.

Perseus had to retreat and the Romans caught up with him at a place named Pydna.

Paullus had never seen a phalanx in action before and privately admitted that the glitter of sunlight on the countless lance points filled him with dread. However, nothing of this fear was allowed to show as he gave out his battle orders. Roman troops must advance and push their way into any gaps that could be seen in the phalanx.

The leading cohort of Paullus's troops was almost wiped out but then the phalanx opposing them reached uneven ground and the gaps began to appear. The Romans, sword in hand, threw themselves into the openings, driving deep wedges into the enemy. The Macedonians could manage no counter move and defeat turned into rout when the disorganised phalanx was attacked by the second Roman legion.

Perseus gave it up as hopeless and rode away with his horsemen, leaving the infantrymen to their fate. 20,000 were killed and more than half that number taken prisoner – to become either slaves or gladiators in some Roman amphitheatre. Perseus himself was later captured and died in a Roman prison.

This was the last known use of the phalanx in battle. Just under 150 years after the death of Alexander, his empire had been mortally wounded. Macedonia was divided into four separate regions paying taxes and tribute to Rome. Twenty years after the battle of Pydna, there was a rebellion in Macedonia. It was put down with great severity and Macedonia became a directly ruled Roman province in 148 B.C.

Two years later, there were similar risings in other parts of Greece. These were crushed even more cruelly. Lucius Mummius was the Roman responsible. Corinth was attacked in 146 B.C. and taken. The city was destroyed and the people killed or made slaves.

The difference between the cultured Greeks and the rough and ready Romans was shown when pack animals were being loaded with priceless art treasures from civilised Corinth. An orderly nearly dropped an exquisite statuette. 'Careful,' said Mummius gruffly, 'if you break that, you'll have to replace it.' He wasn't joking but seriously believed that if a work of art were destroyed, you could always get an identical replacement.

From this time onward, there were no more free Greek city states. Most of the rest of Alexander's old empire fell into Rome's hands, bit by bit. The last piece was Egypt which came under Roman rule when Cleopatra and Marcus Antonius were defeated by Augustus at the battle of Actium in 31 B.C.

The battle of Pydna

203

The Greek legacy

As we have seen, Greece fell prey to Roman empire building. It was almost two thousand years before she regained her freedom – not in fact until 1830, when Turkey, the last occupier, was driven out.

However, the Greek way of life was so attractive to the peoples Greece conquered or was conquered by, that many of the strands of Greek life can still be seen in the modern world.

The list of subjects with a strong Greek influence on our own world is a very long one. We now know that there are many words from Greece connected with the theatre – the word 'theatre' itself, 'scene', 'orchestra' and 'chorus', and it is surely no accident that modern theatres owe a good deal of their layout to the original plans of the Athenian and other classical Greek theatres.

'Odeon' is another Greek word. It was a kind of theatre which staged music and poetry readings. Both 'music' and 'poetry' are from Greek, as are 'harmony', 'rhythm', 'rhyme', 'epic', 'lyric' and 'elegy'.

We've heard about some ancient Greek poetry in stories of the Trojan war but there was much else written in verse. These verses often acted as patterns to later Roman poets such as Virgil and Horace, who in turn influenced English poetry.

'Athlete' is a Greek word; so are 'discus', 'stadium', 'decathlon', 'marathon' and many others. Naturally, we use these classical words because the Greeks were the first to think of the ideas behind them.

When travellers nearer to our own times visited the classical sites, they brought back tales of beautiful buildings and statues. In Europe and America these were copied extensively. There is hardly a major modern city that does not owe something to Greek architects. In England in particular, it was not just the public buildings that were designed to look like Greek temples – even the humble dwelling house of the seventeen and eighteen hundreds might have a temple triangle or pediment over the front door and a doric column on each side of it. Inside, other doors and even fireplaces clearly showed traces of Greek design.

Many terms in science are from Greek, either directly as 'mathematics', 'geography', 'physics' and 'geometry', or they are coined by modern man to name and describe modern discoveries, ideas and inventions. This group includes words such as 'telephone' (distant

The British Museum

Examples of the influence of classical Greek architecture on more modern English architecture.

voice), 'microscope' (small seeing), 'metropolis' (mother city), 'polytechnic' (many arts) and thousands more. Although it is possible to open a good English dictionary at random and not find several words of Greek origin on the page, it is not terribly likely.

It's surprising at times to find out how advanced some Greek ideas were. You may remember Eratosthenes who reasoned that the world was round and who worked out an approximate size: he also drew a fairly accurate map of the earth as known in those days and guessed that it might be possible to sail to India around the south of Africa, or even by going westward across the Atlantic – 'Provided,' he added, in a remarkable glimpse of the truth, 'that there is no large land mass in the way'!

Herophilus of Chalcedon thought that the blood might circulate round the body in the arteries and that perhaps the nerves conveyed sensations to the brain and sent signals back to the limbs. Also strikingly modern is the insistence of some Greek doctors on diet, exercise and hygiene in addition to vegetable based medicines.

Greek styles in pottery and sculpture have been copied in modern times, as have Athenian and Spartan soldiers' helmets – to be seen on the heads of many European mounted soldiers, and even firemen, in the last century.

Probably Greece's greatest gifts to the modern world are to be found in the realms of philosophy, religion and politics. Many patterns of thought laid down by classical thinkers are still followed today.

Although we no longer worship the Olympian gods, their names and deeds are the common heritage of all educated people in the modern world. It's also worth remembering that it was the Greek language which made possible the spread of Christianity and that the Gospels were actually written in Greek.

Undoubtedly we owe the Greeks a great deal – not least in their discovery that it is possible to run a nation on the principle that everyone should have a voice in the government.

'Democracy', too, is a Greek word.

A section of the sculpture from the walls of the Parthenon treasury

Part 3
The Romans

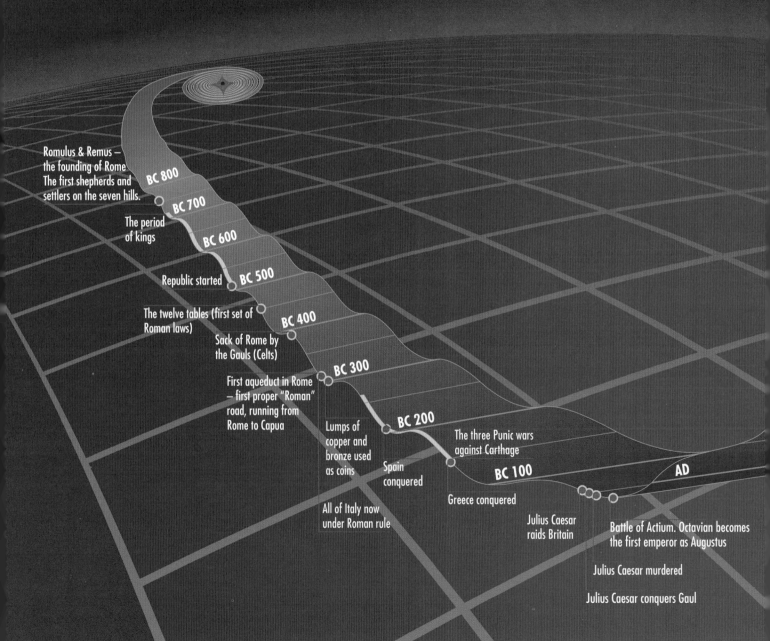

Romulus & Remus – the founding of Rome. The first shepherds and settlers on the seven hills.

BC 800

BC 700

The period of kings

BC 600

Republic started **BC 500**

The twelve tables (first set of Roman laws)

BC 400

Sack of Rome by the Gauls (Celts)

BC 300

First aqueduct in Rome – first proper "Roman" road, running from Rome to Capua

Lumps of copper and bronze used as coins

BC 200

Spain conquered

The three Punic wars against Carthage

BC 100

AD

All of Italy now under Roman rule

Greece conquered

Julius Caesar raids Britain

Battle of Actium. Octavian becomes the first emperor as Augustus

Julius Caesar murdered

Julius Caesar conquers Gaul

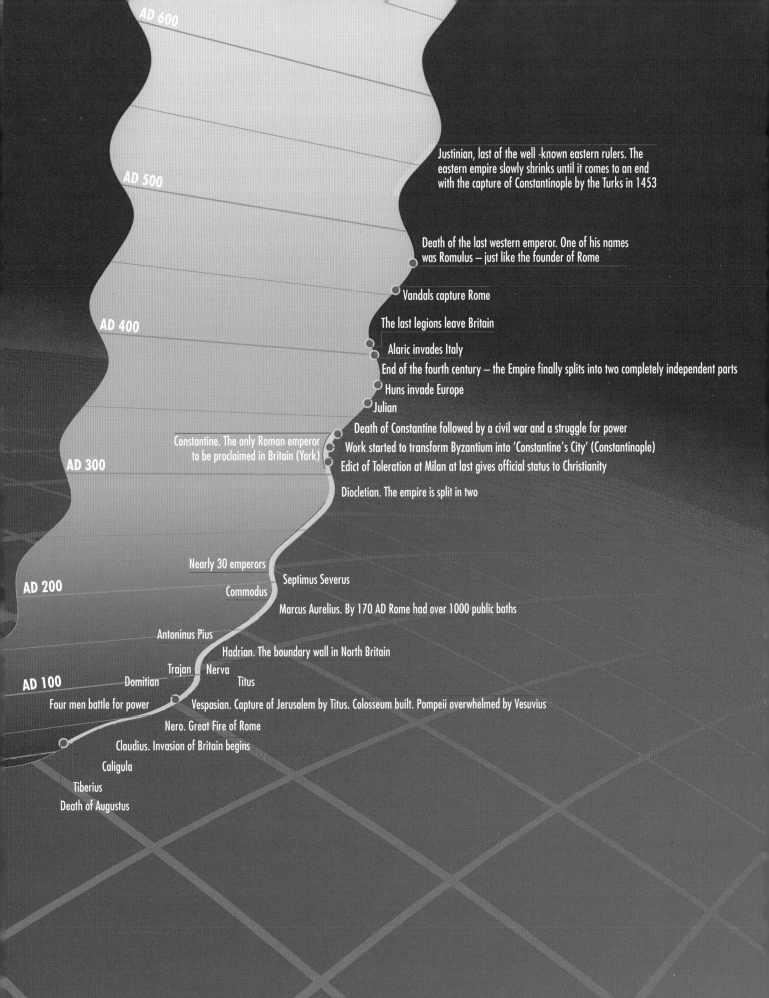

AD 600

AD 500

Justinian, last of the well-known eastern rulers. The eastern empire slowly shrinks until it comes to an end with the capture of Constantinople by the Turks in 1453

Death of the last western emperor. One of his names was Romulus — just like the founder of Rome

Vandals capture Rome

The last legions leave Britain

AD 400

Alaric invades Italy

End of the fourth century — the Empire finally splits into two completely independent parts

Huns invade Europe

Julian

Death of Constantine followed by a civil war and a struggle for power

Constantine. The only Roman emperor to be proclaimed in Britain (York)

Work started to transform Byzantium into 'Constantine's City' (Constantinople)

Edict of Toleration at Milan at last gives official status to Christianity

AD 300

Diocletian. The empire is split in two

Nearly 30 emperors

Septimus Severus

AD 200

Commodus

Marcus Aurelius. By 170 AD Rome had over 1000 public baths

Antoninus Pius

Hadrian. The boundary wall in North Britain

Trajan   Nerva

AD 100

Domitian   Titus

Four men battle for power

Vespasian. Capture of Jerusalem by Titus. Colosseum built. Pompeii overwhelmed by Vesuvius

Nero. Great Fire of Rome

Claudius. Invasion of Britain begins

Caligula

Tiberius

Death of Augustus

Chapter 16   Origins

The legend of Aeneas

On this page and the next are two of the stories that Roman parents told their children when they asked, 'Who were the earliest Romans? Where did they come from?'

There were many legends about the characters who fought in the Trojan War. Virgil, a poet of later Roman times, wrote about Aeneas, a warrior hero, and ancestor of the Roman people. He told the story of Aeneas in a long poem called the *Aeneid*.

Virgil begins by describing how the Greeks attacked and captured the city of Troy. Some Trojans, however, managed to escape. Aeneas, his father Anchises, and his son Ascanius, arranged to meet at Mount Ida, a low hill overlooking the city. Creusa, Aeneas's wife, never arrived. Aeneas sadly concluded that she must have become separated from the family in the stampede of refugees, and had probably been killed in the crush of people.

The family made their way to Antandros, where they managed to get aboard a ship that was fleeing from the doomed city. They sailed to Greece and to the island of Crete, but Aeneas wanted to start building a new city of Troy, and he was sure that neither of these was the right place to do so.

At one point they were attacked by harpies, a flock of birds with human heads who stole their food. The leader of the harpies spoke mockingly to them, saying that they wouldn't find the right place for their new city until they had been forced by hunger to eat the tables on which their food was spread.

They tried to sail from there to Italy, but were blown off course by storms and forced ashore in North Africa. Queen Dido, the ruler of the nearby city of Carthage, took pity on the Trojans. She fell in love with Aeneas and tried to persuade him to marry her. But Aeneas felt he had to move on to look for the place to build the new Troy. When he sailed away, Dido killed herself.

Finally, the wanderers came to the end of their voyage at the mouth of the river Tiber in Italy, where they disembarked.

As they were eating, one of them looked at the meal of pieces of meat laid on slices of wheatcake and exclaimed, 'Aeneas! The prophecy of the harpy queen

Aeneas escapes from Troy with his father and son

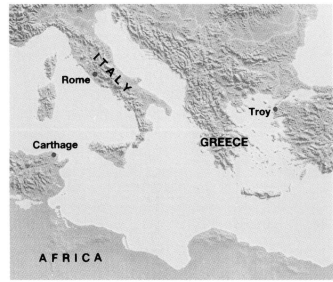

The death of Dido

has come true: are we not eating the tables on which our food is spread?'

They found out that the country was called Latium, and they set out to explore it. Before long, they met Latinus, the king, and Aeneas fell in love with his daughter, Lavinia. Aeneas told the king that he wanted to rebuild Troy, and asked for Lavinia's hand in marriage.

Turnus, the ruler of a nearby land, also wanted to marry Lavinia. When Aeneas wouldn't give way, he challenged him to fight for her. Aeneas had the worst of the duel to start with, but eventually he managed to break Turnus's sword, and the fight was over.

Aeneas built his new town, and called it Lavinium. He and his wife reigned there for many years. After the death of Aeneas, his son Ascanius became king. Ascanius decided to build a new city of his own, called Alba Longa. He left Lavinium and made Alba Longa his capital.

Virgil's account of these adventures ends with the death of Turnus, but other Roman writers tell how the descendants of Ascanius reigned in Alba Longa for over over four hundred years.

Aeneas lands at the mouth of the Tiber

The legend of Romulus and Remus

NUMITOR WAS THE DESCENDANT OF AENEAS. HE RULED IN ALBA LONGA SOME FOUR CENTURIES AFTER THE DEATH OF HIS FAMOUS ANCESTOR.

AMULIUS WAS JEALOUS OF HIS BROTHER, KING NUMITOR, AND RESOLVED TO TAKE HIS THRONE BY FORCE.

AMULIUS DROVE OUT NUMITOR AND REIGNED AT ALBA LONGA IN HIS STEAD.

RHEA SILVIA WAS NUMITOR'S ONLY CHILD, BUT AS A GIRL SHE SEEMED TO PRESENT NO DANGER TO HER WICKED UNCLE.
TO PREVENT HER MARRYING AND PRODUCING A SON WHO MIGHT CLAIM THE THRONE, AMULIUS FORCED HER TO BECOME A PRIESTESS OF A TYPE WHO WERE FORBIDDEN TO MARRY.

IN SPITE OF THESE PRECAUTIONS, MARS, THE ROMAN WAR GOD, MARRIED HER SECRETLY AND SHE HAD TWIN BOYS NAMED ROMULUS AND REMUS.

AMULIUS ORDERED A SERVANT TO DROWN THE TWINS IN THE RIVER, AND RHEA SYLVIA TO BE PUT IN PRISON.

THE SERVANT TOOK PITY ON THE BOYS AND FLOATED THEM DOWN THE RIVER TIBER IN A LITTLE WOODEN CRADLE.

THE CRADLE CAME TO REST AT A PLACE NEAR SEVEN HILLS. A SHE-WOLF WHOSE CUBS HAD BEEN KILLED FOUND THE TWINS. HER BODY WAS HEAVY WITH MILK, SO SHE FED THEM.

FAUSTULUS, ONE OF THE ROYAL SHEPHERDS, FOUND THE CRADLE AND TOOK THE BABIES HOME. HE AND HIS WIFE SECRETLY BROUGHT THE BOYS UP AS THEIR OWN CHILDREN.

ROMULUS AND REMUS GREW UP TO BE STRONG AND ATHLETIC. THEY BECAME THE LEADERS OF THE LOCAL YOUTHS.

WHEN THEY BECAME MEN, THEY FOUND OUT WHAT THEIR GREAT-UNCLE HAD DONE AND THEY ATTACKED HIS CITY. AMULIUS WAS KILLED IN THE FIGHTING. NUMITOR WAS RESTORED TO HIS THRONE, AND THEIR MOTHER, RHEA SILVIA, RELEASED FROM PRISON.

THE YOUNG MEN DECIDED TO BUILD A CITY ON ONE OF THE SEVEN HILLS NEAR WHERE THE WOLF HAD FOUND THEM. THEY COULDN'T AGREE WHICH HILL TO BUILD ON, SO THEY SAT AND STARED AT THE SKY. WHOEVER SAW A VULTURE SHOULD HAVE HIS CHOICE.

ROMULUS STAMPED OFF AFTER THE ARGUMENT, BORROWED A PLOUGH AND OX TEAM, AND CUT A FURROW ROUND THE PALATINE HILL.

REMUS SAW SIX VULTURES BUT ROMULUS CLAIMED TO HAVE SEEN TWELVE. REMUS SAID THAT HE HAD SEEN THE FIRST BIRD BUT ROMULUS DECLARED THAT THE CHOICE WAS HIS, SINCE HE HAD SPOTTED MORE BIRDS.

'THIS IS THE FRONTIER', ROMULUS TOLD HIS BROTHER. 'TO CROSS IT WILL MEAN DEATH.' 'LIKE THIS?' ASKED REMUS CONTEMPTUOUSLY, STEPPING OVER THE FURROW. ROMULUS DREW HIS SWORD FURIOUSLY AND SLEW HIM.

ROMULUS WAS SORRY FOR WHAT HE HAD DONE BUT HIS CITY CONTINUED TO GROW. IT WAS NAMED 'ROME' AFTER ITS FOUNDER.

213

The truth behind the legends

One of the difficulties which faces anyone anxious to discover the truth about early Rome is that most of it may be for ever out of reach. The evidence which might have been unearthed is probably buried beneath the remains of a later, classical Rome. It would take a brave archaeologist to suggest demolishing the Colosseum to see what was underneath it. All the same, some digging has been done and a certain amount of evidence brought to light.

The legend of Romulus and Remus is set by Latin

Warriors beside huts on the Palatine Hill

writers almost eight hundred years before the birth of Jesus Christ – at 753 B.C. This may be fairly near the truth, as the earliest hilltop huts and graves found seem to have been made at about this time.

We know that the huts were small and round because of the post holes left in the soil. In addition, small clay models of houses have been dug up from cemeteries. We believe these were used to contain the ashes of cremations. Beneath the surface of what was later to become the Forum, or market square, were found some even earlier burials.

This kind of arrangement – roughly-built huts on lowish hilltops – appears to have been fairly common on the plains of Latium. No one could have guessed that the settlement on the Palatine Hill near the Tiber would one day become the mightiest city of the ancient world.

The story of Aeneas and his escape from Troy is almost certainly an invention rather than real history. The first dwellers in the earliest Latin towns were not heroic warriors from the Greek world, but simple local shepherds or farmers.

It's even possible that the four centuries that were supposed to separate Aeneas from Romulus and Remus were put into the legends deliberately to account for the time that must have gone by between the Trojan War and the founding of Rome.

Another invention must have been the supposed love of Dido, Queen of Carthage, for Aeneas. In fact, Carthage was only founded about a century before Rome – certainly not at the time of the Trojan War. If Aeneas had left burning Troy and landed in North Africa, he would have found no trace of Carthage nor of Dido.

Latin histories of the earliest city of Rome contain much legendary material and are not very reliable. In any case, the histories are much too late to be of great worth. The first Roman we know of to set down the story of Romulus and Remus was Q. Fabius Pictor and he didn't do so until about 200 B.C. Rome had then been in existence for more than five hundred years.

Some people have said that the word 'Rome' must have come from Romulus's name and therefore his existence is proved. In fact, of course, this is no argument, as no one really knows where the city's name came from. Perhaps the name 'Romulus' was invented to account for the name 'Rome'.

Another mistake in the legends concerns all three of the original Latin cities: Lavinium, Alba Longa and Rome. Archaeology shows that the first two were surely as old as the stories say, but Rome, which should have been four centuries younger, was actually proved to be as ancient as Lavinium and Alba Longa.

Romulus is also credited with the organisation of

Hut urn

local government in Rome – but again, there is no proof. It is said that Romulus chose a hundred 'fathers' to help him rule. They formed the first 'senate', or parliament and their descendants were known as 'patricians', from the Latin word for 'father'. He is then supposed to have divided the people into three main tribes and each tribe into ten smaller units called 'curiae'.

After this, the legend says, he devised a system of recruiting soldiers to defend the city. There were to be 3000 infantry and 300 horsemen, a third of which came from each tribe.

This was most likely to have been no more than a spare time army. The soldiers probably followed their ordinary jobs for much of the time. They were plant or stock farmers, keeping cattle and sheep, and growing wheat, barley, peas and beans. Many could only afford to keep pigs and goats for livestock. The vine and olive were as yet unknown in Italy.

Some farmers also doubled as simple craftsmen, making everyday items in wood, metal or clay for themselves and others. All these were humble occupations.

Later Romans, who knew nothing of their ancestors or the founding of Rome, made up stories about the earliest Romans and their adventures, making them seem more exciting than they actually were. This is how legends sometimes begin.

The early kings

The legends say that the early city was ruled by a succession of seven kings, beginning with Romulus. Some modern historians have cast doubt on the details of their lives and even on whether they lived at all. It's unlikely that they were completely made up, even though we don't really know what they looked like. They were:

1 Romulus (Latin) (753–718 B.C.) Founded the city and began its system of local government. He also started Rome on its process of growing larger and taking in more and more land. He built up the population by welcoming anyone who wanted to move to Rome.

2 Numa Pompilius (Sabine) (717–673 B.C.) A year after the death of Romulus the new ruler had still not been elected. In the area of Rome there were two main tribes of people – Romans and Sabines – and each wanted the honour. The problem was solved when both tribes agreed that a Sabine should be king and that the Romans should do the choosing. Numa Pompilius reorganised the state religion, and founded colleges for priests, the latter being known as 'flamines'. The flamines were taught how to 'take the auspices'. This meant reading the future from the flight of birds and later from flashes of lightning. He also devised a new calendar of twelve months, replacing one of ten months. The last four of our 'modern' months come from Latin words for seventh, eighth, ninth and tenth.

3 Tullus Hostilius (Latin) (672–641 B.C.) He was a military-minded king who believed that his subjects would become soft if they weren't engaged in fighting every so often. He was so successful in his wars that he began to think that armies were more important than ordinary people, or even the worship of the gods. He extended Rome's rule within a circle roughly ten or twelve miles in radius. Among other neighbouring settlements, soldiers under his command attacked and destroyed Rome's original mother city, Alba Longa. At last the gods grew angry and slew the impious king by striking his palace with a bolt of lightning.

Soldiers of the Servian army

4 Ancus Martius (Sabine) (639–616 B.C.) He extended Rome's boundaries to the coast and captured Ostia, which was to become Rome's seaport. He was probably also responsible for the first bridge over the Tiber. This was the Pons Sublicus, just downstream from the river island opposite the Palatine Hill. In addition, he is supposed to have captured and fortified the Janiculum Hill on the far side of the Tiber.

5 Lucius Tarquinius Priscus (Etruscan) (616–579 B.C.) He was the first Etruscan king. He was appointed tutor to the sons of Ancus Martius. When the old king lay dying, Priscus sent the sons away so that he could have himself named as the next ruler. As king, he subdued more of Rome's neighbouring tribes. He built the Capitol temple on the Capitoline Hill but is perhaps more famous for draining the marshes between the Palatine and Aventine Hills. The sewer he had made was called the Cloaca Maxima ('the Great Sewer') and still runs into the Tiber. On the reclaimed land he ordered the laying out of the Circus Maximus, Rome's first chariot-racing course.

6 Servius Tullius (Etruscan) (578–535 B.C.) He divided the citizens into five classes from the richest to poorest. All except the very poor had to provide standby soldiers for the army. The richest groups supplied the cavalry and the rest supplied the infantry. There were also to be corps of specialists such as

carpenters, metalworkers, signallers and engineers. He is said to have built an enormous defensive wall taking in all seven hills, running for about seven miles and enclosing about one and a half square miles. However, archaeologists say that surviving stretches of Roman town wall are much later than was once thought.

7 Tarquinius Superbus (Etruscan) (534–509 B.C.) The name 'Superbus' means 'proud' and, indeed, he was so haughty he took no notice of what his people wanted or needed. He behaved so badly that the people not only drove him out but promised themselves solemnly that they would never have a king to reign over them again.

Rome in the 5th century B.C. surrounded by the Servian walls

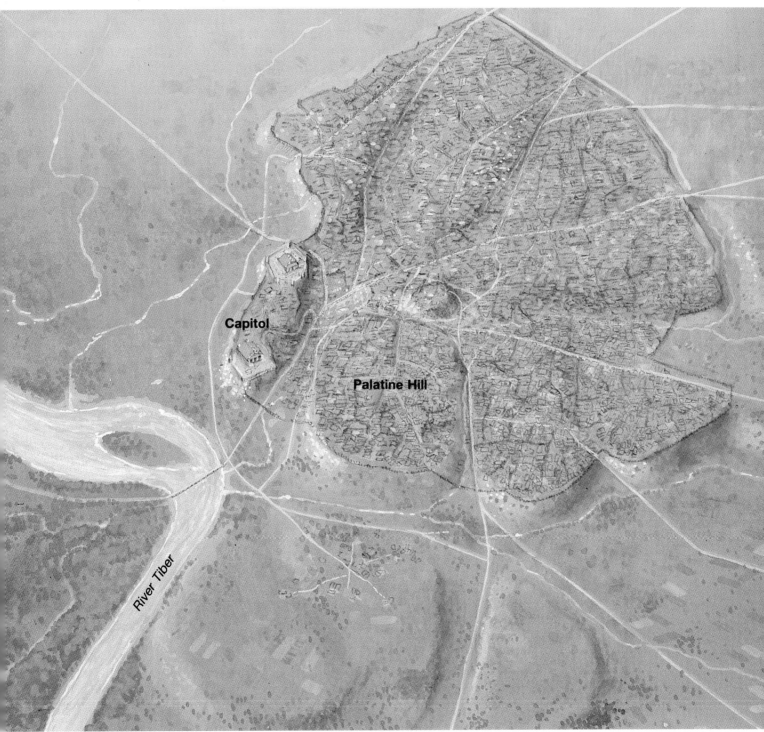

Capitol

Palatine Hill

River Tiber

Sabines and Romans

As we've already seen, the first citizens of Rome had to contend with other inhabitants of the various cities, towns and villages on the plains of Latium. One such tribe was the Sabines, a group which provided Rome with some of its first rulers. The legend telling how they came to co-operate with Romulus and his men is a rather interesting one.

It happened in the first few years after the founding of the city. Romulus had issued a general invitation to anyone who wished to make his home in Rome. The more men it had, the more easily it could be defended. As a result, many men were attracted to the hilltop town: unfortunately, many of them were runaway slaves, petty criminals or even murderers!

Although Rome might have grown fast in the early years, as the newcomers arrived, it couldn't go on growing without a good number of wives and families as well. Lacking these, the men would have aged and then died and without children to follow them, Rome would have died too.

The problem was – where were the wives to come from? The daughters of neighbouring tribesmen were unwilling to marry penniless upstarts like these early Romans. After all, many of them had still risen no higher than cattlemen, shepherds or farm labourers.

Someone had an idea – it may have been Romulus or one of his helpers. It was a very simple idea. The Romans were to organise some games in the form of

Rome and its neighbours

athletic contests. All the nearby tribes were invited.

Of course, the Romans, like the Greeks, only allowed men and boys to watch the contests, which left the womenfolk at home and alone. After the races had started, a secret signal was given and many of the Romans quietly left. They stole away to the Sabine settlements and kidnapped most of the Sabine daughters.

Naturally, the Sabine men soon found out what had happened and were furious. They armed themselves and prepared for battle with the treacherous Romans. Romulus and his men were expecting an attack and they were also equipped with weapons and armour. The two forces met just outside the city and drew up in long lines of men, each soldier facing an enemy.

Before the struggle could begin, however, a strange thing happened. Between the hostile groups ran the Sabine daughters – hundreds of them. When they had filled the space which in modern times would be called 'no man's land', they explained what they were doing.

'We were just daughters a short while ago,' said their leader, 'now we are both wives and daughters. We did not choose our husbands – they chose us. We want this fighting to stop. If it goes ahead, many will be slain. When our fathers are dead, we shall be orphans, but if our husbands die, we shall be widows. We lose either way.'

There was silence while this explanation and plea sank in. Finally it was obvious that the women were right and the battle never took place. At least, that's what the legend says and it does explain how Sabine men were able to become kings in ancient Rome.

Of course, the legend could be quite wrong. Some historians claim that these incidents never happened at all. They point to a long, drawn-out war with no obvious winner as the reason for the alternation of the first kings between Latins and Sabines.

The rape of the Sabine women

219

The Etruscans

No one really knows who the Etruscans were nor where they came from. Some historians have suggested Asia Minor as their homeland and in particular, that part which today we call Turkey.

Their civilisation is more of a mystery than that of the Romans because we can't understand very much of their language. We have thousands of examples of their writing but these are nearly all inscriptions on tombs. As such, there aren't enough words in continuous sentences to make much translation possible. We are, however, pretty sure that Etruscan isn't related to any other European language, as French and Spanish are related to each other, for example.

We do know that they inhabited a part of Italy called Tuscany. This lies to the north and west of the river Tiber and Rome. The Etruscans had their own name for it – 'Etruria'.

Fortunately for us, the tombs can tell us a good deal about everyday life, even if we can't read Etruscan writing. The dead were placed in coffins in stone-cut chambers, the walls of which were often painted in bright colours with scenes from the life of the departed.

In addition to the vivid pictures, there were other things from which we can learn about Etruscan ways. In common with many other ancient peoples, the Etruscans often made their tombs resemble the insides

Stone animal liver from Etruria

of their houses. They also buried many items of everyday use to be the possessions of the dead person in the afterlife.

Some of our knowledge of the Etruscans comes from Roman writers. Unluckily, the most complete account of this mysterious people is missing. It was written by the emperor Claudius early in the Christian era but the history, although running to some twenty volumes, has totally disappeared.

Archaeologists can also provide information and from all these sources a dim misty picture begins to take shape. The Etruscans, at least in their early days, were a cultured people with a love of fine things. They wore brightly coloured clothes patterned on those of the Greeks.

In fact, they admired the Greeks a great deal and copied a lot of their culture. Etruscan painted pottery, for example, can often be confused with that from Corinth or Athens. The Romans imitated many Etruscan things, including the pottery. They adopted a new method of infantry fighting which had come from Greece by way of Etruria.

Many of the ideas which we think of as purely Roman were also borrowed from the Etruscans – for example, the 'triumph' (a procession honouring a victorious general), 'games' (just like the Greek ones), the 'fasces' (axes in bundles of rods as badges of authority) and 'auspices' (telling the future, first of all from birds, then from animal livers and flashes of lightning).

As well as ideas, Rome also imported great quantities

Etruscan writing

of Etruscan art work, since the Etruscans were good craftsmen in metalwork, especially in bronze, silver and gold. As well as small items such as rings, bracelets and ornamental jugs, they also made large metal plaques with designs hammered in, which were intended to decorate furniture and chariots. Among the most sought after treasures were bronze mirrors with pictures of people on the back.

The Romans learnt a good deal about practical matters from the Etruscans and even had a century when they were ruled by Etruscan kings.

Towns in Etruria were laid out on a right-angled grid pattern, with houses, squares, temples and market places. They were often sited on hilltops, as was Rome itself.

Etruscan troops from such towns fought against other tribes in Italy. They were beaten by the Greeks in southern Italy and cut off from some of their lands by peoples such as the Aequi and Volsci. The Romans finally subdued them and they disappeared from the scene.

Romans envied the Etruscans their elegance and tried to imitate it. They also disliked and distrusted the men of Tuscany and fought fiercely against them.

The Etruscan town of Marzobotto was laid out on a rectangular grid pattern.

Placing a body in the Campana tomb at Veii near Rome

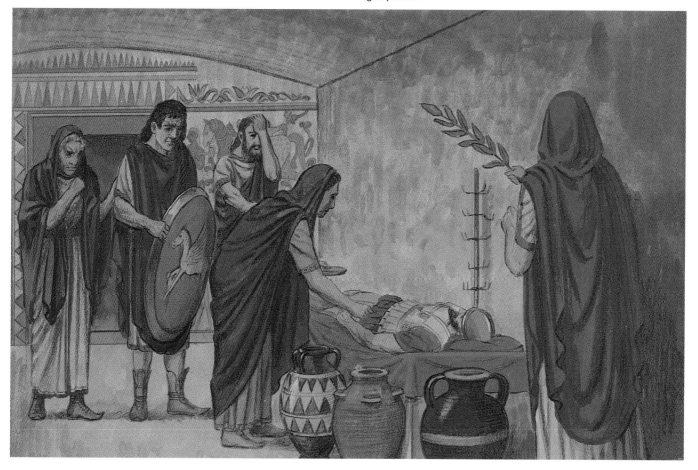

Horatius and the bridge

In the early nineteenth century, Lord Macaulay wrote a poem celebrating a most heroic feat of arms performed by Horatius, as he defended Rome from its enemies.

After Rome's last king, Tarquin the Proud, had been thrown out of the city, the Etruscans decided to avenge this insult. The poem tells how the Etruscan leader, Lars Porsena, first gathered his army together:

'Lars Porsena of Clusium
By the nine Gods he swore
That the great house of Tarquin
Should suffer wrong no more.
By the nine Gods he swore it,
And named a trysting day,

And bade his messengers ride forth,
East and west and south and north,
To summon his array.'

When the soldiers had mustered, there were 'four-score thousand' infantry and 'ten thousand horse'.

As this huge army neared the city, refugees poured into Rome to shelter behind its walls, and sentinels could see a sky made blood-red with the flames of burning villages. Rome's parliament, the Senate, decided that since the Janiculum Hill, on the far side of the Tiber, had been captured, the only bridge over the river must be destroyed. Before this could be done the guards

Lars Porsena orders the attack on Rome

Horatius holds the bridge

shouted that the Etruscan army was already in sight and that it was too late to smash the bridge.

Then Horatius volunteered to go to the far side of the river with two companions and hold up the Etruscans while the bridge was being chopped down. As he says in the poem:

'To every man upon this earth
Death cometh soon or late.
And how can man die better
Than facing fearful odds
For the ashes of his fathers,
And the temples of his Gods.'

The two friends Horatius took with him were Spurius Lartius and Herminius. They prepared for action whilst the working party got busy knocking down the bridge.

'Now while the Three were tightening
Their harness on their backs
The Consul was the foremost man
To take in hand an axe:
And Fathers mixed with Commons
Seized hatchet, bar and crow,
And smote upon the planks above
And loosed the props below.'

All the Etruscan warriors were beaten in turn by the trio:

'Stout Lartius hurled down Aunus
Into the stream beneath:
Herminius struck at Seius
And clove him to the teeth:
At Picus brave Horatius
Darted one fiery thrust;
And the proud Umbrian's gilded arms
Clashed in the bloody dust.'

Spurius Lartius and Herminius darted back just before the bridge fell, thinking Horatius was with them. When they realised that he wasn't, they tried to return but alas! the bridge had fallen and Horatius was alone. He prayed to the gods and then, in full armour, he dived into the Tiber. Some of the enemy cursed him and hoped that he would drown but Lars Porsena rebuked them and said that such a brave man deserved to survive.

Finally Horatius reached the city bank and staggered ashore, bleeding but alive, and Rome was saved. His fame, the poet says, will resound down the ages:

'And still his name sounds stirring
Unto the men of Rome,
As the trumpet-blast that cries to them
To charge the Volscian home;
And wives still pray to Juno
For boys with hearts as bold
As his who kept the bridge so well
In the brave days of old.'

All very stirring stuff about how heroic the young men of Rome were and how glorious Rome's history. However, some historians maintain that the whole story is false: that Lars Porsena actually conquered Rome and ruled there for some years.

It's certainly difficult to sort out the truth from the tales of such early times.

The Celts

The Celts were a very widespread people who lived (at one time or another) in a broad band right across Europe from Ireland in the west, through France, Belgium, Germany, Switzerland, Austria and as far as Turkey in the east. They were the tribes who opposed the landings of the Roman legions in south east England when the emperor Claudius decided to conquer Britain in 43 A.D.

This was not, however, the first meeting between Romans and Celts (or 'Gauls' as they appear in the Latin language). Some five centuries or so before the birth of Christ, tribes of warlike Celts in central Europe had been attracted across the Alps into northern Italy. The rich farmlands along the valley of the river Po were what drew them southward.

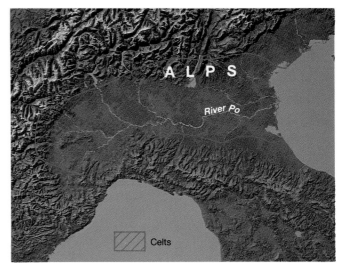
The Celts settled in northern Italy

A Celt touches the senator's beard

Eventually they came into contact with the Etruscans and drove them out. After a time the various tribes settled down on the plains of northern Italy. The Insubres had their capital at Milan, the Boii lived around Bologna, the Cenomani had tribal centres at Brescia and Verona, whilst the Lingones and Senones spread out along the Adriatic coast.

The latter group decided in the year 390 B.C. to raid even further south. A horde of them swept into Etruria and made their way down the Tiber valley.

Alarmed, the Romans sent an army to halt them. Unfortunately for Rome, her soldiers were badly beaten on the banks of the Allia river and the victorious Celts pushed on, unopposed. Three days after the battle, their vanguard appeared before the walls of Rome.

Many of the citizens had fled to other towns and cities – particularly to nearby Caere, leaving a handful of determined young men to garrison the Capitoline Hill. Brennus, the chief of the Celtic Senones, led his men almost unopposed into the rest of the deserted city.

In the Forum, they came upon a line of chairs made of ivory, upon which sat some of Rome's elderly senators. For a while the two groups stared at each other. Then a Celt put out a curious hand and touched a senator's white beard. The old man reacted angrily, so the Celt raised his iron sword and slew him. Soon all the senators were dead.

The Celts turned their attention to the Capitol which was still defended. Although the Celts were bold and daring, they were not keen on long, drawn-out sieges, but this is just what they were faced with. Their attempt to take the Capitol Hill went on for no less than seven months.

At one stage, the invaders tried to scale the cliffs at dead of night and the Romans were only saved by the sacred geese of Juno's temple. The birds cackled so loudly that the defenders were warned and sprang to their positions.

Eventually, the Celts were only persuaded to leave by being bribed with a large sum of gold. Incidentally, there is a legend which relates how a Roman army from one of the nearby cities turned up and drove off the Celts. This is almost certainly an invention, made up to wipe out the shame of the Celtic victory. The story goes on to talk about Rome being left 'a heap of smouldering ruins'.

The Celts assuredly did their share of destruction but it seems unlikely that the fires would still have been burning seven months after the arrival of the enemy. However, practically all the written records, including all mention of the first Roman laws, disappeared with the Celtic raids.

After the Celts had left, there were some Romans who wanted to abandon the city and move to the more easily defended city of Veii, which lay a few miles to the north west of Rome. They were overruled, although there were renewed attacks from old enemies such as the Volsci, the Aequi and the Etruscans.

The Romans rebuilt their city, reorganised their army and beat off their foes. The Celts came back again – several times, in fact, often allying themselves with Rome's ancient adversaries. For all practical purposes, though, the Romans had the last laugh, finally destroying their tormentors in Italy almost exactly a century after the first Celtic attacks.

Celts in the Alps in the 3rd century B.C.

Chapter 17   Rome and her neighbours

The Greeks

Seen through Greek eyes, early Rome was just another shepherds' village. Greeks had founded colonies all over the Mediterranean world, including southern Italy. Some of these settlements had themselves started colonies. It wasn't surprising therefore that Greek ideas should have been known to the pioneer inhabitants of Rome.

It was a two-way process; Greeks knew all about Rome by the fourth century B.C. and it was they who originated some of the legends about the birth of the city. They invented a man named 'Rhomus' after whom they said the city was called, and it was they who said that Romans were descended from Aeneas, the best known refugee from the Trojan war. It wasn't until the second century before Christ that Roman historians began to write down their city's story. When they did, they took the Greek legends and retold them in Latin.

Greek settlers in Italy were not ruled in any way by the cities in Greece from which they had come, but they were still Greeks and in their new homes they began to make a new life very similar to that which they had left behind.

As Rome expanded, it came more and more into contact with Greek ideas and thought. One practical result was the introduction by Greeks of grape and olive growing from their homeland to Italy.

Romans became aware of the fine temples these foreigners had put up to house their gods and in later years tried to imitate them. They also copied the architecture of the Greek dwelling house – at least, the better off Romans did. There were only one-roomed huts in the early days of Rome, but extra chambers were added to the 'atrium', as it was called, in imitation of the best Greek models. Rich Romans went further and included a central garden with fountains and statues and surrounded by even more rooms.

Other borrowings include the alphabet. Romans used it to write in Latin and it came not just from the Greeks but the Etruscans too. In fact, the alphabet was not a Greek invention but had been adapted from letters originally used in the Middle East. The very letter names 'alpha' and 'beta' which we think of as Greek are really near Eastern words for 'ox' and 'house'.

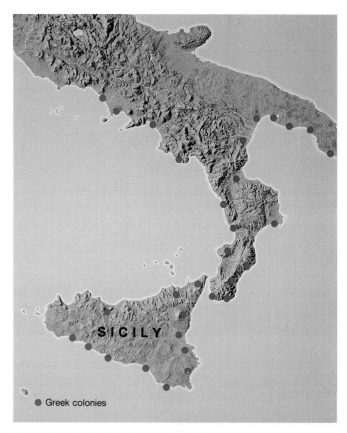

Magna Graecia – the Greeks in southern Italy

Romans cheerfully adopted Greek philosophy and tried to imitate the Greeks' skill as sculptors. Later Roman generals raided the homelands of Athens, Sparta and other city states in order to bear off to Rome countless thousands of original statues.

Latin laws often show a strong likeness to those of Athens. It was also to Athens that Romans owed their ideas of the use of coins to ease trade and commerce.

Greek colonies in southern Italy were known to the Romans as part of 'Magna Graecia' (Greater Greece), probably because in total area they were several times as large as Greece itself. The men of Rome had overrun the Greek Italian settlements by about 273 B.C. Later, in the next century, the legions were to conquer the Greek homelands themselves and thus to include Greece in the new and growing Roman Empire.

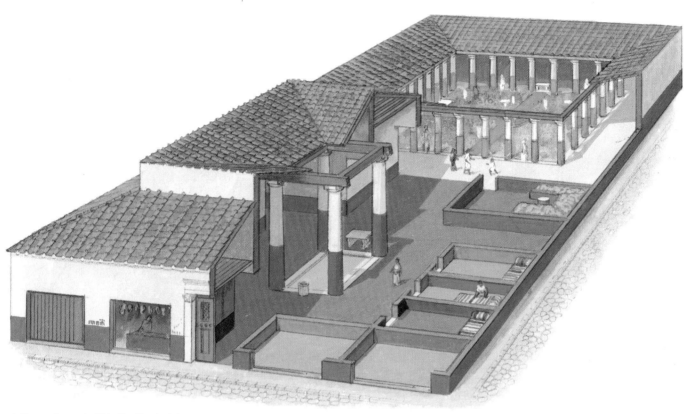

A Roman house built in the Greek style

Greek temple at Paestum, south of modern Naples

Carthage

Carthage was only a neighbour in the sense that the city lay just across the Mediterranean from Rome. She was not a neighbour in any friendly sense, being almost from the first a rival and merciless enemy. The people were known as 'Poeni' (the Latin for 'Phoenician') and anything to do with them as 'Punic'. We could ask a Roman historian to tell us about them and where they came from.

'They were a Middle Eastern people who settled on the coasts of what you call Lebanon about a thousand years or more before Rome itself was founded. Don't you call them Phoenicians?

'Just before Romulus started our own city, colonists from one of their seaports (a place named Tyre) began to build Carthage, or Qarthadasht as they called it in their own tongue. It means "the new capital". You may have heard of Dido and Aeneas, perhaps?'

We nod and he goes on, 'Dido was the sister of Pygmalion, King of Tyre. Her husband, the high priest Acerbas, quarrelled with the king who had him murdered. Dido was told in a dream to escape from

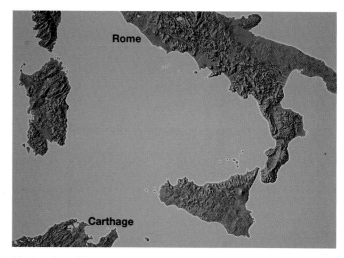

The location of Carthage in relation to Rome

Pygmalion. So with a handful of faithful friends and followers, she sailed away from Tyre and reached Africa where they began to build their new city.

'Now here comes a difficulty. Our poet, Virgil, says Dido fell in love with Aeneas, the ancestor of Romulus

Reconstruction of Carthage from the air

The harbour at Carthage

and Remus. This is a little confusing since the supposed "lovers" lived about three centuries apart. Still, it's only a story.

'Virgil goes on to say that Aeneas did not return her love and set sail for Italy. Dido, in despair, stabbed herself to death and her body was burned on a funeral pyre. Virgil may have a grain of truth here: there is a rumour that the Phoenicians sacrificed babies to their gods by burning them alive.'

'It's more than a rumour,' we say, 'for the burnt remains of hundreds of infants were dug up at the end of the last century. By the way, who were their gods?'

'Baal and Astarte ruled the Phoenician homelands but in Africa Baal became Baal Amon, or Moloch, and Tanith was the new name for Astarte.

'It was really a pity about Carthage. It had to be destroyed after it lost a series of wars against us but it must have been a fine city in its day.

'With nearly a million people, it was easily the largest of the many Phoenician settlements along the North African coast. It was founded by a nation of craftsmen, sailors and traders. It had a nearly ideal situation, being set on a rocky headland, protected both by large lakes on each side and triple city walls.

'These walls were a marvel of engineering. The outside one of the three walls was as thick as a tall man lying down and as high as seven tall men standing one on the other. The three walls ran across the headland for more than three miles. There was a defensive tower every seventy yards or so.

'The really clever part of the defences was the circular harbour, which was big enough to take two hundred warships at once. It was surrounded by another high wall so that an enemy could not tell from the sea whether there were ships there or not. There was a command post for an admiral on a little island in the middle of this lagoon.

'The place where the defenders could make a last stand was the citadel, a fortified hill more or less at the centre of the city. Houses were tall and built alongside narrow streets. It seemed a very difficult town to capture but we Romans not only took Carthage, we destroyed it.'

How they did it you can see in the next few pages.

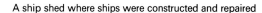
A ship shed where ships were constructed and repaired

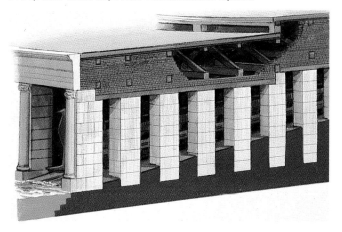

229

A sea fight

As Rome's soldiers conquered the nearby tribes and gradually extended her control over most of Italy, they came into contact with peoples whose homelands were not in Italy at all. Among these were the Greeks and the 'Poeni' from Carthage in North Africa.

The Carthaginians claimed the western half of the Mediterranean as theirs alone to trade in and resented Rome's interference in their affairs. The trouble, as far as Romans could see, was that the men of Carthage were experienced sailors, whilst the men of Rome were landsmen who knew nothing of the sea and its ways.

Roman soldiers crossing the drawbridge to board an enemy ship

The two sides clashed over which one was to rule the islands around Italy, particularly Sicily. War broke out in 264 B.C. The men of Carthage must have thought that it was going to be easy to beat the Roman landlubbers. After all, the Romans not only had no warships, they were not considered skilled enough to make any. Then fate took a hand and a Carthaginian ship was driven ashore in Italy. Roman carpenters were sent to study it.

Within a few short weeks they managed to build and launch over a hundred *Roman* warships. While the actual hulls were being constructed, some benches and oars were made so that the men who were to row the vessels could get some kind of practice on dry land.

The idea was to use oarsmen to move the new ships as it was thought too difficult in the time to learn much about the management of sails. A favourite tactic used by the Phoenicians and other ship-owning nations was to try and ram the enemy vessel with the large armoured beak at the prow.

Because the Romans were good land fighters but knew nothing of warfare at sea, they thought up a new way of fighting a marine battle. As you can see from the picture, each Roman warship had a kind of drawbridge on its deck.

When an enemy vessel was within range, javelins were hurled at its crew and the two vessels were drawn together with grappling irons on the ends of lengths of rope. As soon as the two warships touched, the drawbridge was allowed to fall. The far end dropped onto the enemy deck and a spike beneath it smashed through the planks, thus fastening both ships together.

Roman legionaries then ran across to the opposite deck and proceeded to fight just as though they were engaged in a land battle. Although this method worked well the huge boarding plank made the ship unstable and the technique was quietly dropped when Romans became more experienced at fighting battles at sea.

Hannibal and the Punic Wars

A young boy named Hannibal was taken to a temple by his father and made to swear on the altar of Moloch that he would be Rome's enemy until he died. When he grew up he became the general of the Punic army.

It was reported to him that a city in Spain which he had thought loyal to Carthage had since allied itself to Rome. He attacked the Spanish city and took it after an eight months' siege. This was more than long enough for the news to reach Rome. The government agreed that Hannibal had broken the peace treaty which Rome and Carthage had signed at the end of the first Punic War. Rome sent messages to Carthage demanding that Hannibal be handed over.

A Roman army was sent to Spain to take Hannibal but they arrived at his camp a few days after he and his men had left, heading eastward, no one knew whither. Guesses as to the size of his army varied from twenty to a hundred thousand but everyone agreed that he had with him at least thirty war elephants.

The Romans went back to Italy in ignorance of Hannibal's plans. The Carthaginian general had a very ambitious scheme in mind. He intended to attack Italy from its landward side, in spite of the Alpine ring of mountains which protects its northern frontier.

He led his army up the eastern coast of Spain, crossing the large rivers on rafts big enough to carry his elephants. He skirted the Pyrenees mountains, moved along the coast of France and over the river Rhône, making for the foothills of the Alps.

It was a tremendous achievement to get all his men, not to mention his elephants, up one side of the mountains and down the other – although many of the great beasts died in the attempt. Nowadays we can fly over the Alps, go through them by train in a tunnel, or drive over the top on well-made roads. In those days, the only routes were by way of goat tracks. They also had to contend with sharp rocks, steep slopes, narrow ledges, snowdrifts and ice even in midsummer and countless roaring mountain torrents.

Eventually, they arrived on the fertile plains of northern Italy, hoping that local tribesmen would come and join them. Few did, but the men of Carthage beat off the troops sent to stop them and began raiding towns and villages in the neighbourhood. There was panic in Rome and it seemed that no Roman armies could save the city from defeat. A supreme army commander

Rome and Carthage at the time of Hannibal

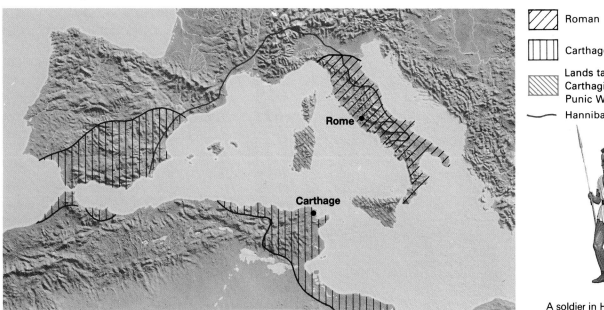

Roman

Carthage and allies

Lands taken from the Carthaginians in First Punic War

— Hannibal's route

A soldier in Hannibal's army.

Hannibal ferrying his elephants across the River Rhône – the elephants panic

named Quintus Fabius Maximus was appointed.

Pitched battles were out of the question from then onward: the Romans were no match for the powerful African army. Fabius had learned from the first engagements that the legions had fought against Hannibal's men what would happen if he were to risk meeting the enemy face to face. If he lost, all was lost, and nothing could save Rome, so he did what he could to annoy and irritate the invader. Raids and ambushes were made on Carthaginian stragglers, retreats ordered when a battle looked likely, food stores and bridges destroyed.

This kind of thing went on for years until the Roman senate got fed up with the tactics of the 'Delayer', as they called him, and appointed another general to command. However, Fabius was proved right when the new man made up his mind to face Hannibal in a proper set battle. His legions were severely mauled.

Eventually the senate sent an army to Spain, largely ruled by Carthage at that time. The commander's name was Scipio. He was so successful he persuaded the senators to give him an army he could take to Carthage itself.

This new army beat a Carthaginian formation in Africa but their main aim was to draw Hannibal away from Italy. The trick worked and Hannibal faced Scipio at Zama near Carthage.

The Carthaginians were trounced and were forced not only to pay war damages but also to cut down the size of their fleet. Rome demanded that Hannibal be handed over to them. He escaped, but after years on the run from fear of Roman vengeance, he committed suicide.

Over fifty years later, the wars broke out again. Carthage lost again and this time refused the terms Rome offered, considering them much too harsh. It was all the excuse Rome needed. The city of Carthage was captured and burned to the ground. The few people left were sold into slavery. The charred ruins were smashed to pieces and the whole area ploughed up.

As a last gesture, orders came from Rome to sow salt on all the farms, so that nothing should ever grow there again.

Thus Rome gained control of the western Mediterranean and began to build an empire in earnest. The fruits of the Punic Wars were North Africa, Spain and the islands of Corsica, Sardinia and Sicily.

What Rome may have looked like

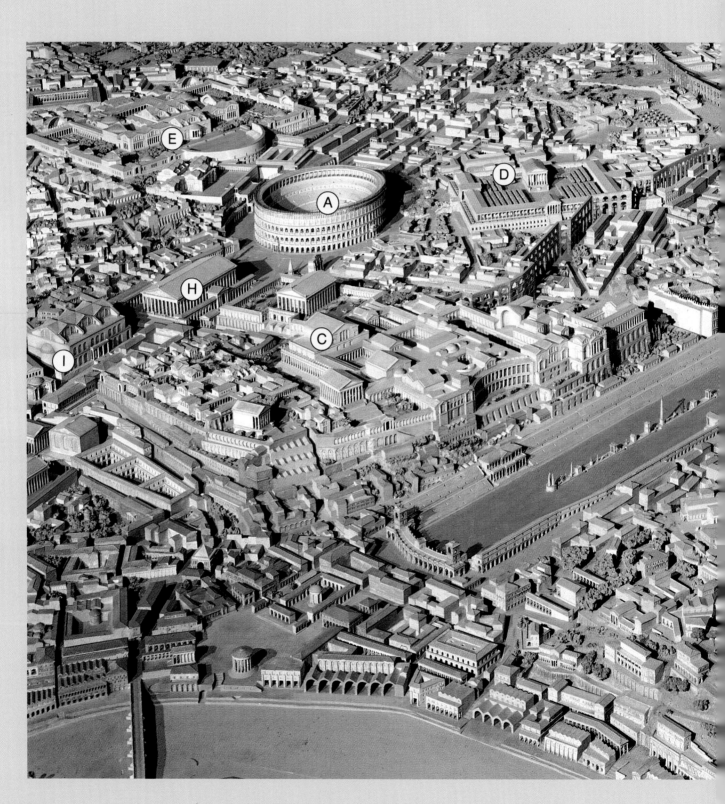

Aqueducts

When a village or town is fairly small, it can be supplied with food, fuel and water from its immediate neighbourhood. Things get difficult when the population increases sharply. No longer will a local stream or well yield all the water required. Not only did the number of Roman citizens increase rapidly, the custom of bathing every day also grew in popularity.

The city authorities decided to bring in water from the nearby hills. They did this by constructing aqueducts. Their engineers would find a suitable stream and make a shallow stone channel to divert its flow. To make sure the water got to the town, the aqueduct had to descend gradually over its entire length. This often meant that a roundabout route had to be chosen.

For instance, the very first aqueduct in Rome was built to the orders of Appius Claudius, in 312 B.C. The water source was only just over $6\frac{3}{4}$ miles away but the final length of the channel was more than ten miles!

Occasionally, the channel had to cross a ravine or a river valley. Then the water had to be taken across on a bridge. Some examples of this still survive. The best known is the Pont du Gard near Nîmes in France.

This was originally part of a twenty-five mile long aqueduct. There are some three hundred yards of it still to be seen. The method of construction was to make a row of huge stone arches, connect them with a flat stone bed, put a second and smaller line of arches on this bed and a third and final row on top of that. The water channel was at the very top. The arches were all solidly built: the ones at the bottom standing on foundations nearly thirty feet across. The middle arches are fifteen feet thick and the top ones ten feet wide. The overall height is about a hundred and sixty feet. A

Pont du Gard Roman aqueduct and bridge

An aqueduct outside Rome

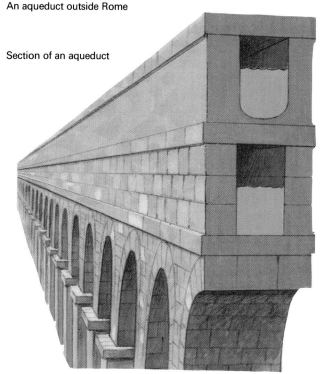

Section of an aqueduct

similar one made of stone blocks but without mortar is still delivering water near Segovia in Spain.

In ancient times, there were eleven aqueducts bringing water to Rome. They had a total length of about three hundred miles and all but fifty of these were either underground or in covered ground-level channels. The stone coverings were to protect the water from insects, birds, small animals and evaporation from the hot sun.

The aqueducts usually ended in reservoirs in the city. Very few private houses had water laid on, although some illegal tapping took place. A civil servant sent by the emperor to investigate found that the five hundred or so slaves who looked after the system had started a business selling the unlawful right to be connected to any who could afford the bribes.

Water supplied public baths, lavatories and fountains, the latter being the source of drinking water for the poor who would collect what they needed in clay pots or goatskins and lug it up to their apartments, perhaps several floors above ground level.

The pressure was never great enough to supply any floor higher than ground level, even for those legally entitled to it. In fact, some parts of the city had to wait decades before they had a water supply at all. The usual reason for this was that some areas were too high: gravity-fed fountains would hardly work on hilltops.

Although the aqueducts delivered plenty of water, the lack of pressure meant that fires could only be fought with buckets of water – never a jet from a hose.

One curious aqueduct called the Alsietina didn't provide drinking water. All its liquid went to a special amphitheatre which could be flooded in order to stage water shows. These gradually came to a stop after Nero's time and the aqueduct was used to water gardens on the slopes of the Janiculum Hill.

Another specialised supply line brought both fresh and salt water from Ostia at the mouth of the Tiber to fill the fish ponds of the city markets. In this way, the Roman shopper could buy his sea food extremely fresh.

The baths

Romans were probably the cleanest of the early civilised peoples. We've seen how aqueducts brought water for fountains and baths – probably somewhere between fifty and two hundred gallons every day for each one of Rome's one million inhabitants.

Of course, the people didn't drink that much water: most of it went to supply the public baths. Many wealthy private houses in the country had their own suites of bathrooms – cleanliness was (from at least as early as the second century B.C.) fast becoming a passion with Romans.

By the time 'B.C.' had given way to 'A.D.', public baths were extremely popular. This was because most poor people lacked a bathroom. Even if they had been provided it would have meant a lot of trips up the stairs with jars of water – and where would the water have been heated?

It wasn't a great hardship to use the public establishments – there was nearly always one close by. In 33 B.C., Rome had about a hundred and seventy of them, but a couple of centuries later the number had grown to over a thousand. In any case, the use of the building and its hot water was either very cheap (less than $\frac{1}{2}$p!) or completely free. Upper-class Romans, seeking election to various posts, often paid the expenses of everyone for an entire year, hoping, no doubt, that such generosity would be rewarded with votes!

Most Roman towns, even small ones, had public baths. Volubilis in Morocco had two grand public baths as well as the private ones in the houses of those Romans who could afford them.

The interior decoration was often awe-inspiring – particularly to someone who had to live in a small flat with very little headroom. The baths provided by the

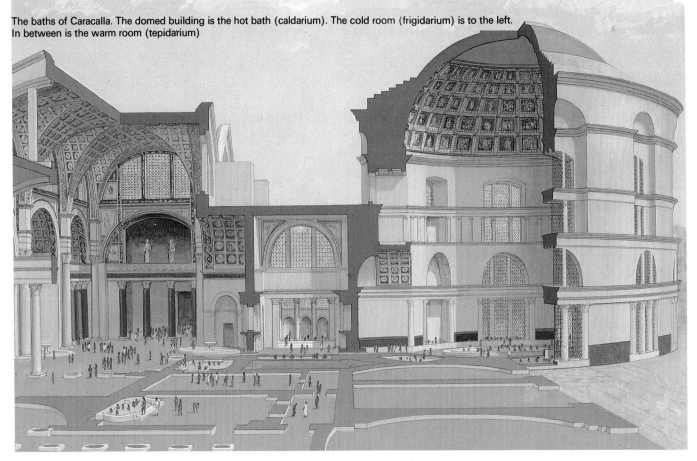

The baths of Caracalla. The domed building is the hot bath (caldarium). The cold room (frigidarium) is to the left. In between is the warm room (tepidarium)

The women's hot bath at Pompeii

emperors were huge. Those of Caracalla measured 750 feet by 380 feet – and that was only the main block. If you included all the walks, gardens and outbuildings, the whole complex covered about twenty-seven acres (equal to about fifteen full-sized hockey or football pitches) and these were not the largest.

The visitor would notice the ceilings a hundred feet above his head and the richness of the decoration. Walls were set with rare stones, corridors lined with marble pillars, whilst floors were often patterned with mosaic designs in pieces of coloured tile called tesserae.

Perhaps we could ask one of the young bathers to tell us what a Roman bath is like.

'My name is Junius. I'm twelve years old and I'm going to bathe on my way home from morning school.'

'Are those your towel and bathing trunks you're carrying?'

'My towel, yes – although you can hire one if you want. But we don't wear bathing costumes. You don't when you take a bath, do you?

'We wait for the opening bell to sound: it signals the end of the women's and girls' time in the baths. Then we go in through one of the four main entrances to the undressing room. It's a good idea to have someone guard your clothes – you might get them stolen otherwise. After that, you can do all kinds of things: you

might go to the hot, dry rooms (we call them "Spartan" baths) –'

'Saunas,' we murmur.

'You sweat a lot and then dive in a cold pool. Or you go to the open air spaces where you can wrestle or play ball games with your friends. Otherwise you work up a sweat by going through the frigid and tepid rooms to the hot steam room –'

'Turkish baths,' we mutter.

'–where you treat your skin to an oiling followed by a scrape down with a strigil. You can hire a slave to do it for you but that's expensive. So is being massaged and perfumed.

'If you're rich, you can afford all these treatments but if you're like me, you splash yourself with hot water from the basin and scrape yourself down before diving into the cold bath or going back through the cooler rooms again.

'You could, if you like, use some of the other attractions. There's a library, laundry, reading-rooms, gardens, tailor's shop, barber's, manicurist, rest-rooms, wine shop, restaurant and gymnasia.

'Most Romans bathe every day – some more than once. One of our emperors, Commodus, is supposed to have bathed no fewer than eight times every day!'

Temples

'I understand you want to look round some of our temples?' We murmur our agreement and the speaker says, 'I'm Lucius Brennius and I'd be happy to show you round. This is our local temple, of course. It's quite old – two or three hundred years, I think.'

'It's very like a Greek one.'

'Yes, but there are differences. To start with, the stone platform on which it stands is much bigger. Greek temples are two or three feet above ground level and you can get on to the platform from anywhere around it. Now, a Roman temple base is often nine or ten feet high and you have to use the staircase at the front to get up.'

'That's right – and your local temple doesn't have columns all round it – only a couple of rows at the front and just a line of half columns down the sides. Are there any at the back?'

'No, they aren't needed. Let's go up the stairs. This is the open part of the temple. At the back is the interior room, or cella. We can't go in, as it's locked. It's where we keep the statue of the god to whom the temple is dedicated.'

'And this one is – ?'

'It's the house of Mars.'

'What's the building made of ?'

'Concrete, stone – things like that.'

'How do Romans make concrete?'

'You take a lot of broken bits of brick or stone, mix them with sand or gravel, adding cement and water. You stir them all together, spread the mixture out wherever you want it and wait for it to set like a rock. With wooden shuttering you can make an arch out of concrete. A long arch gives you a vault. Turn the arch round on its centre spot and you've got a dome. There's a temple in Rome called the Pantheon which has an ordinary rectangular entrance but a round building behind it, surmounted by a huge dome. Hadrian rebuilt it from an earlier model.

'The dome is almost a hundred and fifty feet in diameter and it sits on walls twenty feet thick. There's a circular hole twenty-seven feet across at the top to let the light in. Of course, that's not the only round temple, although they aren't as common as the oblong ones.'

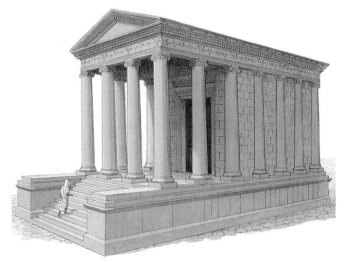

A typical Roman temple

'What does "Pantheon" mean?'

' "All the gods." Usually a temple is the house of just one god but even apart from the Pantheon there are a few places dedicated to two or three different heavenly beings.'

'You didn't finish telling us about what the buildings are made of.'

'Well, the early ones were carpentered from tree trunks but we usually use mined materials now – you know, whatever's available on the spot, perhaps granite, limestone or volcanic tufa. That's a Roman speciality. It's a dull stone but it can be hidden under a coat of plaster or better still enveloped in white marble. A lot of temples are improved with a nice light-coloured paint or decorated with rare stones.

'Some have strong rooms as well. The temple of Saturn in Rome is where the state treasury is situated.'

'That's surprising.'

'Not really. A few temples have large amounts of gold entrusted to them: they even lend money at interest or change cash for foreigners – banks, I suppose you'd call them. In Pompeii and some other towns, the temple is where you find the weights and measures office. There's a slab of stone with scooped out hollows for measuring corn, oil and wine.

'But the chief purpose of the temple is religion. It's the house of the god. I can tell you more about the actual gods, if you like.'

'We haven't time now,' we tell Lucius, 'but thank you all the same.' However, if you want to find out about who the Romans worshipped, turn to p.72.

The Pantheon

Private houses and flats

Block of flats (insula) at Ostia

As in the matter of temples, the better kind of Roman house was copied from a Greek original. But in the beginning, things were very different. The dwellings of the pioneer shepherds on the seven hills were little more than one-roomed huts with a hole in the roof to let the smoke out. As time went on and people became somewhat better off, they added a room or two here and there, around the original hut.

The newer houses followed the same pattern and the 'hole in the roof' room changed into a sort of entrance hall, or 'atrium', as they called it. Below the opening was a shallow trough to collect rainwater. This arrangement continued even into the wealthy times. A rich Roman's house still had its atrium and rainwater pool. Several rooms opened off the atrium – mostly bedrooms.

At the far end were reception rooms and beyond them, a small garden perhaps with statues and a fountain. There was a roofed colonnade running round the garden. Nearby was the kitchen and dining-room. If possible, a bath suite was included.

Walls were plastered and painted with scenes of the countryside, including birds and flowers. The bright colours of the paints were echoed by the different hues of the mosaic floors. Mosaics were made from thousands of pieces of coloured stones or tiles set out in pictures or geometric patterns.

A very large house in Rome might occupy all the space bounded by four streets, thus forming a block, or 'insula' (island), as they called it. Partly to bring in more money and partly to insulate the family from the noise and bustle of the streets, several street-side areas were let off to shopkeepers.

A slave might be stationed at the front door to keep out unwanted callers. A house pet could be chained up nearby to frighten off burglars and similar lawless ones. A mosaic by a street door in Pompeii has a picture of a dog, with the words 'Cave Canem' ('Beware of the Dog') beneath it.

Wealthy houses like these were pretty rare even in Rome. Most people were poor and were forced to live in tenements if they wanted to remain in the capital city. Land was scarce, so landlords had nowhere to expand but upwards. Because greedy owners often used shoddy materials for building, the danger of collapse increased with the height of the building. This caused various Roman emperors to make laws forbidding blocks of flats over a certain height – for example, sixty feet. Even at that, the builders could still get in as many as eight or nine floors. The greater the number of floors, the more extra tenants could be squeezed in and the higher the profits of the block owner.

There were no lifts, of course – nor could poor people afford expensive glazed windows. You didn't need them

Wall paintings from the house of the Vetti brothers at Pompeii

Insula at Pompeii

in a sticky Roman summer but when the weather got worse, the only way to keep the flat's temperature up and the rain out was to close the wooden shutters.

As this plunged the room into darkness, the flat dwellers had to make do with smelly olive-oil lamps. Heating was done by means of a portable metal brazier which burnt charcoal. Rich people had a safer and more efficient system. Main rooms were built over a hypocaust which allowed hot air from an outside furnace to circulate under the floor.

In the tenements, accidents with heaters and lamps were common and – as the apartments were largely made of timber – extremely dangerous. Not only the flat where the brazier accident had occurred was at risk: the whole block could go up in flames. If this happened there wasn't much chance of saving it. There was a sort of fire brigade system under the emperors but there were no mechanical pumps or hoses. All the firemen could do was to form a human chain, passing leather buckets from hand to hand and hoping the water delivered to the block was enough to quench the flames. If this didn't work, they had to try to pull down the building with hooks on long poles, to stop the fire spreading.

It has already been mentioned that there was no water laid on in the blocks. Not only did the flat dwellers have to carry up every drop of water they wanted, but there were no internal lavatories. The tenants were lucky if there was a public lavatory fairly near!

Shops

In the first few years after the founding of Rome, the shepherds and farmers were self-sufficient peasants. If you don't want much beyond the roughest food, shelter and clothing with the crudest of pottery and carpentry, you can do it all for yourself. As soon as the countrymen and their families began to hanker after something better, their standard of living could only rise if there were craftsmen spending most of their time on the special thing they were good at.

A man might make better baskets, spades or shoes than anyone else in his neighbourhood. The neighbours would prefer his products to those they could make themselves and they'd pay him – at first with farm produce and later with coins.

It wasn't long before open areas in the valleys between the seven hills of Rome were used by those with something to sell – either what they had grown or what they had made. Dozens of small stalls were set up at which people could buy whatever took their fancy.

After many years, specially built shops were provided. These might be in rows along a street or the side of a square. Other locations were in odd corners of a rich man's house or block of flats. Glass was known in Roman times but it was only used for fancy containers, drinking vessels or the rare windows in well-to-do houses. It couldn't be made into very large sheets and would have been much too expensive for shop fronts, say, in any case.

For this reason shops were closed at night with wooden shutters and totally open during business hours. In many cases, the man of the family made the trade goods in a workroom behind the shop. His wife and grown-up children sold the goods to the public and the whole family lived in an upper room or an apartment behind the workroom.

Because transport costs were so heavy, there was never any chance of nationwide firms of chain stores with outlets in every large town. So local craftsmen made their wares of local materials to local designs. You wouldn't expect to match the pattern on a favourite piece of cloth in any town but your own. The only goods that seem to have been made and exported on a large scale were some items of pottery.

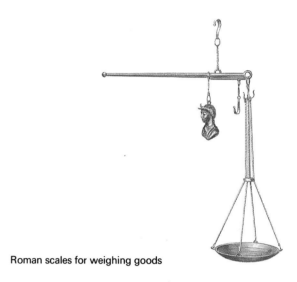

Roman scales for weighing goods

The stalls in the forum, or open square, were where the male slaves did the shopping. Women, particularly rich ones, rarely shopped except for cosmetics, clothes or jewellery.

Market stalls provided meat, fish, vegetables and fruit. The fish was probably dried – if you wanted fresh stuff you went to a proper shop where you could choose your fish live from a tank of water. Other, and more permanent, shops sold shoes, knives, ironware, rope, leather goods, poultry, wine, bread and many more items. Rome, like any large modern city, was a place

Plaster cast of shuttering and door of shop

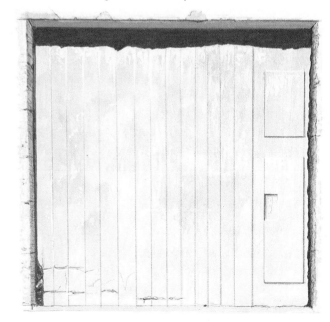

Street scene

where you could buy almost anything.

One service provided, which we don't have anymore, was the public oven. Because of those who lived in flats with nowhere to cook, the baker hired out his ovens. Poor people brought him their dinners and he cooked them for a small fee.

Permanent shops commonly had a name painted outside. It wasn't the name of the owner but that of the product he sold, or the service he provided, e.g. 'oil', 'books', 'shoe repairs' or 'barbers'. If there weren't any words, the shop owner probably had a sign – for instance, tavern keepers draped their doorways with green boughs.

Goods were sold in standard measures and the 'steelyard' type of scale weighed what customers had bought. In earlier days, when things were simpler, a Roman got what he or she wanted by swapping things. It must have made trade a lot easier when (just after 300 B.C.) lumps of copper and bronze came into use to pay for purchases.

Some time before 200 B.C., round metal coins made their appearance – mostly gold and silver for trading abroad and small change of copper, bronze and brass for local deals.

Even the smallest of Roman towns had its share of shops. When St Albans in Hertfordshire was being excavated a few years ago, the diggers found the basements of a row of shops near the open air theatre. It isn't too hard to imagine slaves buying olive-oil, wine or ready-cooked food from the shop assistants or apprentices and paying with bronze coins here in England, at the furthest boundary of the empire.

Nero's Golden House

Such was the method of government in ancient Rome that power was eventually entrusted to one man alone. The emperor, as he was called, had virtually the power of life and death over all of his subjects and the authority to have his every whim carried out exactly.

From the time of Augustus, some of Rome's early emperors lived in houses little different from those of their well-to-do subjects, but as time went on their palaces got larger and more elaborate. Many of these early royal residences were on the Palatine Hill – hence the word 'palace'.

Things were not so bad just as long as the emperor was a fairly sane and responsible person. Unfortunately, not all Roman emperors were reasonable: some were a little odd and others not far from insanity.

Nero came somewhere near the insane end of this scale. He didn't behave in a civilised way and many murders and executions were his responsibility. The same charges could have been levelled at other rulers, but Nero's murders included those of his wife and his own mother.

However, the thing which caused his standing to decline with his more sober and dignified subjects was taking part in public song and poetry recitals. He entered competitions and the organisers dared not let anyone else win.

It was known that Nero wanted a large area of land on which to build a palace, so when a considerable part of Rome caught fire and cleared the region in question, people began to say that perhaps he must have been responsible. Although Nero was not in the city at the time, there was a certain amount of evidence that some of his servants had been seen at the place where the fire had started with flaming torches in their hands. To divert the people's suspicion he accused the Christians and had them tortured and executed by the thousand.

He then took over the burnt-out parts of the city and began to build himself a vast palace. It was called 'the House of Passage' as it led from one hill to another, so extensive was its lay-out. Unluckily for the emperor, it too burned down almost as soon as it was finished. The people groaned, for this meant more taxes to be paid in order that the great work should be redone. They were

right – it was rebuilt and retitled the 'Domus Aurea' ('Golden House').

The Golden House was not one building but several and the whole estate occupied an area of almost a square mile in the very middle of one of the most crowded cities of all time.

Nero had a lake dug out where the Colosseum now stands and surrounded it with parkland, farms, forests and vineyards. Dotted about were rich and elaborate pavilions, some connected by colonnaded paths. Statues adorned the grounds – a few from local sculptors but most taken from Greek cities and temples. On a

single expedition, Nero's servants sent home almost two thousand statues from conquered Greece.

After many years, the people of Rome could stand the behaviour of their murderous, half-mad ruler no longer. The senate turned against him and to avoid punishment and shame, he committed suicide.

After his death, the parklands were broken up and built over. Not only houses and blocks of flats appeared but also many public buildings such as baths and temples. Among them was the Flavian amphitheatre, named from Titus Flavius Vespasian who had it built. It stands where Nero's ornamental lake once was and near where the late emperor's statue once stood. Because of its huge size, Nero's statue was known as the 'colossal' statue. From this word, later generations began to speak of the arena as the 'Colosseum'.

Curiously, the Golden House itself was burnt down some forty years after the emperor's death. Later rulers tried to blot out the memory of this near madman and erected their baths and temples over the remains of his 'folly'. In many cases, these same baths and temples have themselves collapsed into ruin, leaving the buried remains of the Domus Aurea to be found by future archaeologists.

The visitor to today's Rome may be able to see what's left of the splendour – some bits and pieces still remain – for example some sections of decorated wall. There is a high vaulted corridor with painted false windows, through which one can apparently see distant vistas of beautiful landscape.

Alas! there are no longer any traces of the pipes which sprinkled Nero's guests with perfume, nor the ivory ceiling through which flower petals sifted slowly down on the diners. And although there is an octagonal room rather like a small Pantheon, there is nothing left of the cooling system said to have been used in hot weather, i.e. streams of cold water running down the stairs and out through drains in the floor.

Nero's Golden House with the Temple of Claudius and Aqua Claudia (aqueduct) in the foreground

Why the kingdom ended

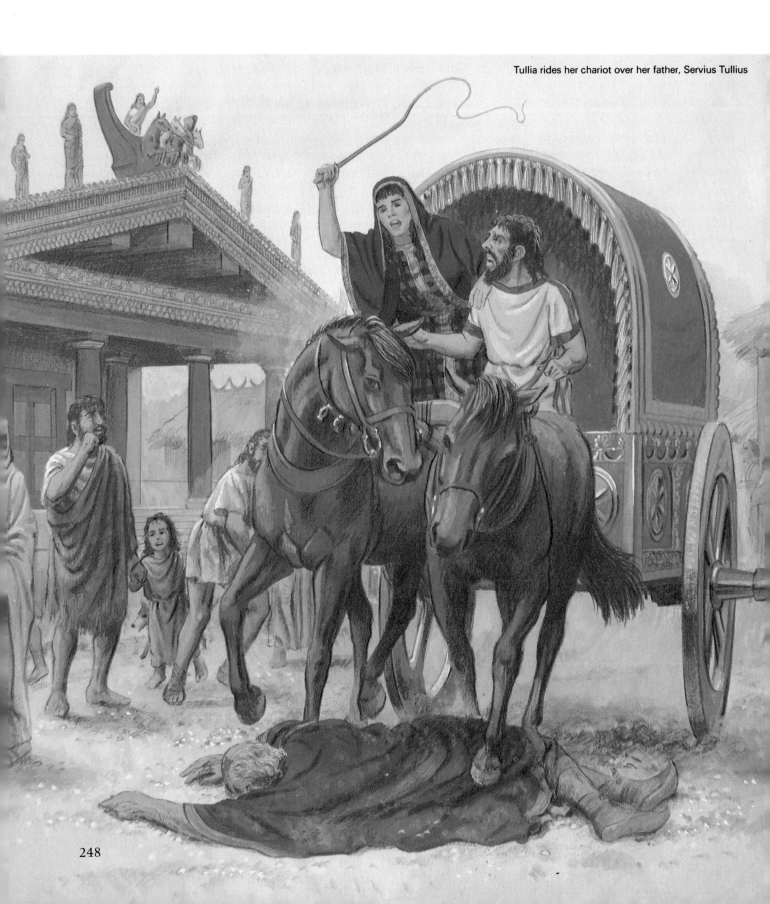

Tullia rides her chariot over her father, Servius Tullius

You could get more than one answer to the question, 'Why did the kingdom end?' The average Roman of about 35 B.C. would tend to believe the legends, whilst a modern historian would have another and more down-to-earth answer. Let's ask both of them what they think: we'll start with Gaius, a citizen of Rome.

'I *know* why we kicked out the kings,' says Gaius, 'I don't have to guess. I suppose you know what our last ruler was called?'

'Tarquinius Superbus,' the historian says, 'Tarquin the Proud.'

'That's right. I believe you've already heard that he behaved so badly as king that he was thrown out? Well, his method of gaining the throne should have warned my ancestors what he was like.

'He married Tullia, the daughter of the king, Servius Tullius, to give himself a claim to the throne when his father-in-law died. But Tarquinius couldn't wait for the king's natural end – he went down to the senate dressed in royal robes, threw the old man down the stairs and took his place on the throne. He sent men to finish him off but Tullia made sure of her father's death by running him over with her chariot.

'From then on, the new king had to have a bodyguard – there were still many Romans loyal to the old king's memory.'

'They hated him because he was an Etruscan,' says the modern historian.

'Perhaps, but he was usually successful in war and gained supporters because of that.'

'What about his sly behaviour with the Gabii?'

'Oh yes. He sent one of his sons, Sextus, to the town of Gabii, one of Rome's neighbours. He pretended he was frightened of his father and wormed his way into their confidence. They gave him command of a small group of soldiers and he led them against a Roman detachment. He waited years but as soon as he was appointed supreme general of all their forces, he rewarded them by surrendering them all to Rome. It was, of course, the plan from the start. None of that family had any second thoughts about breaking promises. No, they were all sly, that lot.

'Take what happened when the king sent two of his sons and their cousin to Delphi to ask the meaning of a vision he had had. The young men decided instead to ask the oracle which of them should reign when their father died. The oracle's answer was "Which ever of you kisses his mother first." Few people heard what the cousin said on their return to Rome. He pretended to stumble full length on the ground, muttering as his lips brushed the soil, "The earth is our mother!" The sly devil was trying to put himself forward as the next king.

Etruscan coin

What a tribe!

'Unfortunately for his chances, the wife of another cousin, a woman named Lucretia, complained that Sextus had, with the king's approval, forced his un-welcome attentions on her. She told all Rome what she had suffered and killed herself in public –'

'I know,' the historian interrupts, 'that what you've said is what is supposed to have made Roman citizens drive the Tarquin family out, but there is another reason.

'The last three kings had all been Etruscans – foreigners as far as Rome was concerned. Etruscans were Rome's biggest rivals in Italy and it seemed that they were about to dominate Rome and other Latin cities by force. They had already taken over much of the trade in northern and central Italy. In any case, I'm sure Romans resented Etruscan culture and success – even in spite of the fact that they had borrowed some of Etruria's best ideas – for instance writing and the use of coins.

'No, Romans were jealous of the Etruscans and their superior ways. *That's* why they were kicked out and why Romans vowed never to have another king. Why, they even passed a law saying that any man who as much as talked about having a king back should be executed! Centuries later, Julius Caesar was murdered – not because he wanted to be king but because he was *suspected* of wanting it!'

The republic and its end

To run the government, Romans elected two consuls who could rule for one year only. Both had to agree before anything at all could be done. It only needed one consul to say 'Veto' ('I forbid') and the matter was dropped.

Other officials were elected – almost entirely from the ranks of the richer citizens. These were the descendants of the first settlers who had had the time to acquire land and become wealthy.

One drawback of the Roman system was that poor people scarcely got a look in. The patricians, as the rich citizens were called, provided all of the three hundred or so senators who ran the affairs of the republic. They were also the group from which came all the priests, army officers and senior civil servants.

The plebeians, as the poor people were called, fought hard throughout the republican period to get on equal terms with the patricians.

They never quite managed it and their struggle was complicated by various military governors who, seeking to restore public order, thought that what Rome needed was to have a single person in charge – each one thinking of himself.

At the time when the Etruscans were expelled, Rome ruled about three hundred and fifty square miles of Italy: just over two and a half centuries later, the figure had risen to ten thousand square miles. Overseas and other territory was added as the result of wars against the Phoenicians of North Africa and Spain; against the Greeks and Macedonians of south east Europe; and against the Gauls, or Celts in northern Italy and southern France.

A number of military adventurers were responsible for extending Rome's frontiers but their ambition to be supreme ruler threatened the peace and order of the republic. Among these men were Sulla, Pompey and Julius Caesar.

Julius Caesar conquered Gaul and raided Britain but he showed no sign of giving up his military dictatorship. A group of conspirators, among them Brutus and Cassius, were afraid that he wanted to be king. Romans had had their fill of unpopular kings in the city's early days, so they murdered him.

Assassination of Julius Caesar beneath Pompey's statue

Outstanding men were often given a division of fighting legionaries to do some special job such as the defence of a frontier, the conquering of a new province or the clearing out of pirate ports. Trouble often followed when such men refused to give up command and used their position to try and take over the government of the empire, as it was rapidly becoming.

Rioting and civil war followed Julius Caesar's murder. On one side were the murderers and the armies they controlled and on the other were the armies of Julius Caesar's great-nephew, Octavian, together with Mark Antony and Lepidus. These latter three ruled Rome together just as soon as they had beaten the armies of the murderers.

They were known as the 'Triumvirate' (Latin for 'three man rule') but it didn't last very long. Lepidus rebelled against Octavian and spent the rest of his life in exile. Mark Antony fell in love with Cleopatra, the last pharaoh of Egypt, and tried to set up a rival empire. His army was badly beaten by Octavian's at the battle of Actium in 31 B.C. Both Cleopatra and Antony killed themselves, leaving Octavian to rule Rome alone.

Although he protested that he was merely restoring the republic, he was in fact the very first emperor.

The republic was at an end.

Pompey, who was defeated by his rival, Julius Caesar

Caesar's troops landing in Britain, 55 B.C.

The early emperors

A Roman triumph

Augustus Caesar. This is the name by which Octavian is known to history. 'Caesar' was his adopted family name and 'Augustus' ('the dignified one') was the title given to him by the senate. He was careful not to seem like an emperor, pretending he was merely 'the first among equals'. The elections of men to the senate and to other public offices were allowed to continue, thus persuading the people that they were still in control, but only those candidates approved by Augustus were permitted to stand.

Augustus himself refused the title 'rex' ('king'), preferring to be called 'commander' or 'chief'. Some people were not fooled but he did bring peace for many years and they were willing to take him as he was because he had ended the decades of unrest and civil war.

Augustus Caesar

He reigned from 31 B.C. and was nearly eighty when he died in 14 A.D.

Tiberius. He was the stepson of Augustus. At the start of his reign he continued the slow, steady progress begun by Augustus. His very slowness was taken by some to be stupidity and several plots against him were discovered. He felt he was being persecuted and retired to the Isle of Capri, leaving Sejanus, the captain of the guard, to run the country.

To justify himself, Sejanus found plots against his master where none existed and many innocent people were executed. He even schemed to get the throne for himself but his behaviour was so suspicious that he himself was arrested and put to death.

Tiberius was almost as old as Augustus had been when he died in 37 A.D. To succeed him, he had chosen a great-nephew named Gaius.

Caligula (37–41). This was Gaius's nickname: it meant 'little army boot', a title he was given as a child because he liked to dress up in a toy soldier's uniform.

The beginning of his reign was uneventful: he was welcomed as a pleasant change from the gloomy and suspicious Tiberius. Unfortunately he had an illness shortly after becoming emperor. It affected his mind and his behaviour became more and more outrageous. Anyone who showed the faintest disagreement with him might find himself thrown to the lions in the arena. He forced the senators to elect his horse consul!

No one knew who would be Caligula's next victim, so it was with relief that they heard he had been murdered. He was the first emperor *known* to have died by violence (although some historians think that both Augustus and Tiberius may have been murdered). However, Caligula was not the last emperor to be assassinated by a long, long way!

Claudius (41–54). The next emperor was the uncle

Caligula

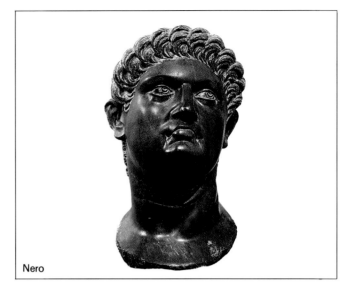

Nero

of Caligula. He had only preserved his life during his nephew's reign by pretending to be a stuttering idiot and therefore harmless. It's possible that he began the successful invasion of Britain to prove he wasn't cowardly or stupid. He was in Britain for just a fortnight in 43 A.D. but Roman legions were here for another four centuries.

Claudius was unlucky enough to meet and marry Agrippina, who nursed a secret ambition to rule Rome herself. As wife of the emperor this wasn't really possible, so she persuaded him to adopt her son by a previous marriage as the next emperor and to cut his own son out of the succession. Agrippina then poisoned Claudius, reasoning that her son as emperor would do as his mother told him. The son's name was Nero.

Nero (54–68). He did as he was bid – at least, to start with – but then began to get impatient. When Agrippina refused to let him divorce his wife, he had his wife murdered. Then to make sure that his throne would not be taken from him, he had Claudius's disinherited son murdered too. Now nursing a bitter hatred of his mother, he made her travel on a special boat which was designed to collapse when it was at sea. Agrippina swam ashore. Later Nero sent his thugs to assassinate her.

We've seen how he was suspected of having set fire to Rome and how his sprawling palaces were resented by the ordinary Roman. His pretensions to be a poet and singer annoyed a lot more people – not least those who found they were competing against him and knowing there could only be a *royal* winner.

Eventually, a number of his military commanders revolted and one of them, named Galba, was made emperor in his place. When Nero heard that he had been sentenced to death by whipping, he took his own life.

The empire expands

At the time of Augustus the Roman empire was almost at its greatest extent. The final conquests took place during the reigns of the five emperors who followed Nero. Maybe this elderly gentleman can tell us something about these five emperors.

'I certainly can,' says the man with the white hair. 'My name is Decius Marullus. I'm eighty years old and I've lived through the reigns of more than five emperors. I was born in Nero's time and now we have Hadrian on the throne.'

'Who were these emperors?'

'After Nero there was a time of confusion when no less than four military commanders raced one another to Rome to take his place. Galba was proclaimed but there was fighting even in Rome itself between the rivals – Galba, Otho, Vitellius and Vespasian.'

'Wasn't Vespasian a legionary commander in the invasion of Britain?'

'That's the man. It was he who came out on top. It was strange really – Nero had favoured his army career and even sent him to Judaea to run the war against the Hebrews. He'd done this because Vespasian wasn't a patrician. Nero thought that no plebeian could ever get to be emperor, so there was no danger in promoting this common soldier.

'Vespasian tried to rule as Augustus had done and to behave as a fair and reasonable person. This was a pleasant change from the madman whom he'd replaced.

'He'd beaten the Hebrews with the help of his son, Titus, so Vespasian chose Titus to succeed him. The emperor gave orders that the conquest of Britain should continue.

Trajan's army crosses the River Danube into Dacia

A scene from Trajan's column – burning a Dacian town

'At home, Vespasian had to increase taxes, as Nero had almost emptied the official money chests.

'Rome was improved with the provision of many new buildings. There were temples and baths of course: there was also a new public square and the foundations of a huge amphitheatre that was to rise on what had once been the bed of Nero's ornamental lake.

'Titus "assumed the purple", as they say, after his father's ten-year reign but he ruled only for two years. During those two years, there was another disastrous fire in Rome and an eruption from the volcano called Vesuvius which buried several towns and villages, including Pompeii and Herculaneum.

'When Titus died, Domitian took his brother's place. During his reign, the conquest of England was completed and the legions moved into southern Scotland. The emperor himself led his troops against the Dacians in eastern Europe. On his return to Rome he rode in triumph through the city. Unkind critics said that he hadn't beaten the barbarians at all but paid them to go away. They accused him of dressing slaves in barbarian costumes and pretending they were Dacian captives.

'He had some success with the opening up of trade routes to India and China but was less lucky in dealing with a "wine lake". The enlargement of the empire had meant that wine from North Africa, France and Spain could now compete with the Italian vintages in Rome, and it flooded in. Laws were passed to limit production – some vines had to be dug up and not replanted – but the laws didn't really work.

'Domitian wanted to be worshipped as a god but many Jews and Christians refused, even at the risk of being thrown to the lions. The emperor was so cruel to anyone merely suspected of plotting against him that sooner or later someone was going to follow a well established pattern and murder him. Those who had planned his assassination then picked an old lawyer named Nerva to be the next ruler.

'He reigned only two years and is mostly remembered for a scheme to look after poor orphans. He had time to nominate Trajan as his successor before he died.

'Trajan was from Spain and reigned nineteen years. He was the first non-Italian to be emperor. He came from a military family so I suppose it's fitting that he should be the one to make the last additions to the empire.

'Unlike Domitian, he really did beat back the Dacians. He reorganised the provinces along the Rhine and added Armenia, Assyria, part of Arabia and Mesopotamia to the empire.

'He also ordered the building of squares, libraries, memorial arches, baths, statues, public halls and theatres, not just in the capital but all over the empire. Here in Rome he had the story of his Dacian campaign carved in a long spiral strip around a stone column!'

The decline of the glory

Our informant, Decius Marullus, who told us about the growing empire on the last page, was living in the reign of Hadrian. This was the emperor who thought it more important for Rome to guard and secure a somewhat smaller empire than that which Trajan had left him.

It wasn't that he was more timid than the last emperor. The fact was that Trajan's adventures had wasted more men and money than Rome could afford. Attacks by barbarians convinced Hadrian that what was needed was not more empire but better defences.

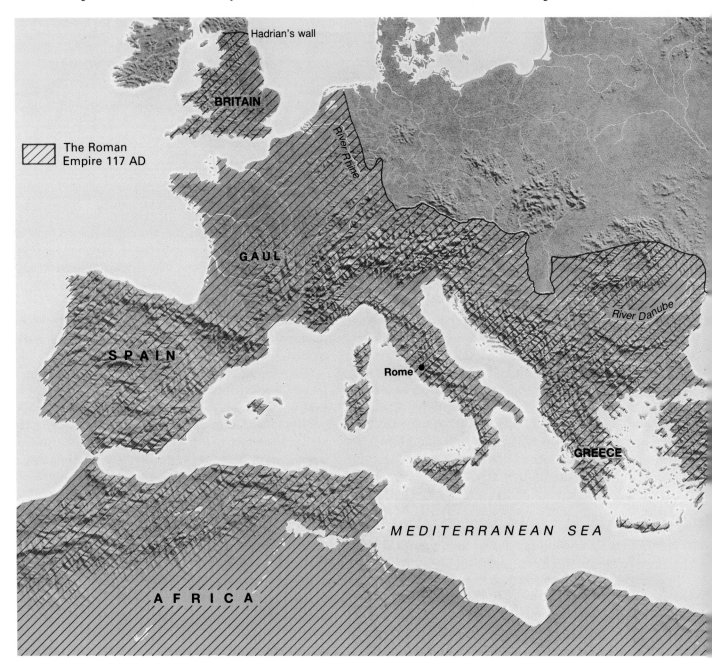

Hadrian's wall

BRITAIN

The Roman
Empire 117 AD

GAUL

River Rhine

River Danube

SPAIN

Rome

GREECE

AFRICA

MEDITERRANEAN SEA

To that end, he abandoned Trajan's conquests in Asia Minor and supervised the setting up of lines of fortresses between the upper Rhine and Danube rivers.

Some five years after he had become emperor he arrived in Britain and ordered the building of a wall from near modern Newcastle right across the country to near modern Carlisle.

Trajan's empire was the largest it was ever to be: from the time of Hadrian it was a struggle to keep things as they were. Later emperors either fought to try and hold on to what they had or for various reasons had to watch while pieces of the empire crumbled away.

The Roman Empire at the beginning of Hadrian's reign, 117 A.D.

ASIA

Antoninus Pius, although a soldier, did very little with the army after he came to the throne, preferring to concern himself with domestic affairs. It's true that his twenty-three-year reign was a better time for the majority of Romans than most other periods of the city's history. All the same, the strain of running such a huge organisation had grown too much for one man to manage.

Antoninus adopted a young man named Marcus Aurelius and gave him the title 'Caesar', keeping the word 'Augustus' for himself. Together they ran the empire and when Antoninus died in 161, Marcus took his place.

Marcus Aurelius would have been far happier browsing in a well-stocked library. Instead of reading, thinking and writing, he was burdened by the cares of an empire he had never sought to rule. A good deal of his time was spent riding the frontiers, pushing back the waves of barbarian invaders, who were themselves being forced towards the empire's borders by wild tribes even further away.

On top of these troubles, there were several epidemics of plague which ran through the native populations like wildfire. Often, the diseases were being brought into the empire by legionaries returning from Asia Minor.

It seemed to Marcus that he was like a swimmer, who, far from moving forward, was energetically treading water to stop himself sinking and drowning. He was glad of the help of his only son, Commodus, who succeeded him as emperor when he finally died, absolutely worn out.

Commodus was as unlike his father as can be imagined. Marcus was thoughtful, kind, educated and well mannered: his son was a selfish, coarse brute who really enjoyed the beast and gladiator fights. He loved to see the blood flow and often boasted that he could have fought better himself.

Soon, idle boasts were translated into action as the emperor decided to take part in the fights himself. To make sure his sacred person was not injured and that the emperor could not lose, his opponents were given blunt weapons made of soft metals such as lead.

His intimate friends were gladiators, animal trainers, boxers and all kinds of people unsuited to court life. When plots against him were uncovered, he couldn't be bothered to hold a long enquiry, followed by proper trials, he merely ordered all the suspects to be executed.

Finally he was murdered by one of his own guards – a fate he shared with quite a few other Roman emperors.

Before we take the story too far, it would be as well to find out a little more of what life was like for ordinary people.

Chapter 20   Daily life

Pompeii

A great deal of our knowledge of daily life in Roman times comes from Pompeii and Herculaneum, two Roman towns near the modern city of Naples, on Italy's south-west coast.

You may remember that Vesuvius had erupted in 79 A.D. No one seems to have been prepared for the devastation, in spite of a previous outburst from the volcano in 63 A.D. Most people were apparently going about their business in August 79 when the first rumbles were heard.

Earthquakes were not uncommon in those parts but these seemed stronger than usual. On the 23rd of that month Vesuvius blew up. The top of the mountain developed a huge cloud shot through with flames. The

The destruction of Pompeii, August 79 A.D.

Plaster casts of a dog, a man, and a loaf of bread found at Pompeii

Wall painting of a religious ceremony from Pompeii

sea drew back from the land, leaving fish flapping on the wet sand. There was darkness during the day time and ash began to fall from the skies.

Some escaped, protecting themselves from the hot ashes by tying pillows over their heads and cutting out the sulphurous smell by winding a scarf over nose and mouth. Others were not so lucky and didn't manage to get away as more lethal gases spilled into the air. The few that were left of Pompeii's 40,000 inhabitants just dropped where they were and died.

The ashes continued drifting down and the buildings slowly disappeared under layers of the stuff, which gradually hardened until it was almost as hard as rock.

The ruins then lay buried and forgotten until the eighteenth century. Then a small group of people interested in history began to uncover the streets, fountains, public buildings and private houses of a Roman provincial town. People have been digging ever since and the town has still not been fully unearthed.

So much has come to light, though, that we can get a new look at the everyday life of ordinary Romans. What did the archaeologists discover?

The remains of countless wall fragments were painted with flowers, fruit, animals, patterns and above all, Pompeian citizens going about their affairs. Pompeii has provided the bulk of all Roman painting known to the experts.

From the foundations and lower wall portions, historians can work out the most popular arrangements for private houses. They can also see that there were understreet sewers, sometimes with inspection covers. The streets they drained were very narrow by modern standards – only about twelve to twenty feet wide, sometimes with wheel ruts in the stone and occasional side pavements, slightly raised and topped with asphalt.

There was a large forum over five hundred feet long and a hundred feet wide, in which were found numerous statues, elegant columns and a triumphal arch.

Pompeii had been both sea port and seaside resort, a holiday haunt for all kinds of people – the emperor Claudius went there more than once. On some of the walls he might have seen the odd graffiti scrawl, an advertisement or an election notice. These various inscriptions show that the people not only spoke Latin but also Greek and a local dialect called Oscan.

There was a theatre seating fifteen hundred people and an amphitheatre which could accommodate at least twenty thousand spectators.

At one place the diggers found the charred remains of actual loaves of bread. These were circular and divided into triangular segments. Some loaves were found with the baker's name formed by the mould which had contained the wet dough.

But perhaps the saddest discoveries were the impressions of corpses. The dead bodies had long since rotted away, leaving hollows in the ash. Excavators pumped in liquid plaster and were able to recover the actual shapes of the once living people when the plaster hardened. One of the bodies was that of a dog with a collar.

Food and drink

One of the phrases often quoted when ancient Rome is being discussed is 'bread and circuses'. This referred to the custom, which had grown over the years, of giving poor and unemployed people food and entertainment to stop them rioting.

The 'annona', as the free food was called, started just over a century before Christ. There had always been shortages and local famines but by about 123 B.C. things had got so serious that poor people were allowed to buy cheap grain from government stores.

Fifty years later, the grain was free and was being supplied to 40,000 families. In another twenty years, the number 'on the dole' had gone up to 50,000 and during the reign of Augustus, almost a third of Rome's population (some 300,000 people) were being fed by the government. By that time, the grain was ground into flour and made up into loaves before being distributed.

Later still, there was free oil, pork fat and even wine. The annona lasted until the central government could no longer afford the huge expense.

Poor people ate bread when they could get it but preferred to boil loose grain into a kind of porridge, which was eked out with goats' cheese, eggs, olives, radishes or onions. Sometimes there was dried or salted fish. Meat was very rare, some poor families only eating it when it was given away after an animal had been sacrificed at a religious ceremony. So, no meat for the poor but a porridge of wheat, barley or millet for the afternoon meal at the end of the working day.

Most Roman tenements had no facilities for cooking beyond a little boiling on a portable brazier. If poor families wanted anything better, they either got the baker to cook for them or bought something ready prepared at a nearby pie or sausage shop.

A main meal at 1.30 or 2 p.m. was so early, that it was often necessary to have a light snack before bedtime. The poor man's breakfast wasn't very different from that of the well-to-do. Many people didn't eat breakfast at all, whether they were rich or not: others had a stale roll dipped in watered wine.

The main meal for the better-off Roman started a little later in the day – perhaps at 2.30 or 3 p.m. This

A cooking stove

A Roman kitchen. The toilet was normally in the kitchen.

may have been because of the growing habit of spending much of the earlier afternoon at the baths. Whatever the cause, the chief meal for the rich began later and later as time went on – and it lasted for several hours.

The banquet was usually given by a man for eight guests. Women and children sometimes ate separately in another part of the house. The guests stretched out at full length on three couches, each holding three diners, around three sides of a table in the 'triclinium', or dining-room.

They supported the upper half of the body on the left elbow, leaving the right hand free to put the food in the mouth. Forks were unknown and even knives and spoons were fairly rare.

A rich household had many slaves to prepare and serve the meal but it was quite common for a guest to take his own slaves with him to a dinner party.

It's probable that some of the stories of luxurious banquets that have come down to us are exaggerations. However, we know that meals could last for hours and consisted of many dishes to each course.

Shellfish, eggs, edible snails and some vegetables might be offered as a first course. The second could be sea fish, small roasted birds such as thrushes, cuts of wild boar, larger birds – not only ducks and chickens but also game birds (pheasants, partridges, et cetera), plus exotic species – cranes, parrots, flamingos or ostriches.

The main course had just as much variety – for example, venison, hare, sow's udders, sucking pig, ham boiled with figs and bay leaves, covered in pastry and baked with honey, plus turbot, salmon or sturgeon and all seasoned with pepper and fish stock.

The diners finished with honey cakes and fruit – not only that grown in Italy but rarer kinds from abroad. The list includes apples, pears, olives, grapes, figs, pomegranates, peaches, apricots, plums, quinces, mulberries, cherries, rhubarb and dates.

Each course was accompanied by wine. Although cider and beer were drunk in parts of the empire, wine was the rule in Rome. It was Italian grown and also imported from North Africa, Spain, Portugal, Germany and even from Palestine, Syria and Babylon.

Dining in a triclinium

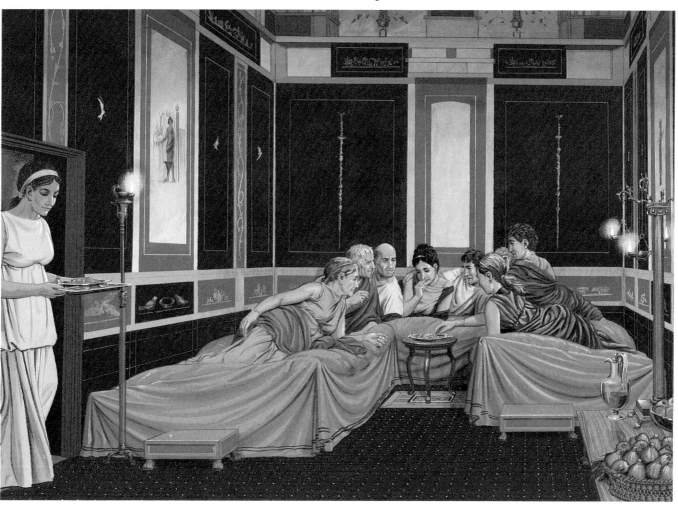

CHAPTER 20

Clothes

From earliest times, the patricians, or rich people of Rome, had settled on a clothing style that continued with little change for a thousand years. Everyone wore a tunic – men, women and children. Plebeians, or poor people, mostly made do with the tunic alone, whilst the well-to-do draped a huge swathe of cloth in folds around the body. This was called a toga.

Togas became more or less compulsory for all free born citizens whenever they went outside the house. The toga was at first always made of wool – and as it was shaped like the edge of a circle over two yards wide and six yards along the straight side, it got very warm in the summer.

After many years of the empire period, it slowly became permissible to leave the toga at home when venturing out. By a very late date, the only use a Roman had for a toga was to cover his corpse before his funeral.

The tunic for men and boys was a simple tube of material with openings for the head and arms. Its lower hem came to about the knees. In cold weather you could wear more than one. The emperor Augustus, who didn't like the short but nippy Roman winters, customarily put on no fewer than four tunics!

In early times, you rose in the morning, having slept in your tunic, with perhaps a toga or cloak as bedclothes. You tied a leather thong round your middle and held the toga's end in one hand, while you arranged the folds round and round your body and over one shoulder.

Romans rarely had much of a wash in the mornings, preferring to wait for the visit to the baths in the early afternoon when work was over. Because the toga always had to look clean, Romans had to have at least one change of clothing.

It wasn't always obvious that garments were grubby for they were made of naturally-coloured sheep's wool. Your slaves could bleach them by laying them out in the sun but there were times when a man wanted a dazzlingly white outfit – perhaps when he was hoping to be elected to a public office. In that case, his things were whitened with wet pipe clay. Our word 'candidate' comes from 'candidus', a Latin word for 'white'.

Working man in tunic

Man in tunic and cloak

Wealthy man in tunic and toga

Some colours were allowed in order to give a little variety. For example, a bride traditionally wore yellow and reddish orange. Young boys sported a thin purple band along the edge of the toga but the only adults allowed the same privilege were senators and magistrates. The emperor alone was entitled to a completely purple outfit.

Women could have their ankle-length tunics and overmantles coloured or patterned. Underwear was not all that popular, although both males and females sometimes wore a kind of loincloth or pants. Mosaics have come to light showing lady athletes wearing bikinis with both bra and pants. In London, archaeologists dug up what looks like a small boy's brief leather pants, fastened at the hips with thongs.

Eventually, cotton, linen and silk were brought to Rome by traders. Linen comes from flax which Romans found they could grow in Italy itself but cotton and silk had to be imported from India and China. The new textiles were rarely used, however, for they always cost more than wool. Indeed, silk, for instance, could only have been afforded by the immensely wealthy – an emperor, perhaps – because in modern terms it must have cost several hundred pounds an ounce.

The founding fathers insisted that their womenfolk spun and wove woollen thread by hand. This continued for centuries in some old-fashioned families. It is well known that hand made things are expensive but it may be surprising to find that they didn't wear too well. This was almost certainly because clothes were washed by being spread on a rock at the riverside and pounded with a lump of stone!

A fuller, or laundryman, could be hired to soak your washing in urine and to jump up and down on it with his bare feet, or to treat it with fuller's earth.

Sandals could be thick-soled and hobnailed for soldiers, workmen, or for ordinary country wear. Shoes of lighter, flexible leather were worn in towns. In rural areas, hats were common but in Rome, a fold of the cloak or toga was held over the head when it rained.

The womenfolk of the first Roman settlers parted their hair in the middle and dragged it back severely. Later on, all sorts of fancy hair styles were permitted. Men started by wearing long hair and beards. They were clean shaven towards the end of the republic and grew beards again in the second century, from the example of Hadrian. Women wore large pieces of gold jewellery and painted their faces. Unfortunately, these paints were often metal oxides which were bad for the skin.

A typical man's hairstyle

Woman in tunic   Woman in tunic and cloak

Women's hairstyles ranged from simple and austere to very elaborate

263

Education

A school room

It's natural to suppose that the children of the first citizens were taught merely by watching their parents and copying their actions and methods. Roman parents continued to educate their own children personally and it wasn't until later that families employed Greek slaves as private tutors or sent their children to the local school.

The elements of reading, writing and arithmetic were taught at the primary stage by a 'magister', or teacher. He was his own boss, running his 'school' in the curtained-off corner of a shop or a disused room of someone's villa. He charged each pupil a few coppers a week and as there weren't usually more than ten to twenty young students, he can't have been very well off.

Lessons consisted of learning things by heart and copying out huge tracts from Latin authors. Rote learning of this kind also included tables of measurement – for instance, length, liquid measure, area and money.

Pupils had to know that there were 'ten asses in a silver denarius'. The 'as' was also a unit of weight. This was a twelve ounce pound, but the word 'as' came to be applied in later years to a copper coin weighing a mere half ounce.

The tables were extremely complicated and a failure to chant the right names and amounts earnt a stroke of the cane.

The copying was done on a writing tablet with a stylus. The tablet was a pair of wooden boards with raised surrounds and hinged together with a leather thong. The flat parts were covered with wax and the letters were inscribed with the sharp end of a stylus, or pen. Mistakes could be removed by smoothing over the errors with the flat end of the stylus.

Roman arithmetic must have been particularly hard to do, since numbers were represented by letters. It isn't impossible to do multiplication and division with these letters but it's very difficult. The chances are that Romans counted on their fingers or used a sort of abacus with pebbles fitting into rows. (Our word 'calculate' comes from the Latin word for a pebble.)

School started at sunrise and went on with no break until lunch time in the middle of the day. The school year began in the autumn and continued until the following high summer when the magister closed up for the annual holiday.

Boys, when they reached the age of about twelve, went on to another kind of teacher called a grammarian. Girls of that age, if they had attended the magister's classes, then went home and had very little further education.

The grammarian concentrated on the Greek language, partly because of Rome's everyday business and administration dealing with the eastern Mediterranean, where nearly everyone spoke Greek. The other main subject was the art of public speaking. No rich man's son could hope to be elected to any important position in the government without a thorough knowledge of how to deal with people and what to say if you wanted to change their opinions.

To round off his education, a wealthy young man might start by taking clients and pleading their cases in law courts. No examination had to be passed. The only requirement was his ability to defend his client properly.

Another route leading to well-paid jobs was to be appointed as an officer in the Roman legions. This often led to men becoming governors or magistrates.

Such was the education of a typical Roman youth of good family.

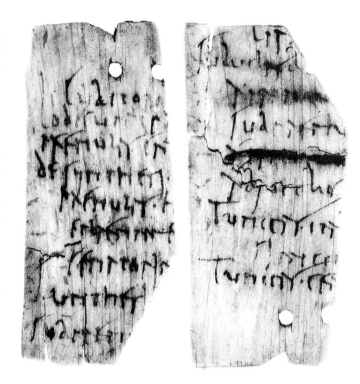

Examples of writing

Boys writing on waxed tablets with styluses

Time and the calendar

A stage direction in Shakespeare's play, 'Julius Caesar', asks for a clock to chime. Unfortunately, these were unknown in Caesar's time, so our great dramatist seems to have made a mistake.

How did they tell the time in Rome? There were, of course, twenty-four hours in their day as there are in ours. The difference was that the Romans then divided the day into twelve hours and did the same for the night. This meant that an hour of a summer's day was a lot longer than one in the winter, for the daylight lasts several more modern hours in June than it does in December.

Romans probably made appointments by saying, 'I'll meet you at the fifth hour', knowing that the time chosen was just less than half-way through the day. You couldn't expect someone to call at your house at exactly two o'clock, if no one knew precisely what the time was.

Romans did have water clocks, similar to the ones used in Egypt. One version of the 'clepsydra', as these clocks were called, had a glass cylinder full of water, which ran out through a tiny hole in the bottom. There were marks scratched onto the outside of the glass (or on the inside, if it was a metal cylinder) so you could see how far the water had sunk down and thus, the hour.

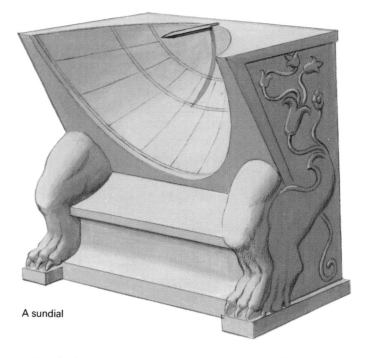

A sundial

Sundials were first brought to Rome from Greek cities but such timepieces have to be made for the place where they are to work and the Romans took time to get their sundials to work properly in Italy.

Nowadays we know that the earth doesn't go round the sun in an exact number of days. The Romans didn't know – nor were they aware of the precise number of whole days involved.

They based their calendar on lunar months (that is, the time from one new moon to the next), but twelve lunar months only made 355 days. The result was a calendar getting farther and farther away from the season it was supposed to tell. If you believed there were only 355 days in the year, you would be starting your second year when there were still ten days to go. In the second year you'd be the original ten and a bit days out, plus another stretch of ten and a bit days. In five years, the calendar would be out of step with the seasons by more than seven weeks and another twelve years later, you'd find yourself celebrating midsummer day in the middle of the winter.

The Roman calendar had twelve months – four named after gods and goddesses and the others known

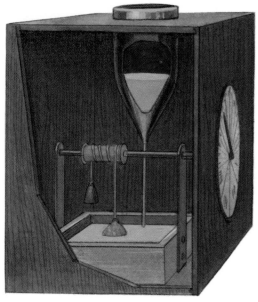

A water clock. In this version the hand on the clock turns when the water level rises

DAYS OF OUR MONTH	JANUARY AUGUST DECEMBER	FEBRUARY	APRIL JUNE SEPTEMBER NOVEMBER	*MARCH MAY JULY OCTOBER
1	Calends	Calends	Calends	Calends
2	a(nte) d(iem) IV Nones	a. d. IV Nones	a. d. IV Nones	a. d. VI Nones
3	a(nte) d(iem) III Nones	a. d. III Nones	a. d. III Nones	a. d. V Nones
4	Pridie Nones	Pridie Nones	Pridie Nones	a. d. IV Nones
5	Nones	Nones	Nones	a. d. III Nones
6	a. d. VIII Ides	a. d. VIII Ides	a. d. VIII Ides	Pridie
7	a. d. VII Ides	a. d. VII Ides	a. d. VII Ides	Nones
8	a. d. VI Ides	a. d. VI Ides	a. d. VI Ides	a. d. VIII Ides
9	a. d. V Ides	a. d. V Ides	a. d. V Ides	a. d. VII Ides
10	a. d. IV Ides	a. d. IV Ides	a. d. IV Ides	a. d. VI Ides
11	a. d. III Ides	a. d. III Ides	a. d. III Ides	a. d. V Ides
12	Pridie Ides	Pridie Ides	Pridie Ides	a. d. IV Ides
13	Ides	Ides	Ides	a. d. III Nones
14	a. d. XIX Calends	a. d. XVI Calends	a. d XVIII Calends	Pridie Ides
15	a. d. XVIII Calends	a. d. XV Calends	a. d. XVII Calends	Ides
16	a. d. XVII Calends	a. d. XIV Calends	a. d. XVI Calends	a. d. XVII Calends
17	a. d. XVI Calends	a. d. XIII Calends	a. d. XV Calends	a. d. XVI Calends
18	a. d. XV Calends	a. d. XII Calends	a. d. XIV Calends	a. d. XV Calends
19	a. d. XIV Calends	a. d. XI Calends	a. d. XIII Calends	a. d. XIV Calends
20	a. d. XIII Calends	a. d. X Calends	a. d. XII Calends	a. d. XIII Calends
21	a. d. XII Calends	a. d. IX Calends	a. d. XI Calends	a. d. XII Calends
22	a. d. XI Calends	a. d. VIII Calends	a. d. X Calends	a. d. XI Calends
23	a. d. X Calends	a. d. VII Calends	a. d. IX Calends	a. d. X Calends
24	a. d. IX Calends	a. d. VI Calends	a. d. VIII Calends	a. d. IX Calends
25	a. d. VIII Calends	a. d. V Calends	a. d. VII Calends	a. d. VIII Calends
26	a. d. VII Calends	a. d. IV Calends	a. d. VI Calends	a. d. VII Calends
27	a. d. VI Calends	a. d. III Calends	a. d. V Calends	a. d. VI Calends
28	a. d. V Calends	Pridie Calends	a. d. IV Calends	a. d. V Calends
29	a. d. IV Calends		a. d. III Calends	a. d. IV Calends
30	a. d. III Calends		Pridie Calends	a. d. III Calends
31	Pridie Calends			Pridie Calends

*In March, May, July and October the days of the Nones and the Ides were set respectively on the 7th and 15th, instead of the 5th and the 13th as in the other months.   'Pridie' means 'day before'.

The Roman calendar after Julius Caesar

as 'the eighth month', 'the fifth month', or whatever it was The calendar seems to have run originally from March to February, hence December was the tenth month. There were additional months put in from time to time to keep the calendar straight. The first of each month was called the 'calends', the mid-month day the 'ides' and the first fortnight thus formed was split in two by days named 'nones'.

Eventually, it was realised that something would have to be done to make the calendar more accurate. It was left to Julius Caesar to make the alterations. These were brought about in the year 46 B.C.

Later still, 'Quinctilis' and 'Sextilis' ('fifth' and 'sixth' months) were renamed in honour of Julius and Augu-stus Caesar (July and August). We still refer to the original seventh month as 'September' and the rest of the autumn and winter months by their Latin numbers. Compare 'October' (eighth month) with 'octopus' (eight legs) and 'December' (tenth month) with 'decimals' (tenths).

Julius's new calendar involved the addition of ninety extra days to 46 B.C. in order to get the calendar in time with the solar year, but his rearranged system lasted until about two hundred years ago, when it had to be reorganised once more. At that time, the year had to lose eleven days and groups of foolish people went about in bands, shouting, 'Give us back our eleven days!' – just as if they had really been robbed of something.

CHAPTER 20

Painting, sculpture, drama and literature

If you've ever visited the remains of a Roman building, you'll have almost certainly seen at least one example of Roman art, namely, a stone-patterned floor. Often, these mosaics are merely geometric designs, made by arranging thousands of little squares of differently coloured stones. Sometimes there are actual pictures –

a human head, flowers and leaves or an animal.

If you want to see proper Roman painting, you'll probably have to go abroad. There are some small fragments of coloured wall plaster in museums, such as the one at St Albans, but the most complete pictures are to be found, for example, at Pompeii in southern Italy.

A Roman theatre in Orange, southern France

Romans occasionally painted on panels of wood but the commonest specimens come from the interior walls of buildings. Wallpaper is a fairly modern invention, so Roman householders had to choose between bare plaster for their rooms, or (if they could afford it), hand-painted illustrations of legends, their own history, sporting activities, landscapes, or perhaps still-life pictures of food and elegant tableware.

Most well-to-do Roman homes had a statue or two in the garden. These might have been made by a local artist as original works but were more likely to be copies of Greek figures, turned out by the dozen in the studio of a man who was more businessman than sculptor.

For their public buildings Romans liked to have the best models that could be had: in most cases, this meant

importing them from foreign countries, now part of the empire. Roman generals plundered defeated Greece and sent thousands of priceless statues back home to grace the walls of the latest temple or bath house.

But it wasn't all a case of Greek figures or nothing. The Greek examples were (and are) very beautiful, no doubt, but local Roman artists could produce a stone head with all its character and oddities so lifelike that the friends of the sitter could recognise it at once.

The examples of statues and busts that have come down to us include portraits on tombs and decorations on triumphal arches and other monuments. Among the latter is Trajan's column in Rome which has some 2,500 figures sculpted in a kind of strip cartoon winding round the pillar from bottom to top in a 215 yard long account of the emperor's campaign in Dacia.

For entertainment, a Roman citizen could go to the theatre but rarely with the chance of seeing the high standard of play the Greeks had enjoyed. The building where the plays were shown, unlike its counterpart in Athens, was completely enclosed within high walls. There was also an arrangement of pulleys and hooks so that the audience could be sheltered from the fierce summer sun by a huge canvas awning which was drawn high over the seats.

Plautus wrote over a hundred plays – mostly musical farces. Terence also wrote comedies. There were also writers of tragedy such as Livius Andronicus, Naevius and Seneca. Unfortunately, the normal standard of drama was never quite as high as that of Greece, most Romans preferring to see low pantomime rather than Greek originals.

For reading matter, citizens had to rely on hand-copied books, for printing had yet to be discovered. Books were in the form of rolls and were usually kept in a container like an umbrella stand.

In those days, a writer could be an expert on many different subjects, although authors such as Cato, Livy, Caesar, Tacitus and Suetonius are known mainly for their history writing. Sometimes, Roman history was not quite as scientific as modern historians would like.

Other authors include poets – Ovid, Horace, Catullus and Virgil. Virgil's poetry could be about almost anything – bees, cattle-breeding, quality of farm soil, weather signs, trees, vine-growing and many other topics. His chief claim to fame, however, was the *Aeneid* which gave Romans an outline of this largely mythical 'history'. Cicero was famous for his essays and speeches.

Although Roman literature, like much of their art, began by copying Greek originals, it eventually achieved a life and status of its own.

269

Earning a living

In some prehistoric villages, there were so few different kinds of life-style that it is possible to describe such a village in a couple of pages. All you have to do is to talk about a typical villager, knowing that his daily experience will be more or less the same for everybody. Rome was no village, though – it was the capital of a great empire, with more than a million inhabitants by the time Christ was born. Life was more complicated and there were thousands of different kinds of jobs to be done. We can't cover all the possible ways a person could earn a living – all we can do is to pick some examples.

If you were rich, you probably owned at least one estate (maybe more), possibly farmed by slaves. You might even employ a superior slave to run your properties for you. From this class of estate owners in earlier times came all the senators and other senior officials, both in the army and outside it.

The next class were called 'knights', as they had once been at least wealthy enough to ride a horse into battle. The Latin word for them was 'equites' from 'equus' (a horse). These were the men who either owned (or could raise) enough money to finance public building contracts, or to fit out ships for overseas trade.

Neither of these activities was allowed to senators. Knights tended to keep out of politics, so that they could run the empire's trade and businesses and make fortunes for themselves. They might be found superintending the building of a temple or an aqueduct: they might be running a spinning and weaving workshop.

To help them in the clothing trade, they employed spinners, weavers and fullers. The last mentioned, you may remember, were also the laundrymen of Rome, using fuller's earth to absorb grease from oily fleeces as well as from dirty clothing.

You might find a knight in charge of a mass production pottery, a mosaic maker's workplace or perhaps a jeweller's shop. He wouldn't, of course, do the work himself but employ others to carry out his orders.

Lower down in the social scale were the owners of small shops. There were no chain stores in the old city and each shop was owned and run by a separate family. Some streets were devoted to one type of shop only – for example, all the harness makers lived and worked within sight of each other as did the glass makers.

As we've seen, the owner of the shop was normally a craftsman who made the product in a workshop at the rear of the premises and sold it from a counter on or near the street. In Rome you could see the shops of shoemakers, tailors, butchers, greengrocers, drapers, carpenters, wine sellers, barbers, herbalists, tanners, booksellers, rope makers, paint sellers, perfumers and many more.

Not all of the above were makers and sellers – some just sold, others provided a service. You could go to a joiner's to buy a table or a cupboard, or you could hire a carpenter to do woodwork in your own house. Other providers of services included fortune tellers, doctors and teachers. There were no specialised lawyers – anyone could speak on behalf of the accused in a law court.

There were also civil servants such as secretaries (often slaves), fire wardens and building inspectors.

More specialised jobs were done by armour makers, horse breakers, trappers of wild animals and owners of gladiator schools (at least in the early days) where fighters were trained for the Colosseum and other amphitheatres.

Some men did their jobs away from the city centre – brick and tile makers, stone cutters, most builders, engineers, shipwrights, sailors and soldiers. If you had no other skill you could always become a porter or delivery man. No carts were allowed through the city gates during the hours of daylight, so the goods they carried had to be unloaded and shouldered on their way by armies of carriers.

If you wanted to make a fortune and didn't mind an element of danger you could always become a paid gladiator or even a chariot driver in the races at the circus.

A shop selling bronzeware, including lanterns, jugs, and lamps

Games and pastimes

The people who lived in Rome spent more time out-doors than we do. This was partly to do with climate. Even today, you won't want to stay in your house when the temperature is high and the weather good.

In those days there wasn't a lot to stay in for: there were no radios or televisions and the light at night in a Roman flat was scarcely bright enough for reading. As a result, Romans got up when the sun rose and many of them went to bed when it set.

It's obvious that most of their pastimes were open air ones. The extremely popular animal and gladiator shows, together with chariot-racing are dealt with in Chapter 22, so little will be said about them here. One point of interest is that the vast majority of Roman men were extremely keen on betting. They would gamble on the result of a fight in the arena or on the outcome of a race in the circus.

Betting was reckoned by the authorities to be such a social sin that it was strictly forbidden – except in the arena or at the circus. It was considered all right to bet on a gladiator or a chariot driver but not on anything else. Not that this worried the average citizen, however. He knew perfectly well that there were a dozen wine shops or taverns almost within sight of his own home, each of which had an illegal back-room betting shop.

The gambling was on the roll of a pair of dice. There are a number of ways of doing this; the simplest being to throw a higher number than your opponent.

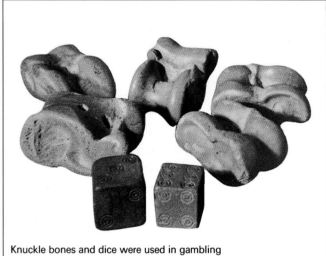

Knuckle bones and dice were used in gambling

Men playing dice

272

At Saturnalia (about the same time as our Christmas), betting was allowed on anything – even coin games. Someone would spin a couple of coins and men would bet on whether they came down two heads, two tails or one of each.

Another popular 'game' was played by two people facing each other. Both hid their right hands behind their backs and at a signal both showed their opponent the previously hidden fist, this time with one to five fingers extended. At the same time, each player called out a number from two to ten. This was supposed to be a guess at the total number of fingers showing. The winner was the one who guessed correctly.

As well as 'micatio', as this game was called, there were more serious 'sitting down' games such as the Roman versions of backgammon, chess or draughts. Board designs, similar to the ones on which we play draughts, have been found scratched into the hard stone pavements of the cloistered walks around Rome's forums.

More energetic were the ball games or wrestling a Roman might prefer when he went to the baths. Some rich citizens enjoyed yachting and those less well off could take part in angling contests. If all you wanted was peace and quiet, a gentle stroll around the public squares after the law courts had finished for the day might be your choice, or even a walk through the grounds of the emperor's palace.

Some popular children's games from Roman times are shown in the pictures on this page.

Miniature chariot

Boys playing 'the mill game' – a cross between noughts and crosses and draughts

Boy playing with a hoop

Chapter 21 The state and religion

Government and the law

This is a reconstruction of the centre of imperial Rome in the mid second century, showing some of the official buildings and temples of the central government.

We may remember how the ruling of Rome began in the early days with the choosing of a monarch – until the very idea of kings became unacceptable. When Tarquinius Superbus had been driven out, two consuls were appointed to lead the citizens for one year at a time, both of whom had to agree before any law was made or scrapped and before war was declared or peace sought.

In time of war, a military dictator was appointed to lead Rome's soldiers against the enemy. He was ex-pected to give up his powers as soon as the emergency was over.

A group of (mainly) ex-consuls formed the city's first parliament, or senate, as they called it. Senators were elected by the landowners and there were usually about three hundred of them. Poor people had their own assembly but it had little power. The two classes were known as patricians (the rich) and plebeians (the poor). A great deal of Rome's history was the running battle between the patricians and plebeians – the former trying to hang on to all of their power and the latter aiming to prise some of it away.

The plebeians chose their moments well: they waited

Looking down on the Roman forum, from the Temple of Jupiter on the Capitol, about 150 A.D. The building bottom right is the Basilica Julia where trials and business matters were conducted.

until Rome was in danger from an enemy attack and then went on strike against army service until the patricians allowed them to elect a tribune to look after their interests.

Towards the end of the republic, those patricians entrusted with high military command tended to forget about the rule asking them to step down when the crisis was over. Then violence was often the outcome. Julius Caesar was murdered because it was thought that he might want to be king.

Eventually one man – Augustus – succeeded in staying at the top, whilst pretending that there was still a republic. But he was, in fact, the first emperor.

Seventy years later, Claudius set educated ex-slaves to run various government departments and the senate was much less powerful than it had once been. The emperor Domitian was so contemptuous of the senate that when some of its members questioned his actions, he had them executed!

Hadrian had to order some patrician rebels to be killed and then, because the senate complained so strongly, he had to promise never again to do so without the senate's consent. Antoninus Pius, on the other hand, always consulted the senate before doing anything important – such as spending public money!

The emperor Pertinax was murdered and the army put the empire up to the highest bidder at an auction. The senate refused to accept the buyer, Didius Julianus, as their emperor. There was yet another civil war; Septimius Severus became the next ruler and Julianus was executed. Septimius had realised that the army was the body which held the gift of power, not the senate. He therefore raised army pay and took away very nearly all of the senate's last privileges.

From then until the final collapse, the emperor's word was law, provided that he could afford to bribe the troops and stay in power long enough to have his wishes respected. Apart from that, the army was the law.

Oddly enough, it was Roman law which survived the empire. To begin with, the law had concerned itself with quarrels between people. Justice was a very rough and ready affair. As time went by, the government took a larger and larger interest in crime. Also, in earlier times, the law's protection in the matter of wills, inheritances, divorce, private disputes and so on was reserved for the upper classes: if you weren't a 'citizen', you couldn't claim anything legally.

For the poorer early settlers, the law had seemed unjust – none of it was written down and only the upper classes had the right to say what it was. After protests, the laws were published – they were engraved on publicly displayed bronze plates. Unfortunately, these disappeared during the Gaulish invasions, so we only know of them from references in ancient writings.

No exams were needed to be a lawyer – only a persuasive tongue. Many young men began their careers by speaking in the law courts.

In spite of the defendant's habit of presenting the judge with a gift (a custom that sounds like bribery!) the Latin system prospered and grew. It was taken all round the Mediterranean and many modern codes of law are based on it. Our own lawyers use Latin words in their everyday work – words such as judge, jury, verdict and justice.

Religion and legends

Early Roman religion was based on a belief in spirits that were invisible. These spirits were called 'numina' and there was a 'numen' for practically everything – a numen for the night, the day, each hill, home, river, mountain, lake, forest, field and almost anything with a separate identity.

Before taking any important step it was necessary to plead with the proper numen, whose shrine might be on a hilltop, in a grove, at a crossroad or in a cavern. A farmer would plead for the numen's help before planting or reaping a crop and a merchant might do the same before taking on a contract to supply bricks.

It was essential to get the words and actions right and to know what offerings to bring the numen. The men who could remember all these things became the first priests. They weren't the spiritual leaders we expect our clergymen to be – they merely knew who to bribe for heavenly help and how to do it.

It may have been the Etruscans who taught Rome that it was easier to think of a deity if a statue was made and set in a specially built house or temple. It was almost certainly they who introduced the gods and goddesses of Greece to the citizens of the seven hills. Many of these were simply taken over, merely changing the name to a Roman one,

In this way, the character of Zeus was adopted as Jupiter and Hera taken over as Juno. The Greek Artemis became Diana and Athena was renamed Minerva. From Ares, the Romans had Mars and Hermes changed into Mercury. Venus started in Greece as Aphrodite.

The most important god of later times was Jupiter, god of light and king of the immortals. The specialities of some of the others were as follows: Juno (queen of the gods), Saturn (agriculture), Ceres (crops), Minerva (wisdom), Venus (love), Vulcan (fire), Neptune (sea), Diana (moon), Apollo (sun), Mars (war), Vesta (hearth), Manes (the dead) and Janus (doorway).

As well as these, there were personal and family gods – the Lares looked after the home and the Penates the store cupboard. The father of every Roman family set up, where possible, a shrine to these protectors and led whatever prayers were said.

Legionaries returning from overseas conquests

Jupiter Optimus Maximus – 'the best and greatest'. There was a temple to him, Juno and Minerva in every Roman town.

brought back the worship of foreign gods such as Mithras from Persia and Isis from Egypt. In later times, as belief in the classical gods dwindled, some Romans took up the study of new philosophies, such as that of the Stoics who were encouraged to ignore both pleas-

Making an offering to the Lares and Penates – the household gods

ure and pain, or of the Epicureans who believed in the pursuit of pleasure as the greatest thing in life.

The custom arose in the days of the empire of making the last dead emperor a god, or even the supreme god. The worship of the departed ruler, as with that of the other gods, was regulated by the government who appointed the priests.

The high priest was known as 'Pontifex Maximus' and the honour normally went to the living emperor. There were other kinds of priests, for example, the flamines who were the burners of offerings and the augurs who could tell the future from flashes of lightning, the flight of birds, or the livers of sacrificed animals.

Romans didn't have regular church meetings with prayers; their visits to temples being more in the nature of bargains struck with the god – 'You protect me on my journey and I'll give you an offering of food and wine.'

In the matter of legends, the Romans were content on the whole to retell Greek myths. Their own history provided some examples of folk tales. These were usually designed to show how brave or noble their ancestors were. We've heard the stories of Romulus and Remus, the adventures of Aeneas, the legend of the Sabine women, to mention only three. Other legendary figures were Cincinnatus, who was made military dictator during a crisis. The period of his authority was supposed to run for six months but he left his plough, beat the enemy in a few days and went straight back to his farm.

In the Punic Wars, a Roman general named Regulus was captured by the Carthaginians. They released him on his honour to return at the end of his mission. This was to go to Rome and persuade his countrymen to surrender. On the contrary, he urged them to go on with the war. Then, because of his promise, he returned to Carthage, even though he knew he was going to torture and death.

Another hero was the magistrate whose sense of duty was so strong, he tried his own sons for rebellion and sentenced them to death.

That was the sort of person the average Roman liked to think he was – brave, stern and dutiful.

The Temple of Vesta, showing the sacred fire

Christianity

The life and death of Jesus passed almost unnoticed in the Roman world. No Roman writer of the time thought it important enough to mention. If they had heard of him at all, they probably dismissed him as another unsuccessful eastern revolutionary.

The followers of Jesus claimed to have talked with their leader after his crucifixion. He had told them to spread the word of God and to tell everyone about the forgiveness of sins and the life everlasting.

His disciples, or followers, started to carry out his request and preached mainly to the groups of Jews scattered throughout the empire. On the whole, however, it wasn't the Jews who were converted but those whose lives were so poor and downtrodden that they embraced Christianity willingly.

The Romans thought (mistakenly) that these converts were all Jews – after all their leader had been one, hadn't he? Not that it mattered much: Rome had always welcomed new religions from all over the civilised world – wasn't this just another new faith? In any case, no Roman thought it odd to believe in more than one god: if a prayer to Jupiter was good then prayers to a couple of other deities were even better.

It wasn't long, though, before the differences became extremely clear. Christians were not like other worshippers – they wouldn't accept office from the government, they wouldn't serve in the army and they refused to bow down to statues of the emperor-god. Neither would they make offerings of food and wine – either to him or to any other of the accepted host of Roman heavenly beings.

St Paul (like St Peter) came to preach in Rome itself. He is supposed to have made converts among the official staff of the emperor. At one stage it was ordered that every citizen must make a sacrifice to one of the accepted gods in the presence of a magistrate. He would then be given a certificate. This, the authorities thought, would make it easier to detect Christians who

Catacombs

Many Christians were killed by lions in the arena. This was a normal method of execution

came before them.

The emperor Nero was suspected (with some reason) of having started the great fire of Rome. Christians were convenient scapegoats and he had them arrested by the hundred. Many were thrown to the lions in the arena: some were burnt to death.

This was only the first of many waves of persecution – strong feelings were whipped up against them, arrests made and executions carried out. Then things would quieten down until the next emperor who felt it was time to make the Christian community toe the official Roman line. Both Peter and Paul perished during the persecutions.

To escape their accusers, Christians often took refuge in the miles of tunnels that ran beneath the city. They were called 'catacombs' and were used to bury the dead. Here the refugees hid, arranged services and held meetings.

Followers of Christ also developed secret signs so they could be sure of revealing their beliefs to friendly ears. A

man might trace the outline of a fish with his finger or the end of his staff. This was because the Greek word for 'fish' was made up of the initial letters of their leader's name and title (Jesus Christ, Son of God and Saviour).

As time went by, the average Roman believed less and less in the official gods. More and more citizens became Christians – not just the poor and lowly but people from every class of society. Even a few of the patricians were claimed for Christ. Many of the latter had tired of an endless round of pleasure and were attracted to what the new religion had to offer.

By the early fourth century, belief in Christ had become respectable and in the reign of Constantine, Christianity was elevated to an official Roman religion. Constantine is reported to have seen a vision of a cross during a battle and to have become converted.

Christian churches were built throughout the Roman world and when the empire eventually broke up, it was the Church which preserved the best of the ancient world and passed it on to the future.

Slavery

Prisoners of war – men, women and children were sold to slave-dealers

'Did you want to speak to me?'

'Yes. We'd like to know about slavery. I believe you are a slave: is that correct?'

'I'm a slave all right. My name is Menenius Lucius Centullus. It's not my real name but one given to me by my owner. I can't remember my proper name but I know my family came from Britain during Julius Caesar's raids.

'I suppose my ancestors must have cost a lot in those days. You see, most slaves are actually captured enemy soldiers or their descendants. If your parents are slaves, then so are you.'

'How were your ancestors bought and sold?'

'Why, in the slave market, of course. It was very undignified being paraded around like a prize sheep so that the public could bid for you. As I was saying, slaves were expensive in the early days but as Rome's empire grew, so did the numbers of prisoners of war. These were auctioned off by the dozen, the hundred and eventually by the hundred thousand.

'Naturally, there were few rich families which could

afford the early prices but as the numbers grew the cost fell rapidly. Nowadays, most citizens who have houses own at least half a dozen slaves. Rich people own hundreds and men like the emperor have thousands.

'The price of a slave also depends on what he or she can do. The better educated and those used to town life fetch the highest amounts and are taken by merchants to act as clerks, book-keepers, secretaries and such like – or they go to be house servants.

'Those with little learning but strong muscles may be sent to work in chain gangs on a farm or down a mine. If the person on sale is a soldier, he can be sent to one of the gladiator schools to be trained to fight to the death in the arena.

'In the old days, slaves were often branded or chained up to make escape difficult. Some slaves were actually kidnapped off the streets of Rome itself: it was very difficult to get away once that happened to you.'

'Were runaways punished?'

'Oh yes; a slave could be whipped, chained, starved or beaten to death – and not just for trying to escape either. If an owner wanted to ill-treat his slave in any of these ways or even to kill him, the owner wouldn't suffer. It was reckoned to be his right to do what he liked with his own "possessions".

'If a slave pretended to be a free man, he could be put to death. So he could if he tried to enlist in the army. Some were employed directly by the government on building or repairing things – temples, roads, aqueducts – that kind of job.

'I suppose I'm lucky. I work as an assistant in the library of the public baths. I'm probably better off than many free citizens. That does worry me a little bit.'

'How so?'

'Well, as time went on, public opinion turned against very harsh punishments. Did you know that the law actually says, "If a slave murder his master, not only he but all the other house slaves shall be executed"? That actually happened about two hundred years ago but I'm sure it couldn't happen now. Then again, I think the growth of Christianity had something to do with it. People are kinder. The trouble is that the kinder you are the more it costs to keep a slave. Then one day your master realises that it would be cheaper to set you free. I don't want to be free – all that would mean is unemployment.

'Once upon a time, a slave would try to save enough money to buy his freedom. The only other ways to escape were freedom under your master's will, rebellion or death. You've heard of Spartacus? He was a gladiator slave who escaped with some of his friends. They defeated the soldiers sent to kill them and took their arms and armour. They released other slaves until they were an army almost 10,000 strong. They terrorised southern Italy for two years. Then General Crassus beat them and rounded them up. He had them crucified – one to a wooden cross, every thirty yards from Rome to Capua, a hundred miles away.

'That's what being a slave was like in the old days!'

Slaves being crucified along the Appian Way after the revolt led by Spartacus

Chapter 22   The arena

The amphitheatre

Romans didn't care overmuch for the kind of play the Greeks supported but they used the Greek theatre ground plan in the construction of their amphitheatres.

There men and beasts fought one another for the amusement of the crowd. Every town of any size at all had an amphitheatre ('theatre on both sides') with rows of seats encircling and rising round a sandy space in the middle. This was called the 'arena' (the Latin word for 'sand'). You can find them all over the Roman Empire – from Portugal to Asia Minor and from Africa to north Britain.

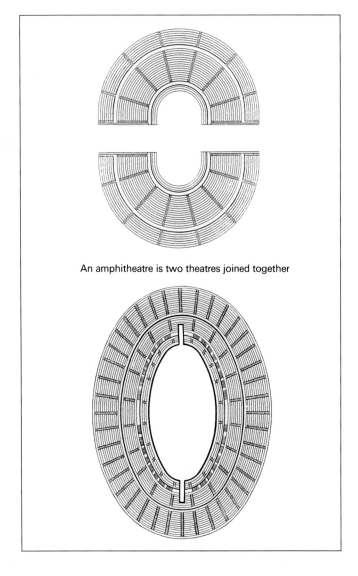

An amphitheatre is two theatres joined together

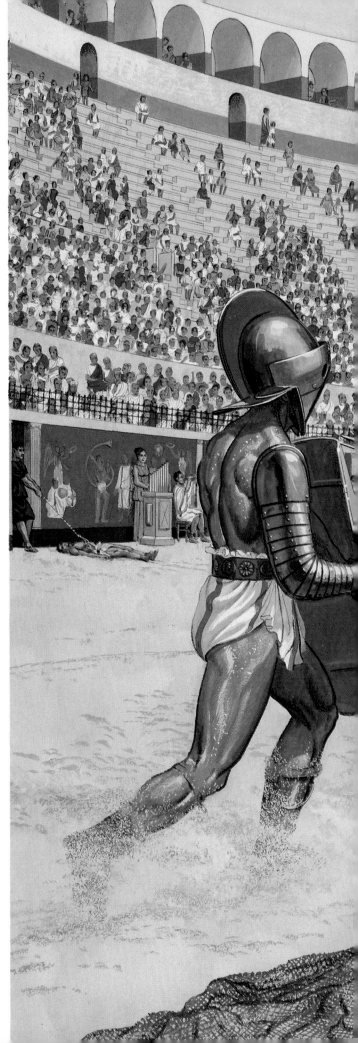

Gladiators fighting in the arena. A secutor fights a retiarius (see page 287)

283

CHAPTER 22

The Colosseum

Whenever the subject of ancient Rome comes up in conversation, it is almost certain that someone will mention the inhuman Roman 'games'. These started in imitation of the customs of other Italian tribes. Perhaps the Samnites or Etruscans had the habit of holding elaborate funerals for their dead chiefs.

At first, the slain leader's slaves were gathered together and executed. Later on in history, they were given swords and paired off so that they could kill each other.

Romans took over this practice but used captured enemy soldiers. With a simple weapon each – perhaps a spear or dagger – they were encouraged to fight to the death, the winner's prize being his own life and freedom.

The fights were held in public squares, armed Roman soldiers forming a ring to prevent escapes. When Rome became the centre of an empire, the emperors began to put up special buildings to house the 'games', as they called them. The greatest of these was the Colosseum.

It wouldn't have been any good asking an ancient Roman to direct you there: the name 'Colosseum' wasn't used until centuries after the empire had passed away. The word comes from the 'colossal' statue of Nero which once stood on the site. When the Colosseum was new, citizens called it the Flavian amphitheatre, after Flavius Vespasian, who began it.

Vespasian had Nero's garden lake drained and the statue smashed to make room for the great building's foundations. It was near the centre of the city and was the greatest project of its kind in Rome. The emperor died before the work was complete and it was left to his son, Titus, to open it to the public.

Even then, it was still unfinished when the first performances took place, the last touches being added later. Finally, it was a gigantic stone oval, three to four storeys high (perhaps 150 feet), with outside measurements of 616 feet along its greatest diameter.

In spite of earthquakes and the pillaging of its fabric in the Middle Ages by those seeking easy and cheap quantities of building stone, enough remains to show modern tourists what might easily be added to any list of 'wonders of the ancient world'.

284

The Colosseum

The arena was formed of stone blocks covered with sand. The blocks rested on top of the walls of underground compartments – cells for the performers and cages for the animals. The oval arena proper was 262 feet by 177 feet and surrounded by a high metal fence to protect the crowd from the wild beasts.

Beyond the fence, there was a corridor right round the arena and then a smooth stone wall thirteen feet high. Above this began the tiers of seats – the first few rows reserved for the emperor and other important officials. Higher still sat the general public in what seem to have been numbered and reserved seats. The Colosseum could seat about 45,000 spectators with room for perhaps another 5,000 standing.

There were many corridors, staircases and exits so that the crowd could be dispersed quickly and safely after the 'show' was over. Many a modern football ground might envy the eighty or so controlled exits.

At the top of the building were the spars and pulleys controlling the canvas awnings which could be drawn across to shield the audience from the intense heat of midsummer.

At first, there was a system of water pipes which could flood the arena and turn it into a lake, on which mock sea fights between galleys could be fought. For the fighters, it was anything but pretence. The boarding parties had swords and spears and there were always soldiers surrounding the 'lake', ready to put an arrow into anyone seen trying to slip away by swimming to the side.

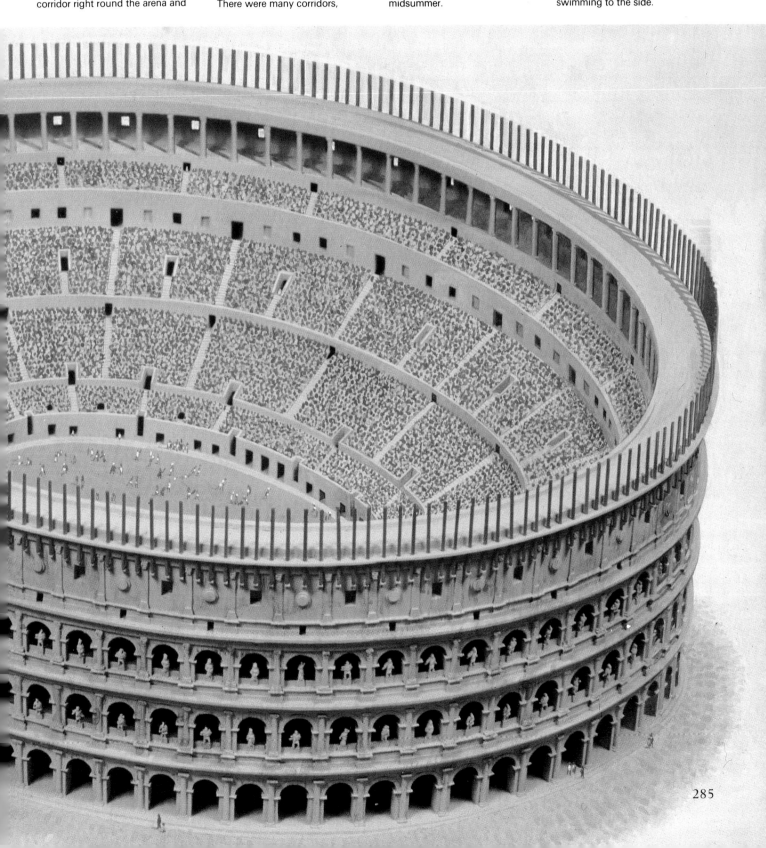

285

Gladiators

It has to be said that many Romans (perhaps a majority of them) were cruel and bloodthirsty. They were like ignorant and brutal peasants who had suddenly become rich enough to give in to whatever beastly passion they liked. Nothing else can explain centuries of men being butchered for sheer amusement.

We know that some prisoners of war were trained as gladiators – the fighters to the death. A few criminals were also taken and there were those who volunteered because they were down on their luck and could earn money if they won.

Why did anyone consent to be a gladiator? If you were a learner and were told, 'Either you kill your opponent or we'll kill you', the chances were that you'd do what you had to, to stay alive.

The learners were kept in small stone cells in training schools and only allowed out to practise. To make sure nothing dangerous happened when they were training with real weapons and that there was no likelihood of escape, the exercise yard was surrounded by guards armed with bows and arrows.

The men rehearsed with wooden swords and spears to start with, going on to blunt metal and then heavier than average ones, so that they'd find the actual swords and spears easier to manage in the arena.

The night before the contests, the manager would lay on a feast for the fighters. In earlier times, the manager or trainer would also have been the owner but then the government took over on the grounds that it was too dangerous to have one man in charge of perhaps 5,000 trained fighting men.

The show started early in the morning but there were purely 'circus' acts to begin with, mostly involving animals doing tricks. After that came the beast fights. Armed men tried to slay the animals without getting crippled or killed themselves. The crowd, however, were impatient for the real 'games' to start, when they could bet on the contestant of their choice and shout or scream their approval as one man after the other was butchered.

There were exhibition contests first, followed by a trumpet fanfare for the parade of the gladiators. They saluted the emperor in his private box and chanted,

Gladiator armour

Mosaic showing gladiators

'Ave imperator! Morituri te salutant!' ('Greetings, emperor. Those who are to die salute you!')

Lots were drawn to see which man should fight which. The opponents could be equally armed and matched but the crowd sometimes liked to see unequal contests. For example, the retiarius had a helmet, dagger and three-pointed fork called a trident, in addition to a large net. The other contestant might be a secutor, with sword, shield, visored helmet, metal leg guards and armour for the sword arm (see page 78).

Each stalked the other, looking for an opening. The retiarius hoped to entangle the secutor in his net. If his throw missed, he could pull back the net with a rope which he kept in his hand. At the same time he must parry sword thrusts with his trident and hope to get in a stab or two with his dagger. Other methods of fighting included chariot battles or contests with lassoes.

The winner received a reward of gold or silver. If the loser was still alive but too hurt or exhausted to go on, he could appeal to the emperor who usually left it to the crowd to decide whether he should be spared or not. A good fighter would be helped out to have his wounds attended, but one who hadn't pleased the crowd was slain where he lay and his corpse dragged out. Fresh sand was sprinkled over the bloodstains and the next fight began.

This sort of thing went on for centuries, the number of public days off gradually growing, so that everyone could revel in the blood letting. At one stage, nearly half the year was 'holiday' for the masses of poor and unemployed. Tens of thousands of men were slaughtered to keep them amused and less likely to rebel. The motto of the government seemed to be 'panem et

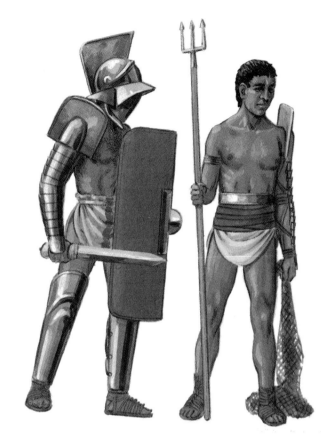
Types of gladiator – the heavy-armed secutor (left) and the retiarius

circenses'. This means 'bread and circuses' and was what the government was ready to supply in the way of food and entertainment for the sake of peace on the streets.

Gradually, however, the spread of Christianity in the empire made these exhibitions less popular and in the reign of Honorius the gladiator fights were banned.

The baiting and killing of animals went on, though, and it is possible that the bull fights which still take place in south west Europe are their descendants.

Bestiarius – animal fighter

287

The Circus Maximus

Romans had always been keen on horse-racing, the more so when the government banned gambling on everything else. The more poor people there were in the capital, the more betting there was; the downtrodden always seem to feel the need to wager more than the rich, even though they can afford it less.

The first races were not arranged or properly organised. Farmers' sons would gather at a stretch of softish ground along the banks of the streams which drained rainwater from the city's hills.

Two wooden posts were driven in the earth some six hundred yards apart and the horsemen galloped from one to the other, round the top post and back again. Anxious citizens cheered on their favourites and made sure the part-time bookmakers didn't run away with the winning bets.

The Circus Maximus started in this way but although the oldest and biggest, it wasn't the only track in or about the city – and, of course, there were many others throughout the empire.

At the 'Maximus', the two wooden posts were replaced with stone and a ridge of earth was set up between them – so like a backbone that the spectators called it the 'spina'. On this spina were set statues of gods thought to be favourable to racing. The spina was rebuilt in stone and temporary wooden stables erected. These were replaced with stone ones, and a set of starting stalls was erected.

Horse-racing was gradually ousted by chariot-racing – each light, two-wheeled vehicle being drawn nor-

Chariot race in the Circus Maximus

mally by four horses, although teams of up to ten animals were not unknown.

Once the spectators had stood or sat on the grassy banks, but another improvement brought rows of seats. The stone ones at track level were reserved for important officials, or even the emperor. Then came the wooden seats and standing room at the back. No one knows for sure but it is thought that there were seats for almost a quarter of a million people.

The fans made their bets and eagerly awaited the appearance of the drivers in their chariots. There were usually four vehicles in each of the twenty-four races, the drivers dressing in tunics coloured white, blue, green or red, depending on the faction, or team, they belonged to.

By this time, the whole complex had been enclosed inside walls like the ones round the Colosseum. This was quite an achievement by the builders, for the walls were about fifty feet high and went right round an area of almost half a mile long and over two hundred yards wide.

Drivers moved their vehicles to the starting stalls, first checking that all was in order. The reins were wound round their waists and tied. In case of an accident, the driver didn't want to be dragged round the arena by stampeding horses, so each one was provided with a razor-sharp knife to cut himself free – that is, supposing he could reach it in time.

Each chariot was led into its place and a rope run across the front of the stalls. The official in charge started the race by dropping a handkerchief: the rope was whipped away and the chariots sped forward.

It was an advantage to get near the stone spine because your turning circle at the far end was shorter than anyone else's. But too near could spell disaster – there were always those who were willing to crowd you into the wall or even to put a hub through your spokes.

Each race consisted of seven laps and the drivers always knew how much more they had to do, because a marshal removed one of seven huge wooden eggs at the end of each lap. Later, the laps were signalled by the turning over of a large bronze dolphin.

Drivers could start on this dangerous profession at the early age of thirteen but few survived to enjoy the huge fortunes that could be won. Although Diocles retired in the year 150 A.D. at the age of forty-two with 3,000 wins behind him, others were not so lucky. Fuscus, Crescens and Mullicius, outstandingly successful drivers, were all killed in racing accidents during their early twenties.

Perhaps only the bookmakers were the winners – as in modern times!

Chapter 23   The army

The citizen soldier and the legion

If we want to find out about the first Roman army we might do worse than ask one of the city's legionaries.

'What can you tell us about the first legions, soldier?' we ask.

'I'm not really a soldier,' he replies. 'Either that or everyone is. You see, we don't have a standing army. Whenever there's danger, everyone who owns property must take his place with the fighting men.'

'Why property owners?'

'Partly because every soldier (even a part-time one) has to provide all his own equipment – a sword, spear, helmet and any armour he cares to wear. Those of us who are well off can afford to have these things made; poorer people can not. Also, because it's thought that those who own farms or estates have most to lose if our enemies win. Therefore they'll fight harder for the city than anyone else would.

'In any case, we all go home and get on with our work when the trouble's over. They do pay a little for the time we spend in the army but our farms provide us with our real income.

'This worked pretty well when all we had to put up with was an attempt to run off some of our cattle or the

Triarii – the rear line of a Republican legion

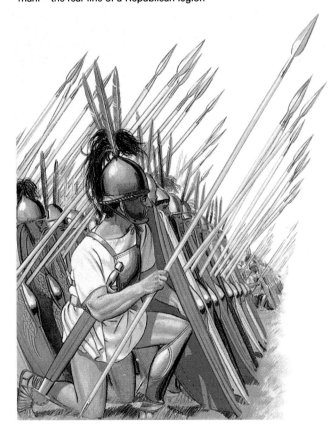

Republican legionaries building siege lines – these were used in the siege of Carthage

occasional raid on the city itself. Unfortunately, things didn't stay like that. We Romans decided that the best way to protect our city from such attacks was to beat our enemies, take their city and make it over to our way of thinking.

'The drawback to this was that our frontiers slowly widened as city after city was absorbed within Roman frontiers. As the borders got farther from our homes, service in the army grew longer and longer. It became harder to recruit men.

'One of our kings, Servius Tullius, reorganised the army. He didn't solve the problem of distance from Rome but some things were different. Before his time, the call-up to deal with our foes resulted in a force of three regiments, each of a thousand men and each commanded by its own officer, or tribune.

'Tullius ordered that all free Roman citizens should be divided into five different classes, the richest at the top and the poorest at the bottom. All were still to supply their own kit but the top group naturally supplied most, and it was from the wealthiest section that the cavalry was recruited.

'The outcome of all this was that Rome now had four infantry legions which fought in a kind of phalanx. This was a formation we copied from the Greeks, each man being armed with a long thrusting spear. The legion was arranged in six ranks of five hundred men apiece.

'The next development was a reduction in the number of lance users. These were called "triarii" and were usually elderly men. The middle-aged (say, 30–40 years old) were the "principes" who formed lines in front of the triarii. The "hastati" were the young men who lined up in the very front of the army. Apart from the lancers, every man had javelins for throwing, plus a sword and shield for close fighting.'

We thank our informant and go on our way. We know that long after his time, the phalanx idea was abandoned. Recruiting had been difficult enough when the soldiers had been compelled to walk long distances before fighting: now they often had to sail abroad before taking part in the war and it proved almost impossible to attract enough men to the legions.

Because of this, entry to the army was thrown open to anyone, however humble a citizen he was. Payment was raised and weapons began to be mass-produced. Now, all the soldiers could be armed and armoured alike.

Thousands of poor men (that is to say, the new recruits) far from wanting release, hoped they'd be kept on as long as possible. Their pay, although small, was more than most of them got as civilians.

At last, all the legionaries came from the poorer classes and the foundations of a paid, standing army had been laid.

Uniform, weapons and tactics

There was little uniformity from man to man in the first legions – soldiers could have whatever weapons and armour they liked and could afford. They had thick leather jackets, or perhaps scale or chain armour, if they were rich enough.

Mail was made from sheets of iron and iron wire. Little quarter inch rings were cut or punched from the sheet iron and joined to others by passing an open ring of wire through the ones to be connected and then closing the ring with pliers. Every ring was thus intertwined with its neighbours on each side and at the top and bottom.

Scale armour was a series of smallish iron or bronze plates, each one wired to its neighbours and sewn on to a stout undercoat – rather like the tiles on a roof, or (as the name suggests) the scales on a fish.

Towards the end of the republic, there were changes in the army pattern. We've seen how legionaries were no longer armed with long jabbing spears, nor were they sorted out into battle formations according to age. Every man was paid adequately and given identical armour and weapons.

The most important difference was the introduction of plate armour. It was made from curved plates of wrought iron or steel. The various pieces went round the chest and over the shoulders, being connected with hinges, or fastened together (and on to the body) with leather straps and buckles – perhaps even with simple hooks.

A charge by an Imperial legion

Helmets were hammered from sheet bronze or iron. With their rounded, projecting neck guards, they looked rather like a modern horse rider's cap worn back to front. Nearly all of them had hinged cheek pieces to protect the sides of the face.

The old oval type of shield gave place to the oblong, slightly curved kind, like a section from a cylinder. The new shields were made from three or four layers of thin laths, glued at right angles to each other and forming a kind of plywood. The laths were probably steamed into shape before they were glued. The whole lot was enveloped with leather and a top layer of linen, and the edges were bound with rawhide or hammered bronze. There was a hollow boss in the centre with a wooden handle behind.

A scarf stopped the armour from rubbing the soldier's neck, and a pair of calf-length leather breeches was worn in cold countries.

Each infantryman had a sword hung on a leather strap which went over his left shoulder. A waist belt carried the sheath for his dagger. The two javelins every man had were found to have a drawback when they were first used. They were designed to be thrown, but unfortunately, the enemy could pull them out of the ground or wrench them from his shield and throw them back. Armourers found the answer. It was to make the second, or lower rivet which joined the handle to the head much weaker – perhaps even a wooden, rather than a metal rivet. This meant that the head of the spear struck and then bent over just below the head, rendering it useless.

It is probably true to say that there were more sieges than battles. However, when a battle was inevitable, the Romans drew up their legions in line abreast with cavalry on either side. The idea of upper-class horse soldiers had long been abandoned: the general concerned preferred to raise local auxiliary horsemen whilst on campaign.

Legionaries had once been organised in centuries of 100 men, each under its own centurion. Later it was found more convenient for a centurion to have in his command only 80 men. Six centuries made a cohort and there were always ten cohorts in every infantry legion. The men lined up side by side and about six feet apart. The line behind them covered the gaps thus formed. The legionaries did nothing until a signal from the commander was relayed by trumpet.

Then they threw their javelins, drew their swords and charged. When in contact with the foe, they closed ranks to plug the initial gaps. The front line fought with sword and shield, the fallen being replaced by men from the second line.

Romans didn't have better weapons or superior commanders but they did have discipline. In a scrappy, hand-to-hand engagement, it would have been easy for the faint-hearted to slip away. This was all but impossible in a legion, where years of training kept the men in rows and in contact with the enemy. In any case, the average legionary had the confidence to smash through the opposing lines, knowing that his sides and back were protected.

Roman generals depended on the infantry to cave in the enemy centre, although they did have cohorts of archers and slingers if they were needed.

A legion cohort of the early empire

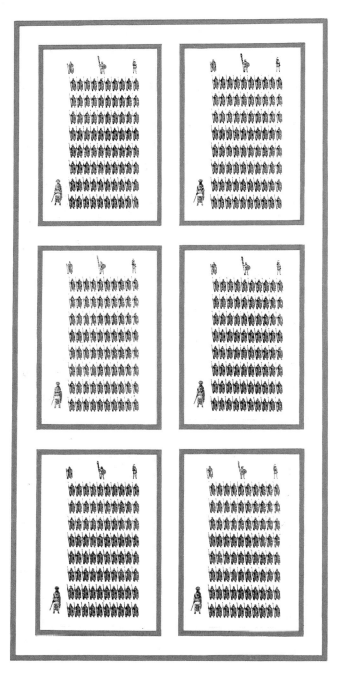

Siege engines

It wasn't only in Rome that sieges were more common than battles. The result was that most of Rome's enemies were familiar with the idea of an army investment of their town and had built stout defensive walls all round it. Army commanders had to know how to reduce an obstinate town or fortress. The emperor Vespasian, when still a legionary commander during the invasion of Britain, stormed and took no fewer than twenty British hill forts in the south of England.

One simple, if boring, way of capturing a town was to surround it and wait for the people inside to starve. Their submission might, of course, take months. Roman officers came early to experience siege methods from the Greeks or from those who had copied them. The ideas had probably originated in the Middle East and they were not improved until the invention of gunpowder in the Middle Ages.

A Roman general, faced with the task of taking a fortress, could order his men to go under, through or over the walls. His choice depended on local circumstances.

Soldiers tunnelled under walls to bring them down, rather than to make a way through for masses of men. Making a hole in the wall could be done with a battering ram. This was often a large tree trunk with one end cased in iron and slung on chains or ropes from

Siege ramp

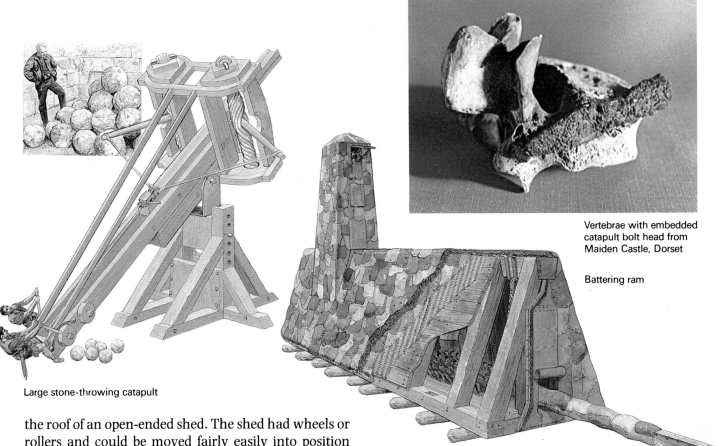

Large stone-throwing catapult

Vertebrae with embedded catapult bolt head from Maiden Castle, Dorset

Battering ram

the roof of an open-ended shed. The shed had wheels or rollers and could be moved fairly easily into position against the walls.

It had to be big enough to hold twenty or thirty men whose job was to swing the log against the bricks or stones. To prevent the defenders setting the shed on fire, it was armoured with metal plates or at least covered with rawhides.

Screens of hides also covered wickerwork frames to protect archers as they fired at the enemy. Galleries rather like the battering ram sheds but not quite so stoutly built, were open at both ends and could be put together by the dozen to make a protected corridor for the attackers to use to get to the base of the walls. The corridor could be long enough to start out of range of the fort's weapons, which was quite an advantage. In an emergency, Roman soldiers could cover themselves, top and sides, with their shields to make what they called a 'testudo' (tortoise), if no other protection was available.

Sometimes a Roman commander would order the building of siege towers to overtop the town walls. These were also protected against fire. They could be wheeled up to the walls as well. If necessary, a protective moat or ditch could be filled in to make a causeway for the towers. The infill consisted mostly of logs with clay in between the layers. Sometimes the earthworks thus formed were enormous. During the siege of Jerusalem, legionaries are supposed to have chopped down every tree within a dozen miles of the operation.

In order to clear the enemy away from the walls whilst the rammers battered, the miners dug or the assault troops crossed to the battlements on the drawbridges of the towers, Roman generals called upon the artillery. The picture shows one of the machines that could be pressed into service. Although such 'guns' could be made on the spot, they were far more likely to have been built elsewhere and transported to the required place.

There were stone-throwing machines varying in size from those able to project a stone the size of a tennis ball to large ones capable of shooting a hundred pound boulder almost half a mile.

Other machines were designed to fire small arrows, or heavier ones up to twelve feet long, as far as the large stones could be slung. One dangerous device was to take something that would burn easily, soak it in naphtha or oil, set fire to it and then shoot it into the enemy fortress.

Evidence of the use of catapult arrows was discovered when Maiden Castle was excavated. This was a huge hill fort, taken by the Second (Augustan) legion during the Claudian invasion of Britain which began in 43 A.D. The diggers found a skeleton with a Roman ballista bolt wedged into the vertebrae of a defender's backbone.

They didn't have gunpowder but Roman artillery was nearly as deadly as any gun of the Middle Ages.

Marching camps

The one thing which could slow down the advance of a legion was the mass of carts and pack animals which carried tents, poles, parts of stone-throwing engines, spare armour, weapons and rations. For this reason, officers in charge of moving the legion gradually transferred a great deal of the baggage on to the shoulders of the ordinary legionary.

As well as his armour, spare boots, helmet, sword, dagger and javelins, each man carried a change of clothing, rations for a fortnight (mostly grain of some kind) and a cooking pot. He also had to sling on his back at least two fencing posts, a spade or entrenching tool, a length of rawhide rope, a saw and perhaps a wooden mallet for driving in tent pegs. In total the load weighed almost a hundred pounds, about as much as a sack of coal.

Towards the end of the afternoon an advance party from the marching legion would go forward to seek a camp site for the night. They looked for a flattish area, perhaps on slightly raised ground or a hillside. The site had to have space for a camp some half a mile square;

A centurion laying out a camp with a groma

there had to be fresh water at hand and grass for the various animals. If at all possible, the chosen spot must not have too many rocks, bushes, trees or broken ground which could give cover for an enemy's surprise attack.

When a site had been found, a surveyor, using an

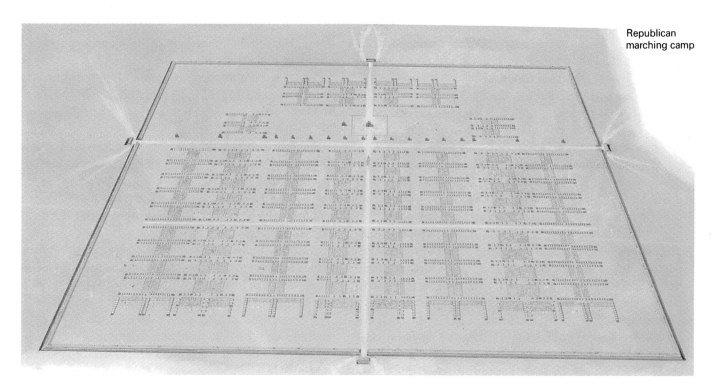

Republican marching camp

Digging trenches for a camp

instrument known as a 'groma', decided where the corners of the camp were to be. These were marked with small coloured flags and the line of the defences scratched through the turf.

Other flags showed the future positions of the officers' and official tents. Another furrow was drawn about two hundred feet inside the defence line. No tent was permitted inside this margin, thus allowing space for the defenders to manoeuvre and keeping tents out of the enemy's artillery range.

When the legion arrived, men knew exactly what their jobs were. Many of them set to work to dig out the ditch. They left a gap in the middle of each side trench for the entrances. A road was laid out between the north and south gateways and another one crossed the camp from east to west. There were no actual gates, the way in being protected by an additional section of trench a little way in front of the opening.

Where the roads met, a space was left for the commander's tent. The space was square, measuring two hundred feet on each side and was called the 'praetorium'. To the left and right of it were two empty areas – one called the 'quaestorium' where some rations were issued and the other a forum for public meetings and parades. Other official tents were nearby.

The ditch diggers threw the excavated dirt just to the inside of the ditch, which was considered adequate if it was seven or eight feet wide and five feet deep. If a serious attack was expected, the ditch was made much

deeper and wider. The soldiers all planted their fencing stakes on top of the new bank of dirt and fastened them together with rope.

The men's tents were put up in lines parallel to the defence works. Often, a small unit had its tents and stables erected on a horseshoe plan, with the centurions camped at the two ends of the formation. The tents themselves might be of canvas over wooden poles but were just as likely to be of thinnish leather.

Even when the ditches were finished and every tent erected and anchored with iron tent pegs, the soldiers' work wasn't done. If they weren't unlucky enough to be picked as guards, the men still had to light their fire and prepare an evening meal. Finally, even the special duty men in tents behind the commander's had their porridge and retired for the night. One man from each group had to report to the commander to be given the password for the night.

If the inspecting officer found a sentry asleep at his post, the offender could be beaten to death – punishments were very hard in the Roman army.

In the morning, the commander ordered the trumpeter to sound a call. On hearing it, the working parties pulled up the pegs around the officers' tents and dismantled them. Then the legionary tents were also struck. On a second trumpet call, the tents were loaded on to what carts there were or strapped to the backs of pack animals. A third signal gave the order to assemble in marching order.

Many of these temporary camps became permanent in some frontier towns. The tents were replaced with buildings of brick, stone and timber, and the earth ramp gave way to stone walls and gatehouses.

The officers

The commander of a legion was called a legate. He was actually a politician, usually appointed by the emperor, but needing army experience before he could advance his civilian career. If he was lucky he might be promoted to a provincial governorship after his time with the legions. A man with such a job would have to be foolish or unfortunate not to become rich, so it was worth roughing it in the army for a few years.

As a legate, he wore an elaborately embroidered tunic in scarlet wool, plus a cloak of similar material. His breast plate was made of bronze and hammered out until it resembled the exaggerated muscular development of a professional athlete.

His second-in-command was a senior tribune. In spite of this description, he wasn't necessarily very old. He was also hoping to be a politician – perhaps a senator – and could not expect to succeed without a spell in the army. His uniform was like his legate's but not so elaborate.

In the legion there were another five junior tribunes. These were not normally aristocrats but came from the same social class which provided a good many local government officials. Again, their uniforms were similar to their superiors', if not quite so fancy. On the whole their duties were more concerned with the running of the legion than active service. However, in an emergency, they could (and did) take command of auxiliary or other troops.

Next in seniority came the camp prefect. He had commonly served at least thirty years, much of the time as senior centurion. His main responsibilities were to see that the legion's equipment of all kinds was up to date and in good repair; that every section was at full strength and properly organised; and that training was being done correctly. At a pinch he could command the legion, if he was the only senior officer present but as an ex-centurion, he couldn't normally expect to be promoted any higher.

The average legion consisted of ten cohorts, each of which was divided up into six 'centuries' of 60–80 men apiece. The non-commissioned-officers, or N.C.O.s,

were called centurions because they had once been in charge of a hundred men – now they looked after a smaller 'century' each. Centurions had a fancier tunic than a common soldier's over which a leather coat was worn. Body protection was provided by scale armour, guards for the lower legs and a legionary-type helmet, except that the crest went from side to side rather than front to back. Over his coat and armour he wore leather straps on which were his medals and decorations.

It was as well for the ordinary soldier to keep on the right side of his centurion. Men signed on for twenty-five years and were given Roman citizenship as a reward when their time was up. This was a prize worth having for there were all kinds of drawbacks to living in the empire without being a citizen.

Some centurions were hard to the point of brutality, thrashing their recruits unmercifully (as part of their training) with a vine stem, their badge of office.

If you were in the centurion's bad books, you might find yourself constantly punished or even dishonourably discharged with no citizenship. The authorities seemed powerless to deal with the frequently made charge that a centurion could be bribed to overlook a man's offences.

Punishments also included stoppage of pay and leave, or reduction in seniority. For serious crimes like desertion, cowardice, theft or sleeping on guard you could be put to death.

The highest rank an ordinary citizen in the army could rise to (apart from camp prefect) was senior centurion – 'primus pilus', or 'first javelin', as he was called.

Other minor officers below centurion rank were known as 'principales'. The 'optio' was the centurion's second-in-command. There were also the standard bearers – either the 'aquilifer', who carried the legion's eagle, their main badge, or the 'signifer' who looked after the century's own standard. At the bottom of the command structure and only just above the lowest rank of legionary were vets, doctors, musicians and orderlies.

Officers in a Roman legion

Left to right:
Standard bearer for century (signifer)
Aquilifer with eagle – the legion standard (behind)
Centurion
Centurion horn blower (cornicen)
Trumpeter (tubicen)
Commander-in-Chief (Provincial Governor – Legate) (seated)
Legion Commander (Legatus legionis) (behind)

Roman roads

Today we take roads so much for granted, we scarcely think about them. If we want to travel about, no matter by what method – car, bicycle, bus or whatever – we don't have to think whether we can get to our destination easily. Of course we can: we can look at a map and pick our route.

Now let's try to imagine that there are no roads at all. Immediately, we realise that we can't travel by car or bicycle but only on foot. If you've ever tried running up the side of a sand dune or through heavy mud, you'll know what a tremendous difference is made by the lack of a hard surface under your feet.

When you went on a bus, coach or car, did you ever cross a river? Would you even have noticed? If you were walking, you'd quickly learn to look for the easiest way to cross even a small stream.

If it's a task for you to make your way through a forest, over a marsh, up hills and across other difficult countryside, just think how much harder it would be to try moving something heavy over the same route.

It's probably true to say that if the Romans had been unable to bring in food and building materials on specially made roads, Rome could never have grown to the size it did.

In the early days, only faint tracks ran from the infant city to nearby towns and villages. Then in 312 B.C., the censor, Appius Claudius had a proper road built from Rome to Capua. Other roads followed as further conquests were made, for example, the Via Flaminia which ran north to Rimini.

Roads were also a military necessity. If there was trouble, troops could get to where it was without delay.

The main roads of the Roman Empire

As we've seen, marching can be much faster on a good hard surface. Every new city conquered had a road built to it – 'All roads led to Rome'.

In the reign of Augustus, a golden milestone was set up in the 'Forum Romanum', the market place and main square of Rome. The distances of all other towns were measured from it. There were occasional milestones on the new roads. These were cylinders of stone standing five feet or so above ground level, showing how far the next town was and which emperor had ordered the stone to be erected.

Roman roads were as straight as possible. If a high cliff or a mountain was in the way, the road was angled round it – but if the obstacle was merely a hill or a fen, then the engineers went straight ahead.

They would pick a spot on the horizon – a tree, perhaps. If there was nothing to see, an advance party would be sent ahead to light a fire in the distance to provide a point towards which the road must be driven.

The roads were made both by civilians and soldiers but perhaps the last named did most. A lot of the heavy labouring was done by slaves.

The outline of the proposed road was marked with poles and the road bed cleared by pick and shovel. Then various layers of mortar, stone, clay and gravel were laid bringing the surface up to about three feet above the old level. In places where traffic was heavy – for example, near large towns – the engineers ordered flat slabs of stone to be laid on the top. Most roads had a slight hump or camber in the centre of the highway. When it rained, the water trickled into the ditches running on each side. The drainage ditches were about twelve or fifteen feet apart, although some roads were wider and others narrower. The rule seemed to be that there must be room on a main highway for two legions to pass one another.

Along the roads travelled not only soldiers but ordinary people and goods on all kinds of journeys. If the emperor wanted a message sent, his messenger rode a horse: if he rode furiously, changing mounts every few miles, he might cover two hundred miles in a day. He couldn't keep it up however, but if he had been able to, it would still have taken nearly a fortnight to get from one end of the empire to the other.

This may sound slow going but after the empire collapsed, it was to be thirteen centuries before man could move as fast again.

Roman roads covered most of Europe and the lands around the Mediterranean in a complete network. There were enough main roads to have gone round the Equator twice and sufficient roads of all kinds to circle the world ten times!

Troops of Emperor Augustus building the road over the Great St Bernard Pass

303

Chapter 24   Barbarians at the gate

Barbarians settle inside the frontiers

The groups of men in front of us are not speaking Latin, although we are several miles inside the frontiers of the Roman Empire. Not only that – they are armed to the teeth with spears and swords slung from leather baldrics or shoulder straps, and they are wearing conical helmets and sheepskin jackets.

We know that for centuries, the Roman army has recruited men from anywhere in Italy and finally from anywhere in the empire: but these men aren't dressed in uniform and they don't look like legionaries from a standard unit. Perhaps we could ask where they are from? We beckon and one of them strolls over, his hand resting lightly on the hilt of his sword.

'We'd like to know who you are and what you are doing inside the empire. You obviously aren't in a legion – or are you?'

The man laughs. 'No, we're not Roman soldiers. We come from the north and east. The Roman authorities let us come in and settle this side of the frontier.'

'Why should they do that?'

'I can't really say for certain. All I can do is guess. You see, we were living peacefully – well, as peacefully as anyone can in these troubled times. Then, only a year or so ago, our neighbours began to raid more often than they'd ever done before.

'Once upon a time, all they wanted to do was to make a surprise attack and run off some of our horses and cows. Then they began to press us back – not just a cattle raid, you understand, more like an all-out attempt to push us out of our territory.

'We captured some of their horsemen and demanded to know why we were being thrust back. They told us that they had already lost almost half their own north-eastern lands to a people which had come from the far

The Rhine/Danube frontier of the Roman Empire, showing incursions by barbarian tribes

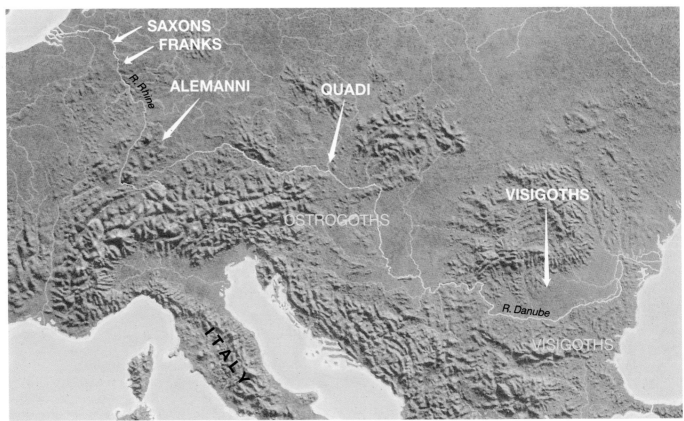

Gothic archer and horseman

Hunnish horseman

east. These people all rode on horses and used short but very powerful bows. Captured bows revealed that they were made of thin strips of bone, glued and pinned together. One of our prisoners swore that he had seen one of the arrows go straight through a shield.'

'Do you know what these invaders were called?'

'They called themselves Huns. They were quite strange looking. They had brownish-yellow skins, almond shaped eyes and high cheek bones. They also carried wickedly sharp sabres. A new feature was their use of murderous lances – from horseback, naturally – but they couldn't have been effective without stirrups. You look surprised?'

We nod, so he continues, 'If you hit something with a spear when you're riding, you're more likely to come out of the saddle without stirrups.

'Anyway, these Huns were driving our neighbours back; our neighbours attacked us, so we asked the nearest Roman governor to let us settle on the south side of the Danube. The land we wanted was only thinly populated so we thought we had a good chance.

'To start with, the Romans wouldn't listen – until we made them an offer they could not refuse. We offered to

defend the banks of the river ourselves and keep out any other "barbarians", as the Romans call us.

'It was obvious that the governor was at least interested. He told us to go away while he consulted with his colleagues. So we waited. We found out later that other tribes from beyond the empire had put forward the same kind of proposal and in some cases the Romans had accepted.

'Finally the governor gave us his permission – but there were conditions. Some of us had to join their regular army and the rest of us were divided into smaller groups and kept apart from each other.

'I don't think the Romans are too happy about the arrangement, though, and I know that in some instances, they preferred to pay us savages just to go away. But there certainly are similar tribal groups settled on the "wrong" side of the Rhine-Danube frontier in several areas. They do say that there are more of us inside the empire in other areas. I can't swear to that but I must say that if I were a Roman, I wouldn't feel too secure relying on what to them must seem like enemies to guard their precious empire.'

Some provinces are abandoned

The first reason why Rome had expanded was that other cities had attacked her. The best defence is attack and early Romans might have said, 'I'm not a bully, nor am I greedy: all I want is the land that touches mine!' This motto might have been the reason why Rome went on growing.

However, during the reign of Trajan, the empire had become as vast as it was ever to be. Hadrian, the emperor who followed Trajan, thought that it was already too big and voluntarily gave up a large part of the eastern provinces. This meant that the expansion had at last come to a halt and that from then on a slow shrinking had begun.

The barbarians around the frontiers pressed forward more and more often. The defence of Rome wasn't helped by the fact that there was no satisfactory way of getting rid of a bad emperor, short of killing him. Soldiers, rather than the senate, were the emperor makers and if they weren't rewarded by the man they had chosen, they murdered him and looked around for someone else.

In our own twentieth century, there have been no more than four British rulers during the last seventy years. During the same length of time at the beginning of the third century, Rome had twenty-three, only one of whom died a natural death.

Among the barbarians now battering at the imperial frontiers was a group of Germanic tribes, including the Franks, the Alemanni and the Goths. These were crossing northern and north-western Roman lines, whilst other outlanders were doing the same in the east.

To make matters worse, the empire was rapidly becoming harder to govern, as law and order collapsed and street riots became more common. At times there was even civil war within the empire. To deal with this, legions were withdrawn from the fighting and sent to Rome to keep the peace. As a result, the defences were considerably weakened and in Dacia, to the north of the river Danube, there were hardly any legionaries left. The Goths poured across the abandoned lines in their thousands.

One Roman emperor fell in battle, one was captured

Aurelian

and many others assassinated. They came and went swiftly as various army commanders vied with each other to take the throne. At one stage, no less than nineteen senior officers strove to be the next emperor.

Among the crowd of would-be rulers, a few names are outstanding in the fight against the outlanders. The emperor Aurelian, for example, actually defeated a Gothic army, although he did allow them to settle on the Roman side of the boundaries, perhaps hoping that they would keep out any further adventurers. He beat back another invasion of the Alemanni, put down rebellions in the east and generally restored law and order. It is a pity there were few emperors such as Aurelian. But in spite of his good record at protecting the empire, he too was murdered, as were both of the next two emperors.

No wonder provinces were abandoned under the pressure of waves of advancing barbarians – there was hardly a Roman ruler who lived long enough to think up a reasonable defensive plan and put it into operation.

Emperor Aurelian built walls around Rome in about 275 A.D. They had square towers every 100 feet and were 12 miles long.

305

Constantine, his town and the division of the empire

When Diocletian ruled Rome at the end of the third century, Rome was already more than a thousand years old and much too large to govern properly. The emperor therefore decided that everything would be easier if the whole area was split in two.

He promoted one of his men to be co-ruler. This was Maximian who would rule the western half from Milan, while the emperor would run the eastern part from what is now Turkey. Many of the citizens of Rome must have found the new arrangements very strange. Let's go back to the fourth century and ask someone about the changes.

'Excuse me, are you a citizen of Rome?'

'Of course I am. Everyone knows me: my name's Marcellus.'

'But do you live in Rome itself?'

'Yes, I do have a home there but I've two or three other homes as well. I began work as a sailor, rose to be a ship's captain, and after a while bought a ship of my own. Now I've got a fleet of 'em. We carry some passengers but mostly we take cargoes such as timber, wool, wheat, iron ore, pottery and even wild animals for gladiators to fight.'

'What happened when the empire split?'

'A blow to the pride of those who live in Rome, perhaps, but no great differences in day-to-day matters.'

'What exactly were the alterations?'

'I suppose you already know that Diocletian and Maximian shared the ruling between them? Yes? Well, each man was called "Augustus" – after our first emperor, of course – and each had an assistant known as a "Caesar".

'Diocletian and Maximian did something rather surprising a few years later. The year 305 it was.'

'What did they do?'

'Why, they resigned. Sensible really. No point in waiting about to be stabbed to death, eh? Yes, they retired and Diocletian went to live in what you call Yugoslavia. He built himself a fine palace at a place called Split and became interested in growing cabbages, of all things.'

Constantine defeats Maxentius, son of Maximian, at the Battle of Milvian Bridge

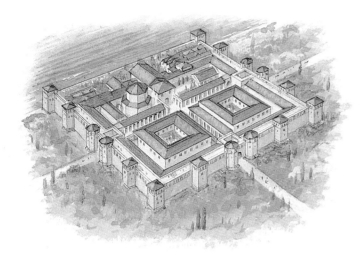

Diocletian's palace at Spoleto (now Split) in Yugoslavia

'Who took over from them?'

'At least half a dozen men struggled for power. One of them, a man named Constantine, won in the end. He was put forward by his troops – "proclaimed" is the word they use. It happened at York in Britain, as a matter of fact. He was the one who is said to have seen the vision of a cross in the sky during one of his battles. I don't know if that's true but from then on, people were allowed to be Christians openly.'

'Didn't Constantine make a new capital city?'

'He certainly did. Maybe he wanted to get away from those men in Rome who still thought they ought to have some say in the government. The emperor didn't want his word to be questioned so he made the new chief city at a place just about as far from Rome as he could get. Byzantium was his choice. It's an old Greek city standing on the narrow strait which divides the Mediterranean from the Black Sea. It must have seemed a miraculous place to Constantine: it was already a Romanised town with the usual temples, market place, baths, theatre and so on – but what astounded him was the fact that it even had seven hills, just like Rome itself.

'Constantine began enthusiastically in 326 to change it into a great city. It was called "Constantinople" from then on. I suppose that must be a sort of Greek word meaning "Constantine's town".'

'I think we call it "Istanbul" nowadays', we say.

'A lot of people called it "New Rome". It was half in Europe and half in Asia, with a good anchorage for ships. Not just naval ships, you understand, but merchant vessels like mine.

'I suppose the biggest difference it made to me was the easing of trade between east and west. And, of course, more profit,' he smiles. 'But whether it'll be a good thing in the long run, I can't say. It's still rather odd to feel that Rome is no longer the most important town in our empire, and that's a fact.'

Constantinople from the air

CHAPTER 24

Alaric and the sack of Rome

We've seen that some emperors sought to preserve the frontiers by allowing in some of the barbarians and bribing them to keep out any others. The leader of such a group was Alaric, the chief of an east European tribe of Visigoths (western Goths). The Visigoths had probably been forced westward and into what we now call Bulgaria by another barbarian tribe called Huns. Alaric was born about the year 376 into an important family then living on an island at the mouth of the river Danube.

As a young man he was appointed general of a group of irregular troops who helped the emperor Theodosius to crush a rebellion. He was hoping to be given a proper commission in the regular Roman army as a reward but the old emperor died and the new one, Honorius, did just the opposite. Not only did he refuse any reward, he also cut off the 'presents', or bribes, which had bought the service of the Visigoths.

Alaric's men then proclaimed Alaric King of the Visigoths and together they swore to carve out a new

kingdom for themselves. Alaric led them towards Constantinople only to find the place was far too well defended to fall to their attacks. They headed for Greece, capturing and looting one city after another and selling the inhabitants into slavery. A Roman regular army cut off their retreat and they had great difficulty in fighting their way free.

This was almost the last victory of proper Roman legionaries fighting on foot with javelin, sword and shield. In the old days, such men were very nearly unbeatable. At the time of Alaric however, Rome now depended on legionaries who – far from being citizens of Rome or dwellers in Italy – were not even born within the boundaries of the empire. They were, in fact, largely

Alaric and his Goths sack Rome. The Basilica Julia (right) and the Temple of Divine Julius (left) were burnt.

recruited from the very tribes of barbarians which threatened Rome's existence.

In the old days, Romans had fought for their own families and homes, but now the empire was being defended by men bribed to fight for others. Woe betide Rome if the bribes were not handed over.

At one stage, Alaric and his men seemed so dangerous to Romans that they were bribed to protect the lands which lay between the western and eastern empires, now no longer on friendly terms with each other. Alaric played off one Augustus against the other, even managing to get official government factories to provide weapons and armour for his men.

Still smarting from the refusal of the authorities to give him respect in the form of an army commission, Alaric decided in 400 to attack Italy itself. He was defeated after a couple of years but the strange thing was that the army which drove him away was also led by a barbarian. His raids had the effect of causing the emperor to move his capital and (rather more important as far as Britain is concerned) to bring back a legion from Britain in order to defend the heart of the empire. In addition, the tying up of Roman armies in this struggle had allowed other tribesmen to sweep across Europe, occupying both France and Spain, which then passed out of Roman control for good.

Twice more Alaric attacked the city of Rome and on his third attempt, his Visigoth warriors broke through the gates and into the streets of the old capital. As a result of the attack, Romans in North Africa cut off supplies of corn to the city. Alaric thought that the only way to deal with this was to attack the North African provinces in order to get the grain ships sailing again. During the voyage across the Mediterranean, a fierce storm arose, most of the ships were wrecked and the Visigoth army they were carrying was almost wiped out.

Alaric himself died shortly afterwards – some say of a fever – and his body, together with his weapons and armour, was buried in the bed of a river which had been temporarily diverted. When the funeral was over the river was allowed back in its old course and the slaves who had done the work were slaughtered to stop them telling anyone where the grave was.

All this should have been good news for the Romans, but during Alaric's life, Rome had been attacked repeatedly, the central part of the empire lost, France and Spain overrun by other barbarian peoples and the eastern and western halves of the old empire reduced almost to a state of war with each other.

It wasn't quite the end of the Roman Empire, but it was the beginning of the end.

More barbarian attacks

There was more trouble after the death of Alaric. Rome tried hard to stem the inward flow of wild tribesmen but in 429, Vandals captured Carthage and the rest of the North African Roman provinces. In 410, the Roman-ised inhabitants of Britain had appealed to the Roman emperor for help against the hordes of barbarians that were attacking Britain. The emperor's message was to the effect that they must look to their own defence as

Rome was unable to send troops to fight off the attacks. In fact no troops were ever sent again.

Some towns and cities in Britain were still standing after the invading Angles and Saxons moved in but the outlanders had little knowledge of building or civil engineering and so allowed the places where Romans had once lived to fall slowly to pieces. Even if the newcomers had wanted to use villas and temples they

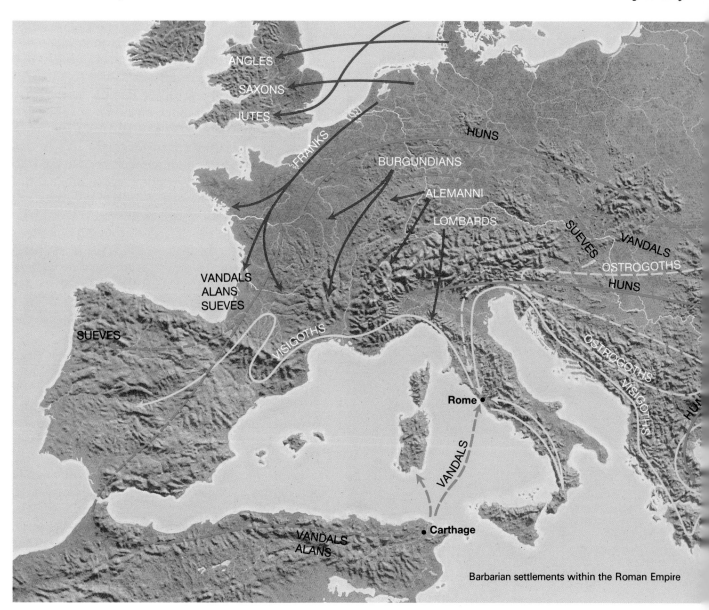

Barbarian settlements within the Roman Empire

had no way of repairing and protecting them.

The same thing applied to roads. Roman engineers had left Britain with a fine network of highways and lesser roads, which the incoming Angles and Saxons were happy to use. This was fine provided that nothing went wrong – but if a flood washed away a surface or a tree fell across the road, the local people who lived nearby felt no need to go and make good the damage. Travellers coming to the obstacle did nothing either, they merely walked round it.

Such authorities that were still in existence in Rome had more pressing problems than what to do about the outlying province of Britain. In March 451, more than 70,000 of a new tribe of barbarians crossed the Rhine into France capturing cities such as Paris, Metz and Orleans – burning, killing and pillaging as they went. These were the Huns. The only way such outlanders could be stopped was by another army of outlanders who might still be faithful to Rome.

The leader of the Huns was a man feared throughout the civilised world. His name was Attila and he was described by a writer of the time as being 'short and thick, swarthy with grey hair, deep-set eyes and an upturned nose. He walked with a proud swagger as though he was the greatest lord who had ever lived.'

This time the Huns were turned back but they returned in the spring of the following year, laying waste to much of northern Italy. They captured many cities including Padua, which they burned. However, the Pope came out to meet Attila at the head of his army of hard-bitten horsemen. No one knows what was said when they met, but the Pope apparently talked the Hun leader out of attacking Rome. Perhaps Pope Leo reminded Attila what had happened to Alaric, the last barbarian to do so. It may be that Attila was superstitious and didn't want to die immediately afterwards, as Alaric had done. It's more likely that he feared that famine and plague then affecting Italy would weaken his army until they were unable to fight their way back over the Alps. At all events, he turned his back on Rome and headed north once more.

Death of Attila

The next year, Attila got married. He ate and drank so hugely at the wedding feast that he burst a blood vessel and died. The menace of the Huns faded away, never to rise again.

But Rome's end was very near. Another band of Vandals sacked Rome in 455. The looting lasted a fortnight. Barbarians were now permanently in charge of Rome and her affairs.

In 476, the very last Roman emperor was deposed. Oddly enough, his name was Romulus, the same as the first king and founder of Rome over 1200 years before.

By the end of the 400s, both Italy and the rest of the western empire had been shared out between the various barbarian tribes – the Suevi and Visigoths in Portugal and Spain, the Franks and Burgundi in France, the Saxons and Angles in England, the Ostrogoths (eastern Goths) in Italy and the Vandals in North Africa. The *western* empire was at an end.

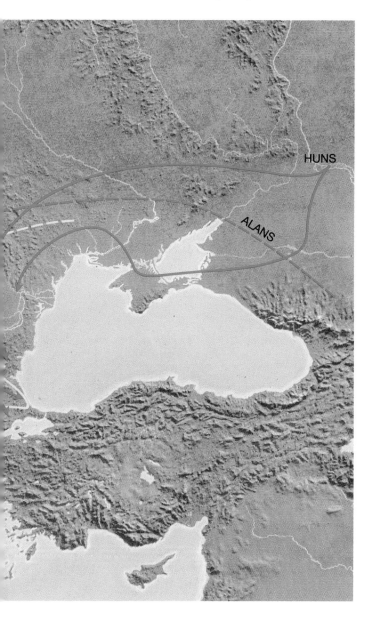

HUNS

ALANS

CHAPTER 24

The Byzantine Empire lasts another thousand years

To get some idea of what happened to the rest of the Roman world, we'll ask a historian to give us some facts.

'The western empire was all but dead,' he says, 'overrun and occupied by tens of thousands of outsiders. The eastern part was luckier. There, the emperor

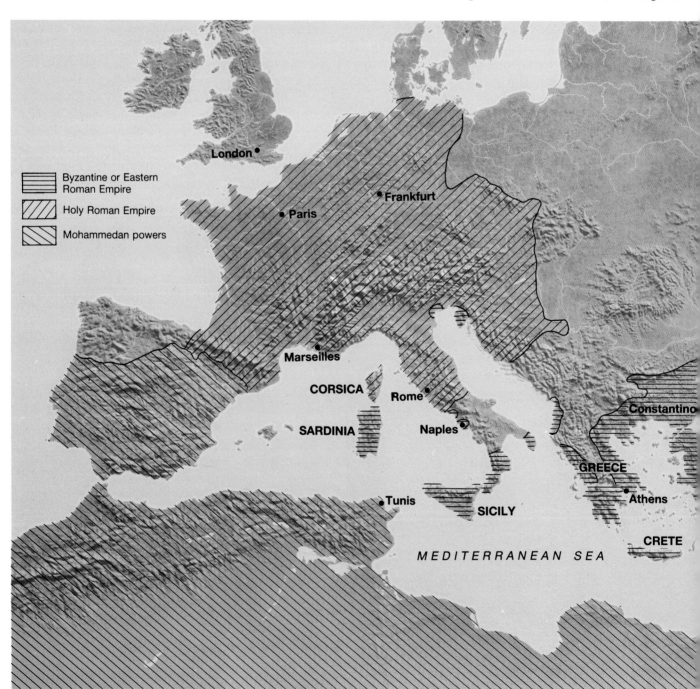

Byzantine or Eastern
Roman Empire

Holy Roman Empire

Mohammedan powers

London

Paris

Frankfurt

Marseilles

CORSICA

Rome

SARDINIA

Naples

Constantino

GREECE

Tunis

SICILY

Athens

CRETE

MEDITERRANEAN SEA

was able either to beat off really serious attacks or to absorb some of the invaders into his territory. He began to build up the army and then finally abandoned the idea that only foot soldiers could be effective.

'Instead, he had his men trained as horse soldiers. They rode into battle in mail coats and were armed with spear and sword. Cavalry of this kind found it easier to deal with the incoming waves of enemy tribesmen, many of whom were also mounted on horseback.

'So well did the eastern empire do at first, that the emperor Justinian in the sixth century was actually

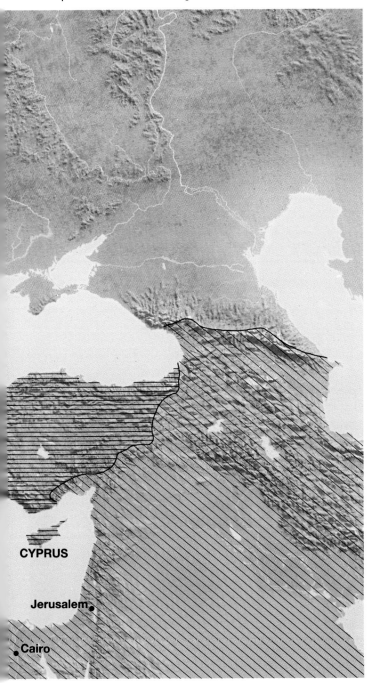

Europe at the death of Charlemagne

CYPRUS

Jerusalem

Cairo

able to recapture some parts of the west that had been lost.'

'The Roman Empire got bigger again?' we ask.

'I'm afraid it was only temporary,' replies the historian. 'The reconquered Roman lands were taken back by the barbarians only three or four years after Justinian's death. Even the eastern empire itself was slowly crumbling away as a result of more barbarian assaults.

'Mohammedans, intent on spreading their religion, overran lands to the east of the Mediterranean such as what are now Egypt, Israel and Syria. Then in the seventh and eighth centuries, they swept through the old Roman provinces of North Africa and across the sea at Gibraltar. They occupied Spain where they were to stay for more than another seven hundred years. They even tried to conquer France but were finally driven out by Charles Martel.'

'Who was he?'

'He was the King of the Franks, the barbarian tribe who then lived in France and from whom the country gets its name. You may be interested to know that his grandson was Charles the Great, or Charlemagne, as we usually call him. Charlemagne ruled almost all of mainland north western Europe and was pleased to call his vast lands "The Holy Roman Empire".'

'But it wasn't – is that what you're saying?'

'No, it wasn't. It was neither an empire nor Roman. I suppose the word "holy" might be excused, since many of the tribesmen that Charlemagne ruled had become Christians.

'It's strange really to think that when they overran what we now know as Germany and France, they probably spoke a language rather like modern German. Those in the German part kept and developed this tongue whilst those in the French part began to speak a common form of Latin which slowly changed through the centuries into French.

'Another group of Mohammedans called Ottomans, or Ottoman Turks, gradually pushed westward into Asia Minor and the Holy Land. Several crusades, or wars of the cross, were begun by Christians of the west to try and drive them out of the Bible lands but all failed in the end.

'Finally in 1453, the Ottoman army, led by by Sultan Mohammed, besieged and bombarded Constantinople until it fell.

'With its capture the last traces of Roman rule in Europe disappeared. The so-called "Holy Roman Empire" of Charlemagne went on – at least in name, if in nothing else – until 1806 when Napoleon did away with the title. Thus was the very last link broken.'

Postscript

The legacy of Rome

When we talk about a 'legacy', we are normally referring to some money or property that has come to us in a relative's will. We are usually pleased to have whatever the will maker has decided to leave us. In the case of Rome, it isn't money or property but rather a legacy of ideas and ways of thinking and behaving.

What are the things that Rome has left us? It would be as well to list them (although not in order of importance) as follows:

1 *Law* In the early days, this was mostly the result of traditional public wisdom. Laws dealt with civil matters such as land tenure, trespass, inheritance, contracts, etc. Only later did republican magistrates publish the rules – on bronze plates known as the 'Twelve Tables'. During the time of the emperors, criminal activities also came to be recorded with proper punishments. Justinian collected the laws, sorted them out, discarded a number which were out of date and published the rest. Roman law was taken to every part of the empire and forms the basis of the legal systems of many modern countries, including those nations whose existence wasn't even suspected in Roman days – Australia, for instance, and the United States.

2 *Cleanliness and water supplies* Once the empire was overwhelmed, these things which had been taken for granted were swept away, not to return, even to the developed countries of the world, until the last century.

The White House, Washington D.C.

3 *Roads* The legions constructed thousands of miles of roads all over the empire. In many cases they are still being used – either as the base of modern highways, or at least, as 'easiest route' markers for roads and perhaps even railways.

4 *Towns* Many towns began as army camps or as important sites, perhaps at a crossroads or a ford. Rome itself 'just grew', but later 'planned' towns often follow a more geometric square pattern. Some north American settlements have copied the idea in modern times. Many cities have been provided with the equivalent of the Roman forum, i.e. an open space surrounded by imposing buildings, such as Trafalgar Square in London or the Place de la Concorde in Paris.

5 *Buildings* Techniques of various kinds were either invented or at least developed by the Romans, for instance, the self-supporting arch of bricks or stones. Multiple arches made a barrel vault whilst a groined vault was formed from two barrel vaults crossing at right angles. A simple arch turned through $180°$ produced a dome. Some huge arches were constructed to make bridges and aqueducts.

Other advances include the use of structural

Trafalgar Square, London. The National Gallery is on the left.

concrete, stonefaced walls banded with thin red bricks and packed with rubble.

A lot of eighteenth, nineteenth and twentieth-century buildings are copies of the Roman style – for example, the National Gallery and the British Museum in London, the Arc de Triomphe in Paris and the White House, Washington.

6 *Government* Government systems at national and local level have been copied in numerous places, as has the idea of a well-trained civil service. Some of the original Roman civil servants almost certainly used a form of Latin shorthand.

7 *Calendar* Our arrangements of months and weeks, including the names of the months (and Saturday) come from Roman sources.

8 *Sport* The Romans invented the sports arena with tickets and numbered seats: the word 'sport' itself is from Latin.

9 *Weights and measures* Some British imperial weights and measures were based on Roman ones. The idea of standard lengths, sets of containers and weights was a Roman one.

10 *Miscellaneous* Many other things were first tried out or adopted on the banks of the Tiber – for example, a postal delivery service, hospitals, our own alphabet, central heating, glass windows, blocks of flats, the organisation of the army, banks, etc.

11 *Latin* The language survived the barbarian invasions because it was used in the church and then at universities or schools and in law courts. The local Latin slang developed into what we call the 'Romance' languages – e.g. French, Spanish, Italian, Romanian and Portuguese. An interesting illustration of the way a legionary's slang became the basis of a modern language is provided by the everyday word 'testa'. It meant (literally) a 'pot' but was used to mean 'head', just as we might say 'napper' or 'bonce'. It was used instead of the proper word 'caput'. Then 'testa' changed into 'tête', which is modern French for 'head'.

We still use some expressions which come directly from Latin such as 'cave' ('beware'), 'tempus fugit' ('time flies'), 'et cetera' ('and so on') – and a good half of English words are descended, directly or indirectly from the tongue the Romans spoke.

12 *Numbers* Roman numerals are used in books for chapter headings and volume numbers, on some clocks and occasionally at the end of television programmes.

13 *Remains* There are still Roman ruins scattered the length and breadth of the old empire. Rich young men in the last couple of centuries finished their education by touring to see what the Greeks and Romans had left behind them. European rulers of all periods thought it was quite the thing to have a portrait or a statue made showing them in classical dress (tunic and toga, or Roman officer's uniform), rather than their normal attire.

It's very true that our world would have been a totally different place if the Romans had never existed.

Index

Acknowledgements

The publishers would like to thank the following for permission to reproduce copyright material:

Part 1

Aerofilms p. 88 (both), p. 89, p. 91 right, p. 95 btm; British Museum p. 22 btm, p. 23, p. 39 top, p. 56 btm left and right, p. 58 btm, p. 68, p. 69, p. 70; C M Dixon p. 87 left, p. 94 left; Egyptian Department of Antiquities p. 53; Werner Forman p. 47, p. 66 top; Robert Harding p. 39 btm, p. 59 top, p. 61 top left, centre, top right btm left; Hirmer Fotoarchiv p. 29 right, p. 30 left, p. 39 centre, p. 74; Michael Holford p. 10, p. 27 (both) p. 36, p. 44, p. 50 btm, p. 51, p. 56 top left, p. 72, p. 73 left, p. 83, p. 85; Chris Honeywell p. 54 left; Impact p. 17; Illustrated London News p. 11, p. 54 right, p. 60 (both); Metropolitan Museum of Art, New York p. 62, p. 63 top and bottom; National Museum of Antiquities of Scotland p. 87 right; Ronald Sheridan p. 22 top, p. 29 left, p. 30 right, p. 34, p. 50 top left, top right, p. 59 btm, p. 61 btm right, p. 73 right, p. 90 top, centre left, centre right, and btm; John Topham Picture Library p. 25 top left, top right, p. 95 top right; Roger Wood p. 66 btm

Illustrations are by Steve Ashley. Chapman and Bounford. Peter Connolly. John Fraser. Peter Kesteven. Chris Molan. Tony Morris. David Salariya. Graham Smith. Tony Smith. Techniques. Michael Whittlesea and Maurice Wilson.

Part 2

American School of Classical Studies at Athens p. 132 right; Archaeological Museum of Thessalonika p. 187 left & right; Ashmolean Museum. Oxford p. 102, pps. 102–3, p. 105; John Boardman p. 147; Mensun Bound Maritime Archaeological Research Oxford p. 141; The Trustees of the British Museum p. 138 left & right, p. 139 bottom right & top left, p. 154, p. 161, p. 182 top left, p. 193, p. 205; Nobby Clark p. 167; Peter Connolly p. 121, p. 123; C M Dixon Photo Resources p. 107 right; Fitzwilliam Museum Cambridge p. 114; Sonia Halliday Photographs p. 104, p. 106; Robert Harding Picture Library p. 131; Hirmer Fotoarchiv p. 107 left, p. 111 top, p. 112, p. 115 top & bottom, p. 135, p. 142 middle & right; Michael Holford Photographs p. 132 middle, p. 168 left, p. 172 top, p. 182 top right; Malta High Commission p. 168 right; Mansell Collection p. 120, p. 142 left; Musées Nationaux p. 177 top; Museum of Fine Arts Boston p. 139 top right & bottom left; National Archaeological Museum of Athens p. 111 bottom, p. 155, p. 176; Ronald Sheridan's Photo-Library p. 132 left, p. 172 bottom, p. 173, p. 182 bottom right & bottom left, p. 204 left & right.

The illustrations including the map models are by Peter Connolly, except for p.59 (top) which is by John Batchelor. Handwriting is by Elitta Fell.

Part 3

Robin Birley/The Vindolanda Trust p. 265; Dorest Natural History Society, Dorset County Museum, Dorchester, Dorset p. 295; Robert Estall p. 315; Michael Holford p. 236; The Hutchison Library p. 314; Ny Calsberg Glyptotek, Copenhagen p. 251; Rheinisches Landesmuseum Trier p. 264; Scala p. 215, p. 216, p. 227, pps. 234–235, p. 241, p. 242, p. 249, p. 252, p. 253, p. 259; Ronald Sheridan's Photo Library p. 253 bottom, p. 304; Weidenfeld and Nicolson Ltd./Galleria Borghese p. 287

The illustrations including the map models are by Peter Connolly. Handwriting is by Elitta Fell.

Cover illustrations are by Peter Connolly.

Timelines by Stephen Hawkins of Oxprint.

320